D0867295

BANDIT INVINCIBLE: BUTCH CASSIDY

A Western Story

BANDIT INVINCIBLE: BUTCH CASSIDY

A Western Story

SUZANNE LYON

Five Star
Unity, Maine

Five Star Western
Published in conjunction with Golden West Literary Agency.

Cover photograph courtesy of The Denver Public Library, Western History Collection

December 1999

Standard Print Hardcover Edition.

First Edition, Second Printing.

Five Star Standard Print Western Series.

The text of this edition is unabridged.

Set in 11 pt. Plantin by Minnie B. Raven.

Printed in the United States on permanent paper.

Library of Congress Cataloging-in-Publication Data

Lyon, Suzanne.
   Bandit invincible : Butch Cassidy : a western story /
by Suzanne Lyon. — 1st ed.
     p. cm.
   ISBN 0-7862-1843-6 (hc : alk. paper)
   1. Cassidy, Butch, b. 1866 Fiction. I. Title.
PS3562.Y4459B36 1999
  813′.54—dc21   99-41704

For my mother,
who always loved a good story

Prologue

1934

The old man paused along the shore of the crystalline lake. Removing his battered, broad-brimmed hat, he lifted his face to the morning sun and concentrated on being still. Inhaling the familiar smells of the forest, he lost the sense of himself as separate from his surroundings. The mountain silence was broken only by the wind swaying the tops of the pine trees in a rushing rhythm that felt like the blood coursing through his body. Before him, Mary's Lake lay unruffled by the breeze. *Like her,* he thought, *smooth and deep and calm.*

It had been on a day much like today, in a place much like this place that he had found the courage to give up his old ways, to disappear, to abandon the map of his former life and draw a new one.

The new course he charted had led him, a grizzled old man of sixty-eight, to the Wind River Mountains of western Wyoming. Anxiously, he awaited the arrival of a woman whom he had not seen in thirty-eight years but whose face remained as clear and sweet to him as this pristine mountain lake that bore her name. Instinctively, he reached inside his faded, cotton shirt and fingered a cross that hung from a gold chain around his neck. Gertrude had pestered him mercilessly about that cross, begging him to tell her where it had come from and why he refused to take it off. He had never told her, and it lay between them, one of many things that divided him and his wife. Like this trip to the mountains.

★ ★ ★ ★ ★

"I don't understand, Bill," Gertrude had said when he had told her of his latest plan to visit Wyoming. "There's nothing there for you any more. Why can't you accept the fact that it's lost? You'll never find what you're looking for."

"It ain't just the money, Gertie, never has been," he said. "It's just being there, being there in the mountains. . . ." He trailed off, unable to express to her the need he had for the rugged, unforgiving land, as tangible to him as his need for food and drink. "You knew how it would be, Gertie. I never told you no different. You knew up front what kind of life I'd led, and I told you I didn't know if I could change. I've done my damnedest, Gertie, and you got to admit it's worked out pretty good. But sometimes I just get so. . . . I just got to get out . . . out to where I can see farther than my own god-damn' front door." He sank down in the nearest chair, the upholstery faded and threadbare, and ran his hands through his sandy hair.

Gertrude was silent, gazing around the living room of their small home. They had moved three years ago, when the business at Bill's machine shop had dried up, lost to the ravages of the Depression. She had tried to cram all of her possessions into the tiny house—things that had displayed so well in the big, beautiful house on Providence Street but in the new place just looked like so much clutter. Clutter that was closing in on her handsome, free-spirited husband.

And to Gertrude he was still so handsome, despite advancing age and waning health. Nothing could dim the light in those startling blue eyes—the color of a sun-speckled mountain lake—or soften the line of that square jaw that spoke to her of character and determination. She had been lost to him years ago, from the moment he had wandered into the Baptist church in Adrian, Michigan, drawn, he had

8

said, by the sound of her piano playing. Gertrude Livesay, thirty-two years old, skinny and asthmatic, had been so taken with the handsome, mysterious stranger that by the time he had confessed his past to her she had been beyond caring. And what had he confessed, really? His true name and a few well-chosen details of his previous outlaw existence. The fact that he now desired to "go straight" and live a virtuous life with her at his side. He had "come clean" all right, but she had come to know he had revealed nothing of true importance. Nothing of the essential man.

Gertrude had lived her entire life in small-town Michigan. While she had not been so sheltered that she had not heard the name he had told her, it had been hard to connect this charming, well-mannered gentleman to that purveyor of crime and mischief. He had sworn to her that he had never killed, or even badly hurt anyone. If he had in the past "redistributed the wealth" a little bit in a place so far away she could barely imagine it, did that really matter? God had brought him to her for a purpose that she could not ignore—the chance to help guide a lost soul struggling toward the light—and if in the bargain she gained a good-looking, lively husband who would deliver her from a life of sickly spinsterhood, so much the better.

So she had married him after a shockingly short courtship, and they had embarked on a life together in that faraway place known as the Wild West. They had lived well, for the most part, finally settling in Spokane where "Bill," as he preferred to be called, had built a successful business and where they had raised their adopted son.

She had endured much over the years. Bill's gregarious nature had needed an outlet she alone could not provide, so he had begun to spend more and more time away from home in the company of friends and, she had suspected, a mistress or two. Furthermore, he had a wanderlust that he had periodically indulged, leaving her and their son at home while he went God-knows-where to do God-knows-what. He had always come back to her, his sunny nature restored, charming her all over again, shutting down only when she had queried him too closely about his long absences. He had finally admitted that he was hunting a stash of money buried somewhere in the Wind River Mountains but that he had been unable to find it. She had been furious with him, accusing him of lying to her about his desire to go straight, vowing that she would never live off of stolen money. He had brushed aside her anger with his quick smile. "Looks like you ain't going to have to live off of nothing but the fruits of my honest labor, honey, 'cause I can't find the loot."

"Oh, Bill, don't you see, that's not the point," she had said. "It's the principle of the thing. If you truly wanted in your heart to be the God-fearing man you promised to be, you wouldn't even think of searching for that money."

His grin fading, he had spoken quietly. "I get a little uneasy when you start talking principles, Gertie. I got certain principles, and you know it. But that money out there ain't got a life of its own. It ain't virtuous, and it ain't sinful. It's just money. And it ain't going to hurt nobody nor help nobody long as it stays buried which it appears likely to do."

She had sighed, resigned to her love for him in spite of everything. "I just want you to be satisfied with your life, Bill, with our life as it is, not as it could be."

"I am, girl." He had reached out and touched her arm, then drew his hand away. "I am."

But she didn't really believe him and she knew as he sat before her, head in his hands, that she had merely been a resting place for him, a safe harbor from the storm that had been his previous life. Yet even now, old and failing, he could not leave behind the past. The memory of those thrilling, wild, free days was all he had, his only reality. His life with her meant nothing to him. It had been simply a way to escape detection from everyone but himself.

Gertrude rose from her chair and placed a trembling hand on his shoulder. He looked up at her, ready to receive forgiveness and understanding as he had so often before. Her voice surprisingly steady, she said: "It would have been better if you had been killed in that shoot-out. You haven't really been alive since then anyway."

He recoiled from her touch. "That's a hell of a thing to say!"

She turned her back on him, shaking her head. "Go on, Bill. Go on to Wyoming or wherever you please. I can't stop you, and I don't even want to any more."

So in May he had left, reassuring her of his return by the end of the summer. She had said nothing, but disbelief, and worse, apathy, occupied her eyes.

Short of funds to finance such an extended trip by himself, he had asked a well-off friend from Spokane, Ellen Harris, to accompany him. An adventurous widow excited by the prospect of traveling with a former outlaw, for she was one of the few people who knew Bill's secret, she had accepted, and brought along her son Ben. Once in Lander, Bill had arranged for his old friend Bill Boyd to pack them into the mountains where they had set up camp by Mary's Lake.

The summer was perfect, one of those rare times when everything seemed touched by magic. One brilliant day followed another, and Bill's mood quickly improved until he was once again his genial, good-natured self. Several of

Bill's old-time friends came to visit them at their camp: Bill Boyd and his wife, Minnie, their nephews Roy Jones and Herman LaJeunesse, Bert and Jesse Chamberlin. All of them knew about Bill's past, yet they treated him with a loving respect more suited to a bank president than a bank robber. Around the campfire at night, Bill, or rather George, as he was known to his friends, regaled them with stories of his exploits. Ellen was at first shocked by some of these stories, but she soon accepted what everyone there seemed to believe—that George had been falsely accused and goaded into outlawry by greedy and unscrupulous cattle barons.

George spent his days hunting—he was an expert marksman—prospecting, and wood-working. Ellen marveled at his craftsmanship with tools and insisted that he take back to Spokane the beautiful furniture he created. "Nah, you take it Ellen, if you think any of it's worth saving," he said. "Gertie's got a houseful of furniture, and she don't want this rustic-looking stuff anyway."

He seemed content, but as the summer started to wind down, something appeared to nag at him. He would go off by himself for a day or two with no explanation. He would stop in the middle of a story as though he had lost his train of thought. Once, Ellen came upon him out in the woods writing something, but, when she approached him, he crumpled the paper and stuck it in his pocket. He was still happy-go-lucky George, always ready to tell a joke or play a game of cards, but he began acting like a man with a decision to make.

Finally, he took Bill Boyd aside for a private word. After breakfast, Boyd harnessed up the empty buckboard and left camp, promising to return sometime the following week. George's agitation increased with each passing day until one morning Roy Jones rode into camp and announced that Uncle Bill and Aunt Mary would be there within the hour. Ellen turned to ask George about this mysterious "Aunt Mary" but held her tongue when she saw his face.

Without a word, George rose slowly and walked off into the woods. There, by the side of Mary's Lake, with the crisp mountain air already touched by autumn's tingle filling his senses, he made his decision. Thirty-eight years had passed since he had last seen this woman, some of them glorious but most of them lonely and unfulfilled. The time had come to make one last bid for happiness. He returned to camp and calmly awaited the arrival of Mary Boyd.

An hour later, the sound of a creaking buckboard reached the campsite. Ellen put down the book she was pretending to read, eager to satisfy her curiosity about the approaching visitor. She had found out that Aunt Mary was Bill Boyd's sister, but why her presence in camp should cause such a stir remained a mystery. George sat silently in one of his home-made chairs, whittling on a piece of wood. He, too, heard the noisy wagon coming up the trail, and his knife stopped in mid-stroke.

The buckboard rounded a bend in the trail and jolted into the clearing. Bill secured the reins and hopped down, assisting his sister to the ground. She was a small woman although sturdy-looking. Her pretty, lemon-yellow housedress draped a figure that was just beginning to thicken around the middle, and on her feet she wore delicately beaded moccasins. She put her palms on her hips and stretched this way and that, working out the stiffness of the journey.

"Them wagon seats don't get no softer, do they, Aunt Mary?" Roy said, pecking her on the cheek.

"Isn't that the truth. Especially not the way Bill was driving, jouncing me all over the place. I'd surely like to know what got the burr under your seat, brother," Mary said, removing her straw hat and wiping her forehead with a large handkerchief she kept tucked under her belt. Bill turned away and busied himself unloading boxes from the back of the wagon.

"And how come you took off so fast, Roy? You must have gotten here a good hour ahead of us."

"Why, I just wanted to let everyone know you was coming."

"Everyone! Who's everyone? I thought it was just us and the Chamberlins on this camping trip, and Lord knows Bert and Jesse don't much care what time I show up!" Mary spoke forthrightly but not sharply; she seemed to enjoy teasing her nephew a bit.

"Mary, we got some new friends for you to meet," Bill said, guiding her over to Ellen and Ben Harris. "I wanted to surprise you, that's why I didn't mention it on the way up." Bill made the introductions, and Mary shook hands, polite but puzzled at the presence of these strangers. Ellen noticed the resemblance between Mary and Bill; the high cheekbones and deep-set dark eyes that, in Mary's case, were hidden behind round, wire-framed eyeglasses.

Just then Bert Chamberlin and his son Jesse strolled up from the lake, carrying their fishing poles. They greeted Mary, and the group fell into small talk. Bert inquired about Bill and Mary's trip up from Riverton and then offered as how the fish just weren't biting. Mary asked Ellen if she were enjoying the sunny weather they'd been having, and Ellen allowed as how it sure beat the climate in Spokane. Suddenly everyone fell into an awkward silence.

"Bill," Mary said uneasily, "why don't you show me where I'm going to bunk. Unless you expect me to pitch my own tent which I could do, mind you, if I had to."

" 'Course not. We'll put you in with Ellen," Bill said. He slapped his hat nervously against his thigh. "But first, Sis, there's someone else here for you to see. This ain't no stranger, though. This is somebody you know right well."

"Billy, what are you up to? You've been acting funny every since we left Riverton, and you, too, Roy, for that matter. What have you got up your sleeve?" She poked playfully at Bill's arm, trying not to let his agitation affect her, but her stomach suddenly felt all fluttery.

He led her to the edge of the clearing, to a small tent set partially among the tall pines. A broad-shouldered, slightly bowlegged man stood, hat in hand. Shadows from the surrounding trees fell across the man's face, but she would have known him in near dark from fifty yards away. She knew his stance—one booted foot slightly forward, chest out, head up. She knew his hands—strong, blunt-tipped fingers covered with traces of sandy hair. She knew, if she turned his left hand over, there would be a tiny scar on the ball of his thumb. She knew how the muscles knotted under his shoulders, how his earlobes tipped up when he smiled. She knew how the cowlick on his forehead made his hair grow straight down in front. She knew this man's body as well as she knew her own, although more than half her life had passed since she had last seen him. *Knew his body,* she thought sadly, *but never his mind.*

George took a half step forward and stopped. His eyes wandered over her face. She wondered what he saw there. Did he see traces of the beautiful half-breed girl who had spent many a stolen hour in his arms? Or did he see only a wrinkled, bespectacled old woman who had gone on to build a life without him?

"Look who's here, Mary," Bill said. "You recognize him, don't you?"

" 'Course, I do. I heard you were still alive, but I never figured on seeing you again. Heard you were living up northwest somewhere." How normal her husky voice sounded, fashioning words that made sentences that seemed to make sense.

"That's right. Spokane, Washington. But you know me, Mary. I can't stay away from these mountains for long." George grinned at her with that old, familiar smile that lighted his whole face, and she felt like slapping him and hugging him at the same time.

"Long enough," she said roughly. "Been nigh on to forty years since I saw you."

"I know, Mary, and I'm right sorry about that. I can't lie to you . . . I've been back to Wyoming a time or two, but I never got the nerve to see you till now. Believe me, I wish I had, because you are a sight for sore eyes, just like always."

"Still a sweet-talker, aren't you? Well, come on, let's catch up on old times. Like to hear how you got out of that jam down in South America, for one thing."

Rejoining the group, they spent the rest of the afternoon filling in the details of two lives spent apart. Mary knew George was leaving out parts of his story, but she didn't press him—it had always been that way.

Later that evening, when Mary was fixing up her bedroll, George appeared in front of the open tent flap. "Come, walk with me a little," he said. Mary had been dreading this moment. She had succeeded in keeping the conversation at a superficial level all day, and now, she feared, George wanted to offer excuses and explanations. Well, she wanted no part of it. Long ago she had made her reckoning with the past, and she had done it alone, with no one to confide in or ease her way. Let George find his own peace of mind, dammit, without dragging her through it all again! Her

16

thoughts played out on her face, for George laughed and said: "You know, I always loved you best when you got ornery! Come on now, girl, I'm too old to try any sparking with you, even if you are the best-looking widow woman I've ever seen."

"As though I'd worry about taking up with you again after all these years," she said. "It's just that I'm awful tired after bouncing around in that wagon all day."

"I reckon you are, honey. Just sit with me a spell by the lake and help me count the stars. It's better than counting sheep for getting a body all relaxed and ready for a night of dreamless sleep."

Mary put her hands on her hips and looked at him askance. "All the major trouble in my life has come from letting you sweet-talk me into things," she said.

George threw back his head and laughed, then held out his hand to her. They were silent as they walked, arm in arm, enjoying the smells and sounds of the forest. The late August night was cool, and Mary was glad for the warmth of his body next to hers. By the side of the lake they sat on a couple of overturned logs. Many minutes passed, each lost in his or her own thoughts, comfortable with the silence. At length, a full moon crept over the horizon, huge and tawny as a mountain lion's coat.

"This seems familiar, don't it . . . gazing at the moon together? We should've done a lot more of that," George said. Mary closed her eyes and said nothing.

He shifted on the log and stared at his hands clasped in front of him. "I know I didn't do right by you, Mary. I ain't done most of the right things in my life. Fact is, 'most everything I ever did was wrong. But the biggest mistake I made was not holding on to you." He paused, but still she was silent. "I had no cause to expect you to wait for me while I was in the cooler, but somehow I thought. . . ." He sighed and tossed a rock into the lake. "Hell, Mary, I thought you loved me. Jailbirds don't make for much of a future, I admit, but you never gave me a chance."

"Stop it! Just stop it now! What's the point of all this? What's past is done with. Why are you dredging it all up? Why'd you make Billy drag me all the way out here to listen to this foolishness?"

"Jesus, I'm sorry, Mary. I ain't never been good at this. I never really told you how I felt about you when it counted, and now that I've finally got around to it, I'm making a mess of it." He unbuttoned the top button of his shirt and pulled out the cross he wore around his neck. "Look, honey, look at this. You gave it to me to remember you by, you said. Well, I ain't never taken it off, Mary, not in thirty-eight years. That's how long I been remembering you."

Mary fought the tears that crowded her eyes. She wanted to shake him, to shout at him: *You bastard, if you only knew what I went through for you, what I gave up for you! And now you come to me and say you've been pining after me all these years.* But she was, after all, half Shoshone and too proud to let him see how she had suffered.

"I never forgot you either, George," she said quietly. "I won't deny we had something special. But it's like that moon yonder. It starts out all big and golden and full of promise, but, little by little, it goes away till there's nothing left."

"You got that wrong, Mary." He crouched in front of her and took her hand. "The moon don't start out full. You can't see a new moon at all. But every day it reveals a little more to you until one day you can see the whole thing."

Mary turned his hand over and touched the tiny scar she knew was there. God help her, she had never stopped loving

18

him. He pulled his hand away, removed a ring from his little finger, and pressed it into her hand. "This is for you, Mary. I'm a broken-down, poor, old man. I got nothing left but this, and I want you to have it."

She recoiled and pushed it back at him. "You can't think I'd take your wedding ring! What about your wife?"

"I ain't got no wife!"

Mary stared at him, speechless.

"William T. Phillips is married sure enough, but *I* ain't got no wife! I never wore a wedding ring, 'cause in my heart I'm pledged to you. This ring here is real special to me." He held it up to the bright moonlight; a large fire opal glinted in a shiny silver band. "You can't see it in the dark, but it's engraved . . . 'George C. to Mary B.' Take it." He pressed it back into her hand. She looked at it, turning it over and over, feeling the indentation of the engraved words. Finally she slipped it on her finger and took both his hands in hers.

"I never understood you, what made you the way you were," she whispered. "You could have been anything you wanted to be . . . a rancher, a businessman, a teacher. Why, I often thought you would have been a first-rate preacher, the way you could lead people and make them feel good about things. So much brains, so much natural talent, so good with people, and yet you spent your life running and hiding. A waste . . . a wasted life."

He tried to pull his hands away, but she held on tightly. "Why did you do it George? You were still so young that first time, in Telluride, and you never had no cause that I could tell for turning against the law. What made you do it? What made you become Butch Cassidy?"

Chapter One

1879

Robert Leroy Parker sauntered down the road, half asleep atop the plodding dun-colored horse. The warmth of the summer sun and the rhythmic movement of the big horse had a soporific effect on the thirteen-year-old boy. Every now and then, to keep himself awake, he shifted position, leaning forward to caress the horse's neck or wiping the grime from his face with his faded bandanna. Despite the heat and dust of the road, he was in no particular hurry to return to the ranch where he hired out. He was perfectly happy to while away time, feeling solid horseflesh between his legs and mulling things over in his sleepy brain.

Bob loved horses. He spent most of his waking hours riding, feeding, grooming, talking to or about horses. Many of his sleeping hours were spent dreaming about them. When his father told him that, to help with the family finances, he had been hired out to Pat Ryan for the summer, he was secretly thrilled, in part because it meant temporary escape from the Parkers' over-crowded log cabin and the drudgery of farm chores on their hundred-and-sixty-acre homestead, but also because it would give him a chance to work with Mr. Ryan's horses. His father owned one plow horse and one buggy horse, but Mr. Ryan kept a stable full of fine horses, including one or two not yet broken to the bit. Ryan's foreman soon noticed Bob's natural affinity for horses and assigned him as a permanent stable hand, but the boy was not yet allowed to try his hand at breaking one of the beautiful, wild animals rounded up by the more experienced cowboys. As he ambled along, Bob daydreamed of slipping into the corral with a wild horse, letting it get used to the smell and nearness of him, then walking close enough to touch it, uttering soothing words until it let him gently stroke it and lay his face against its flank, feeling with his cheek the creature's skittering heart and smelling its moist, fearful, untamed smell.

He came to with a start and, glancing down, realized his dream had aroused him. Dismounting, he pulled his canteen from the saddle and washed out his mouth, spitting into the road. From behind him came the sound of galloping hoofs, fast approaching. He wondered who could be in such a hurry on this lazy stretch of road between Milford and Hay Springs, a remote location even by Utah standards, and considered that whoever it was might be up to no good. But before he could take cover the rider was upon him, reining up sharply as he saw the boy in the road.

"Whoa there, Buck," the rider quieted his winded horse, and squinted at Bob from beneath a preposterously oversized hat. "Are you Robert Leroy Parker?"

"Who's asking?"

"Deputy Marshal Bullock," the man said, elbowing aside his worn leather vest to reveal a star pinned to his shirt. "I followed you from Milford, son. Weren't too hard, seeing as yours was the only set of tracks coming this direction. Looks like you been just moseying along. You want to tell me what happened back there? Reckon I might as well get your side of the story before I take you in."

"Take me in! What are you talking about? I ain't done nothing!" Bob stood his ground, although he hated that his voice squeaked.

"Now, son, it won't do you no good to lie. I got this complaint swore out against you by Orson Peabody that says you stole a pair of overalls from his store this morning. You ain't calling Mister Peabody a liar now, are you?" The lawman removed a piece of paper from his shirt pocket and dropped it at Bob's feet. Bob picked it up and looked at it. He didn't understand it all, and some of the big words he couldn't read, but he got the gist of it—Orson Peabody, owner of the general store in Milford, was accusing him of being a thief. Angrily Bob slapped the paper with the back of his hand. How could anyone accuse him, the oldest son of Maxi Parker, of being a thief? It must be a misunderstanding.

"Marshal, what this paper don't say is that I left a note for Mister Peabody, explaining that since he weren't there I'd pay for the overalls next time I came to town. It ain't stealing when you leave a man your I.O.U."

"That ain't how Mister Peabody sees it, son. Where are you headed for?"

"Pat Ryan's ranch. I'm a hired hand there."

"That right? Well, seeing as we're a lot closer to Ryan's place than Milford, I'll take you on in to see Mister Ryan. Maybe he'll vouch for you."

Bob didn't like that plan at all. Pat Ryan was a good man and a fair employer, but he tolerated no misbehavior by his ranch hands. While Bob didn't think he had done anything wrong, he did not want to take the chance that Mr. Ryan would see things differently. That would surely be the end of his job at the ranch.

"Here, Marshal," Bob said, scrambling for bills in his pocket. "I got the money for the overalls right here. Like I said, the only reason I didn't leave it at the store was there weren't nobody there, and I was afraid it would get lost or that somebody it didn't belong to would take it. Why don't you just take the money to Mister Peabody, and we can forget the whole thing." He thrust the money at Deputy Marshal Bullock who sat his horse without moving.

The lawman looked at him pityingly. "Son, I can't do that. Peabody wants his money, all right, but he also wants to learn you a lesson about respecting other people's property. A person can't just go waltzing into a store what's all closed up and take what they want, even if he leaves his I. O. U. Now come on, mount up."

"Does Mister Peabody want me to go to jail?" asked Bob in a thin, scared voice.

"I don't think so, son. I think we can straighten this out, if you tell him you're sorry and pay him the money . . . maybe do a few chores for him around the store. It'll probably help, if Mister Ryan vouches for you. Let's get going."

Scared and worried, Bob fell in step behind the deputy marshal. He could not see what he had done wrong. When he had arrived at Peabody's store that morning, there had been a sign posted on the door: **Back in Five Minutes.** He had waited five minutes, then five minutes more, and no one had come. To kill time, he had wandered down to the town's livery stable to admire the horses there and chat with the stable hand. When he had returned to Peabody's, the sign was still up. He tried the door—it was unlocked. What the hell, he couldn't wait all day and it could be a month or more before he made it back to town. He needed those overalls now—the ones he wore were too short and out at the knees—and his mother had sent him the money especially to buy new ones. So he had entered the store, picked out what he needed, and left his I.O.U. by the cash register, underneath a heavy inkwell so it wouldn't blow away.

What had he done wrong? The merchants in Circleville

would accept his father's I.O.U. without question. Why would Mr. Peabody doubt his word? This was all Peabody's fault. If he didn't run such a slipshod business, none of this would have happened. *Damned if I'm going to apologize or do any chores for that lazy, no-good geezer,* Bob thought. By the time they rode into the ranch, he had worked himself into such a huff he didn't even notice the curious looks of the other hands. Eyes flashing and jaw set, he swung himself off his horse, threw the reins around the hitching rail, and stomped up the steps to the big house. Hands on hips, he waited while the deputy marshal knocked. Pat Ryan answered the door.

"Mister Ryan? Deputy Marshal Bullock from Milford, sir. Does this boy work for you?"

Ryan was a big man, thick around the middle, and ruddy faced. Puzzled, he glanced at Bob. "Why yes, Marshal. Leroy Parker's his name. Been working here all summer. He in some kind of trouble?"

They entered the house, and the deputy marshal explained, showing Ryan the complaint against Bob. Ryan gave the boy a chance to tell his side, but in the end, as Bob had feared, he agreed with the deputy marshal that Bob had been wrong to enter Peabody's closed store. But Maxi Parker, Bob's father, was a friend of Ryan's, so to spare Maxi embarrassment, Ryan talked the deputy marshal into leaving Bob with him, promising that the boy and his father would return to Milford and make it right with Mr. Peabody. Bullock had Ryan sign an acknowledgment that he had received the complaint, then, glad to be done with such a minor matter, rode back to town.

Pat Ryan spoke to the boy sternly. "Leroy, I'm disappointed in you. You've done good work here, and I thought you had some sense, but that was a foolish thing you did.

Under the circumstances, I'm sure you can see I can't let you stay here. The other boys would think I'd gone soft, if I kept you on. You go get your things together and ride that dun-colored horse on home. You and your daddy can bring him back when you go to Milford to straighten things out with Peabody."

Angry and too proud to beg, Bob turned on his heel. Ryan let him get as far as the door, then called out to him: "If it means anything to you, I've never seen anyone your age handle horses like you do. You got a real gift, son. Don't squander it by being stupid."

Bob went back to his family's small farm south of Circleville. When he told his parents what had happened in Milford, his mother cried and his father gave him a stern lecture. He accompanied his father to Milford to apologize and make restitution to Orson Peabody who, when he realized Robert Leroy Parker was the grandson of Robert Parker of Beaver, Utah, one of the church elders, was inclined to drop the matter. They returned Pat Ryan's horse to him and apologized there as well, and that was that. Maxi seemed more put out at losing a day's work than by Bob's minor transgression. Even though his punishment had been minimal, Bob still seethed. He felt he had been treated unfairly and had barely been able to mouth the words of apology to the sanctimonious Peabody.

But he buried his resentment and busied himself with the never-ending chores around the farm. Things were not going well on the Parker homestead. Maxi and Annie Parker and their six children had arrived in Circle Valley only that spring, moving into an old, two-room log cabin. Enamored by the notion of working his own land and tired of living in the shadow of his venerable father, Maxi had left his job as a mail carrier in Beaver. Although he tried hard, he was neither an experienced nor an accomplished farmer. Mother Nature refused to co-operate that first year, as well. Twice, the inexorable wind blew Maxi's wheat seed right out of the ground. The third planting took, but, as luck would have it, there was a drought that summer, and the crops stood withering in the fields. The family desperately needed another source of income, but Bob was the only one of the children old enough to hire out, and he had managed to get himself fired.

One late summer evening, Bob sat alone just outside the cabin, listening to his mother clean up from supper and get the younger children ready for bed. Her life was unceasing drudgery, it seemed to him, a constant effort to keep her large brood fed and clothed, but she was rarely cross, seeming to accept her lot with equanimity. Her devotion to the Mormon church sustained her, and, if she had one major disappointment in her life, it was her inability to instill the same level of spiritual commitment in her husband and son.

Maxi walked up from the shed where he had been trying to repair one of the wagon traces. He was a compact man, normally quick on his feet, but tonight his shoulders drooped from fatigue. Farm life had worn him down. He reached in his pocket for the makings of a cigarette. Bob quickly glanced in the window to see if Annie were looking; smoking was strictly forbidden by the church.

"Ah, maybe you're right, son," Maxi said, dropping the makings back in his pocket. "No point in flaunting it, is there? I'll go down to the creek for a smoke later on."

He gave his oldest son a wink, and Bob grinned back. They both knew that Annie knew of Maxi's smoking, but as long as he was circumspect she chose to ignore it. Bob and

Maxi had an unspoken agreement to help each other avoid the strictures of the church. On Sundays, one of them would harness the buggy for Annie to take into town, but, when it came time to leave, Maxi would suddenly be busy with an important chore, one that absolutely required the help of his eldest son. Occasionally Annie insisted that Bob go with her and the rest of the children, but more often than not she simply shook her head and drove off. It wasn't that she had given up on her oldest child's spiritual education exactly. It was just that she didn't have the energy to argue about it, and, with Maxi's taking the boy's part, she was outnumbered. Besides, it wasn't as though he was a bad boy. He was a perfectly lovely boy, a hard worker, and kind to his brothers and sisters who adored him. Smart as a whip, too. Perhaps if she didn't force it on him, he would come on his own to appreciate the wisdom and beauty and order of the Mormon faith.

Maxi rested his hand on his son's shoulder. "Leroy," he said, using the name both parents used to address him, "go see if you can mend that broken trace. You're better at fixing the horses' tack than I am."

"Sure, Pa," Bob said. He ambled down to the shed and lit the lantern. The two horses swung their big heads toward him and snorted at his familiar smell. "Hey, Babe. Hey, Cookie," he greeted them softly. He picked up the currycomb and brushed them gently, speaking to them all the while in a hushed voice, before turning his attention to the broken trace. It lay on the bench where Maxi had left it. After studying it for a moment, he fashioned a makeshift repair. But he would have to tell Maxi to buy a new one next time he went to town because it was sure to break again. *Where will the money for that come from?* he wondered.

He doused the lantern and walked back to the cabin, lingering outside to watch the stars shimmer in the endless sky. *Guess them people across the ocean are looking at these same stars,* he thought. *It ain't fair. Ma and Pa were born in England and crossed an ocean and half of this country to get here, and I ain't ever been anywhere outside of western Utah. Some day, though, I'm getting out. Some day.*

His parents' voices came to him through the open window. He listened quietly, not consciously eavesdropping; the Parker family was so large and their living space so small that privacy was simply never expected by any of them.

"We've got to do something soon, Annie," Maxi was saying. "We just aren't making it on this measly homestead."

"It's a shame Leroy didn't bring in more wages this summer," she said. "We could try to hire him out again, but all the ranchers are letting people go for the winter, not hiring them. I asked around town if anybody needs help with cooking or cleaning, but nobody does. Anyway, I've got my hands full with this brood and another one on the way."

This was the first Bob had heard of Annie's latest pregnancy, but it didn't surprise him—his mother seemed to enlarge the family every year or two.

"I wouldn't have you working in some other man's home," Maxi said proudly. "I've got a plan to get us through the winter. Come spring, we'll plant again and with any luck have a decent crop next summer."

"What's your plan?" asked Annie.

"I've found work over in Frisco, cutting railroad ties and studs for the mines."

"But, Maxi, Frisco's so far away, you'll hardly be able to get home all winter. How will we get by without you?"

"You'll manage. Leroy can do just about everything

around here I can, and some things better. Be good for him to have some responsibility . . . maybe it'll cure him of his never-ending daydreaming." Bob heard Maxi's chair scrape and then the sound of his boots pacing the length of the tiny cabin.

"That's not fair. Leroy already does a huge load of work around here, and I don't want to wear him down to where he stops dreaming. He's a smart boy, Maxi. He's going to do big things in his life. Why, I was hoping he could go to school some this winter." Bob appreciated his mother's praise, but hoped she wasn't serious about school; he had had three years of schooling and didn't much want any more. He found it dull and confining.

"Not this year, Annie. He'll be needed here at home. But you haven't heard all my plan yet. This job in Frisco's just temporary, just to get us through the winter. Like I said, we'll plant again in the spring. But we're never going to get anywhere farming just this spread. We need to expand our operation . . . start grazing some cattle and get us some more horses." Maxi spoke excitedly, although in a low voice so as not to wake the sleeping children. "I know just the property, too . . . a hundred and sixty acres down the valley, just north of the Marshall place. It's a beautiful piece of property . . . borders the river, and it's more protected by the hills than this place, so maybe the wind won't be blowing my dirt and seeds to kingdom come. Can't believe it ain't been homesteaded yet, but it's free for the taking!"

Annie finished putting away the dishes, then sat down at the long pine table. "Are you sure about this, Maxi? Seems to me we've had trouble enough making this place pay. How are we going to handle two?"

"It's the only way we're ever going to improve our lot, honey. Small ranchers just get swallowed up in this country.

You got to be big to survive. We'll never make it selling a few acres of wheat, but, if we could start a cattle herd, why that's the easiest money there is. Did you know you can get forty-five dollars a steer at the market these days?"

"Maybe you're right. I trust your judgment in these things," Annie said, although Bob thought she sounded unconvinced. "You're sure no one else has claimed this property?"

"Yes, ma'am. All we got to do is start working the land, and five years from now it's ours, free and clear."

They continued to discuss the details of Maxi's ambitious plan, but Bob had stopped listening. While he didn't relish the idea of additional farm chores, he had heard his father say something about acquiring more horses, so a new Parker homestead sounded just fine and dandy to him. Eventually, Annie called him to come in. He fetched some blankets from the small bedroom where his brothers and sisters slept and told his mother he would bunk outside. She merely nodded. Her oldest son slept outdoors in all but the most inclement weather, and she couldn't blame him. Six children sharing two small beds made for awfully cramped sleeping conditions.

Bob arranged his blankets underneath a tall row of cottonwoods not far from the house. He lay down and gazed up through the leaves at the night sky. *This sure beats sleeping in that durn cabin,* he thought. He almost never went inside it any more except to eat his meals and change his clothes. He loved his family, but he couldn't stand being confined to two small rooms with all those people. And soon there would be one more person sharing the space. Another baby coming, and Annie still with two in diapers. Maxi might not follow the church in other matters, but he sure liked its partiality to large families!

Living in such close quarters, Bob had often heard his parents making love, but he had never associated the sounds coming through the thin cabin walls with the subsequent appearance of a new baby. That is, not until the older ranch hands at the Ryan place educated him. After a summer of bunkhouse tales, Bob knew enough to be embarrassed by the closeness of his parents and was ashamed that his father's need resulted in such a harsh life for his mother. He resolved never to become beholden to such a weakness. If he could control that part of himself, he could stay free forever.

He rolled over and searched for the old hoot owl that lived in the cottonwood. His expert eye soon spotted the dark mass, clinging to one of the highest branches. "Hey, you old owlhoot, you," he whispered. "What's it look like from up there?"

As though answering his question, the owl hooted back, a full-throated, comforting sound. Smiling to himself, the boy gathered his blankets around him and slept.

Chapter Two

Spring of 1880 came none too soon for Bob Parker. The winter had been particularly severe, forcing him into extended periods of confinement with his large family in their tiny cabin. Worse than that, the harsh weather wiped out all but two of their cows, making Maxi's dream of becoming a cattle baron all but unattainable. To top it all off, Annie went into labor in the midst of a March blizzard. Unable to go for the doctor in town, Bob fetched the nearest neighbor woman, but by the time they returned, Annie had already delivered, assisted only by her young children. Sickened and shamed by the bloody mess, Bob turned away, but, when he saw his tiny new sister, he picked her up and cuddled her to his chest. Another burden, perhaps, but what a perfect little doll she was, flaxen-haired and blue-eyed like the rest of the Parkers.

Maxi returned from Frisco in April, in time for Bob's fourteenth birthday. The bad winter and disaster with the cattle had not dampened his enthusiasm for homesteading additional property, so, at the first thaw, he and Bob and Bob's brother, Dan, harnessed their old draft horse and plowed a few acres of the new property. At the end of the long, hard day, Maxi looked back over the freshly furrowed field, put his arms around his sons' shoulders, and said: "Don't it make you feel proud, boys, to work your own land?"

"It ain't ours yet, Pa," said Dan, always a wiseacre.

"It's as good as ours," Maxi explained, "now that we're working it. Five years ain't long to wait . . . then everything will be legal."

"When are we going to get them horses you talked about?" Bob asked.

"One thing at a time, Son. We got to get back on our feet, get in a good crop, and buy some more cattle. Maybe in a couple of years we'll be ready for another horse or two. Till then, old Babe and Cookie are going to have to do us."

Later, Bob thought. *Everything always happens later. Well, I'll be damned if I'm going to be stuck pushing this plow the rest of my life.*

The next day, Bob was out in the yard chopping wood, when Maxi rode back from town, breathless and red-faced.

"What happened, Pa?" Bob said.

Maxi didn't answer. He threw the reins to his oldest son and marched toward the cabin. Just as he reached the door, two year old Eb came toddling out, and Maxi tripped over him, catching himself but causing the child to fall. "Dammit, woman, can't you keep these children out of the way?" he yelled.

Bob stared, amazed to hear his father speak coarsely to his mother. Eb started to cry, more from fear at Maxi's tone of voice than from any real hurt. Annie came bolting out the door. She picked the child up and held him close.

"I'll thank you not to swear in front of these children again, Maximilian Parker!"

"I'll swear if I god damn want to!" he shouted, and kicked at a milk can sitting on the doorstep. Annie slammed the door in his face. He stood there for several minutes, clenching and unclenching his fists, listening to the crying child inside. Finally, he caught Bob's eye, and the boy could see the fight go out of him. With sagging shoulders, he turned and quietly opened the door.

Annie sat in the rocker, holding Eb in her lap. Maxi took him from her. "Poor Eb. Papa's sorry." He walked back and forth, jiggling Eb in his arms until the child quieted.

"What's wrong?" Annie asked.

"Our claim on the new homestead's been jumped," Maxi said.

"How can that be?" Annie said. "I thought you checked it out!"

"I did. Of course, I did! It must be a mistake." Maxi put the baby down and ran his hands through his hair. "The property, our property, is next to John Otto's homestead. Today, I ran into Otto in town, and he asked me what I thought I was doing, plowing up his field."

"His field?" Annie said. "John Otto's too lazy to plow the fields he's got, much less a new one."

"That's what I'm thinking, of course, when he tells me this, but all I say is . . . 'John, that property looked unimproved to me'. Then he tells me that five years ago he filed papers on it and built a shed for storing hay, but that it collapsed under the heavy snow this past winter. Come this June, he says, he'll have homesteaded that property for five years, and it'll be his, fair and square. The liar! I checked and double checked, and there ain't no papers filed on that property. He never looked twice at that land till he saw me plowing it!"

"Did you notify the bishop?" Annie said. The custom in their Mormon community was for the local bishop to settle land disputes.

"Yes, for all the good it'll do me," Maxi said.

"The bishop's a fair man. He'll do what's right."

"I wish I had your faith, Annie. The problem is . . . I hear John Otto's a regular church-goer . . . never misses a Sunday." He looked at Annie sheepishly. "I'm afraid that'll weigh heavily with the bishop."

"That may be true, but there are other virtues, besides

34

regular church attendance, like industriousness and honesty. Not that going to church isn't important"—she frowned at Maxi—"but I just don't think that's the only thing the bishop will consider. The church has an interest in seeing this valley prosper . . . I can't believe it would reward John Otto's slothfulness!"

"I hope you're right."

But two weeks later, despite Maxi's new-found interest in attending church, the bishop awarded the property to John Otto. Maxi was summoned to town to receive the news, and on the way home he picked up a bottle of whiskey. When he didn't show for supper, Annie sent Bob to find him. Bob followed Cookie's tracks to the edge of the creek at the far end of their property where he found his father sprawled over a log, drunk and bitter.

"She sent you to find me, eh?" Maxi drawled. "A man can't ever be by himself around here. Can't think for himself. Always somebody tellin' him what to do. God-damn church doesn't own me!" He took another swig from the bottle. "Never seen your old man drunk before, have you, Leroy? 'Course not, the church don't allow drinkin' or smokin' or cussin'. 'Bout the only thing it does allow is screwin'. Guess I'll have to stop that, too, seein' as how I can barely feed the kids I got."

"Come on, Pa, everyone's waiting for you at home," Bob said, embarrassed by Maxi's rambling.

"Let 'em wait. Sit down here, Leroy. Lemme tell you a few facts of life." When Bob hesitated, Maxi roared: "Sit down!"

Morosely he rambled on. "They tell a man that, if he follows the rules, does what's expected of him, he'll be rewarded in the end. Don't you believe it, Son. Rules are for god-damn' sheep who can't make up their own minds about what to do. Like me."

"Pa, don't say that. You ain't no sheep. You don't follow hardly any church rules."

"I ain't talkin' 'bout those kind of rules, Son. I mean the rules 'bout who decides things in life. Why should some idiot Mormon bishop have the right to take away my land? 'Cause I gave him the right, that's why. I never questioned the church's authority, so now, I guess, I got to live with its decision. They're wrong . . . John Otto's a liar, and everyone knows it . . . but I can't do nothin' 'bout it." He eyed Bob unevenly. " 'Member that, when you grow up, Son. It's better to make your own rules than be a damn' sheep."

Bob plucked at a blade of grass. "Ma says the meek and mild shall inherit the earth."

"Your ma's a good woman, but she don't know much 'bout the ways of the world. Women like all those rules, 'cause they're what keep the men tied to 'em. Aw, hell, Son, don't listen to me. I'm just a sorry drunk." Maxi pitched the empty bottle into the creek.

"What do we do now, Pa?" Bob said.

"Reckon I better not go home in this condition. Tell your Ma I got tied up in town tonight. I'll be back in the mornin'."

"What I mean is . . . how we gonna live?"

Maxi put his arm around Bob's shoulders. "One day at a time, Son. I'll go back to cuttin' ties this winter. We'll have to hire you out somewhere, and, maybe, your mother, too. The Parkers will survive, even if they have to do it by workin' for wages."

"Come on home, Pa," Bob said. "Ma'll be madder at you for staying away all night than for getting drunk."

Maxi looked at Bob, sadness, love, and a touch of envy in his gaze. "Son, you got your whole life ahead of you, and you got the tools to make somethin' out of yourself. You're smart . . . you're good at everything you do. What's more, you got that spark about you, makes people want to be around you and do what you tell 'em. God knows I love you, and I love this valley, but you got to get out of here, Leroy. This place is too small for you. You ain't going to be able to get much of an education, but don't let that hold you back. You're smart enough to learn what you need to on your own. Make me proud of you, Leroy, you hear?" Maxi's head fell back, and he lapsed into a sodden slumber. Bob unsaddled Cookie, propped his father's head on the saddle, and covered him with the saddle blanket. He kept watch over him until he came to a few hours later, then helped him back to their cabin where Annie, silenced by her worry, put Maxi to bed.

Chapter Three

The wild horse crow-hopped around the corral, vainly trying to buck off the foreign saddle attached to its back. Circling the nervous animal, sixteen-year-old Bob Parker followed its every move, alert for signs of tiring. After several minutes the horse stood still, chest heaving, eyes rolling. Slowly Bob approached, speaking softly, letting it become accustomed to his presence. The horse let him get to within a yard, then shied away. Bob stopped in his tracks and resumed his crooning until he sensed the horse relax. Again he approached. This time the horse held its ground. Bob stood close to the animal's neck, not touching it, whispering assurances. Finally the horse's quivering ceased, and it swung its head toward the boy and smelled him. Unmoving, Bob let the horse take its time getting used to him, then ever so slowly placed his hand on its neck and stroked gently. The horse did not flinch. The boy stroked and talked for fifteen more minutes, then slowly unbuckled the saddle and slid it off. As he turned to throw it over the corral rail, he saw for the first time the man leaning on the fence, watching him.

"Ain't you going to try to get aboard?" the man said.

Bob eyed the man warily. "Not yet. Just letting him get used to the saddle today."

"He looked all tuckered out. If it had been me, I'd have tried to mount him."

"Been my experience it don't pay to move too fast breaking a horse. It's best to give them plenty of time to get used to the whole idea of being rode." Bob slipped off the rope from around the horse's neck, and watched the beautiful animal dance away.

Chuckling, the man swung open the corral gate for Bob. "Your experience, eh? Just how much experience you got, young fella?"

Bob bristled. "This is my second season here at the Marshall Ranch, if that's what you mean, but I been around horses all my life. I know one end from the other." He hauled the saddle off the rail and started toward the horse barn.

"Ain't no doubt about that," said the man. Bob turned back to look at him. He was still smiling, but he didn't seem to be making fun of him. "Fact is, I never seen a wild horse gentle so fast. You got some mighty fine horse sense."

"Thanks." Bob examined the amiable stranger more closely. He was shorter than Bob, who at sixteen was five foot nine inches and still growing. He appeared to be in his mid-thirties, although his road-weary face with its several days' growth of beard may have made him look older than he really was. His smile looked genuine enough, but there was something about the look in his small, dark eyes that made Bob uneasy. He turned again toward the barn.

"You mind telling me who I'd talk to about a job around here?"

Once again Bob paused and considered this shifty-looking, little man. He'd bet a month's wages that Jim Marshall would never hire him. Bob nodded his head in the direction of the big house. "Mister Marshall ought to be showing up for supper soon. Talk to him."

"Much obliged, son. You got a name?" the man said, extending his hand.

Annoyed at being called son, Bob hesitated to introduce himself, but good manners won out, and he shifted the weight of the saddle onto his hip and shook hands. "Bob Parker."

"Mike Cassidy," the man said. "Pleased to meet you, Bob. Well, I'll let you get on about your business. Maybe I'll see you in the chow line." He touched two fingers to the brim of his hat and sauntered away.

Bob watched him go, thinking that Mike Cassidy seemed friendly enough despite his shifty eyes. He shrugged and carried his load to the barn.

Ordinarily Bob ate his meals in the messhouse with the other ranch hands, but tonight he had told his mother he would eat with her in her small cabin. As Maxi had predicted, losing their second homestead had necessitated as many family members as possible hiring out. Maxi, therefore, continued to work in Frisco during the winter months, while Annie got a job managing the dairy at Jim Marshall's ranch, twelve miles south of the Parker homestead. During the summers, she lived at the ranch with her younger children, while the older ones stayed at home to help Maxi with the farm. Bob was hired by Jim Marshall, too, but he slept in the bunkhouse with the rest of the hands. Annie was not pleased with the arrangement—she would have preferred to have Bob living with her so she could prevent him from being influenced by the older, more worldly men—but Bob would have none of it, and, once again, Annie gave in to her oldest son.

This evening, as Annie prepared supper, Bob rolled around on the floor with his younger brothers Eb and William, letting them pin him down in a pretend wrestling match. The little boys screamed with delight at their big brother's antics. Annie made no attempt to quiet them. These moments of family togetherness were precious to her because she knew the time was coming when Bob would leave Circle Valley. When, or under what circumstances, she did not know, but every day she saw signs of his increasing desire for independence. Her son had grown into a skilled ranch hand, yet because of his youth the other cowboys often tried to order him around or assign him the least desirable chores. He chafed under this treatment, and Annie was afraid the day of his rebellion was not far off. *He's like one of them wild horses he loves so much,* she thought. *Only maybe he'll never be broken.* Part of her, she had to admit, wanted her talented, free-spirited son to escape the confines of their small valley. But they needed him—she needed him. Not just for the wages he earned, but for his cheeriness and optimism that seemed to lift the heavy load from her shoulders. He was the family catalyst, and she feared what would happen to them all when he left.

"Sit yourselves down, kids," Annie said, placing plates on the table. The newest Parker, born the previous winter, started squalling in its crib. "Oh, Lord," sighed Annie. "Why does that baby always decide to wake up right at suppertime?"

"I'll tend to her, Ma," Bob said. "You go ahead and eat."

"Thank you, Son, but I don't think you got what it takes to quiet her down." Annie unbuttoned the front of her dress and settled in the rocker with the baby. "Tell me about your day."

"Ain't much to tell. Andy had me out cutting hay, but I quit early so I could work with that new horse. He's a beauty, Ma. I think I got him used to the saddle finally."

"Now, Bob," Annie said—at his insistence, she no longer called him Leroy—"don't you go disobeying Mister Marshall's foreman. If he says to cut hay, you cut hay!"

"I've done more'n my share of hay-cutting around here," said Bob testily. "Anyway, he won't get mad, when he sees how good that horse is coming along."

"I wouldn't be so sure, Son. People don't like to be crossed, no matter if the outcome's good or not. You'd do well to follow orders and stay out of trouble." She set the baby on her shoulder and vigorously patted its back.

"Ran into a new fella out by the corral this afternoon," Bob said, wisely changing the subject. "Said he needed a job, so I sent him up to Mister Marshall."

"He from around here?" Annie asked.

"Didn't say, but I doubt it. I'd never heard his name, and he looked like he'd rode a far piece to get here. Kinda scruffy-looking but a nice enough fella."

"Well, he may get a meal or two, but I'm sure Mister Marshall won't hire him. We've got plenty of hands around here," Annie said dismissively. She placed the satisfied baby in its crib and came to the table. "Listen, Son, I need some help tomorrow out in the dairy barn. That roof's been leaking something awful, and it's got to be patched. I spoke to Andy today and asked if he could spare you to work on it tomorrow, and he said that'd be fine."

Bob threw his fork onto his plate and glared at his mother. "You could have checked with me first! I was planning on working with that new horse all day tomorrow."

"Don't you get all high and mighty with me, Son. That horse ain't in no hurry to get broke, and I am in a hurry to get that roof fixed."

"Well, why do I have to do it? I ain't the only hand around here."

"Pardon me, if I thought you might enjoy helping out your mother," Annie said, tears coming to her eyes.

"Oh, Ma," Bob sighed. He hated to see her cry, which she seemed to do more and more frequently these days. " 'Course, I'll help you. Just next time ask me first, OK?"

"Certainly, Son," she said, composed again. They finished their supper in exaggerated politeness, and Bob left for the bunkhouse. She watched out the window as her fair-haired boy, soon to be a man, headed to the barn for a final check on the horses. Her heart ached, although she couldn't say exactly why.

The next morning Bob was eating breakfast in the messhouse, sullenly anticipating his day, when Mike Cassidy slid in across from him. " 'Morning, Bob. Didn't see you in the bunkhouse last night." Smiling, he shoved a biscuit in his mouth, crumbs dropping down his shirt front. Freshly shaved, he looked a little more presentable, although his clothes were still dusty from the road.

"I slept outside," Bob said, in no mood for conversation.

"There's a boy after my own heart," Cassidy said. "Nothing like sleeping outdoors on a fine summer night. 'Course, when you been on the road as long as I have, a bed and a mattress look pretty damn' good!"

"Where you come from, Cassidy?" asked Pinky Gibbs, one of the older hands.

"Oh, here and there . . . no place in particular. Like the looks of this country, though. Might stay for a while, now that Marshall's hired me. How 'bout you, Bob . . . you from around here?"

"My folks got a homestead just north of here," Bob said, pushing food around his plate.

"His Ma runs the dairy operation right here," put in Pinky. "She and a passel of young 'uns live in their own cabin up by the big house. 'Course, Bob, he's too much of a man to stay with his momma." The veteran cowboy elbowed Bob good-naturedly.

"Shut up, Pinky," Bob said.

"Whoo-ee, ain't we touchy today," Pinky sniggered.

Bob started to give Pinky a piece of his mind, but just then Andy Barnes, the ranch foreman, stepped into the messhouse. "Listen up, boys," he commanded, and read out their assignments for the day. Bob's name was the last on his list, and, when he assigned the boy to do repairs on the dairy barn, a few of the men chuckled. Red-faced, Bob picked up his plate and threw it in the slop bucket. He was almost out the door, when Mike Cassidy spoke up.

"Say, Barnes," he said, "if it's all the same to you, I'll work on the dairy barn today." The room was suddenly silent as all eyes stared at Cassidy. No one ever disputed the foreman's orders, and it was inconceivable that a cowboy would ask to do roof repairs. Unruffled, Cassidy rose from the table as though the matter were settled.

"Forget it, Cassidy. You're riding fence today," Barnes replied gruffly. He turned to leave.

"Not today, I ain't," said Cassidy calmly. "Today I'm working on the dairy barn. This boy here," he clapped Bob on the shoulder, "he's got a horse needs breaking. Yes, sir, I watched him working at it yesterday, and he's this close to having himself one fine saddle horse. Or should I say Mister Marshall's close to having a fine horse. Which I'm sure he would appreciate a lot more than having some roof patched. But he can have both, don't you see, 'cause I'm a master roof patcher." Cassidy grinned insolently at Barnes. Bob stared, too stunned to speak. What had got into this strange little man to stick up for him like this?

Barnes started to say something, then clamped his mouth shut. He looked around at the other men uncertainly. Through clenched teeth he said: "If you want to work on a hot roof all day, it's fine by me. But Parker ain't going to waste all day on that horse. Finish with the horse by noon, Parker, then go help Cassidy with the roof." He stomped out, slamming the door behind him. The men all started talking at once, but Cassidy merely winked at Bob and left to do his chores.

Walking with Pinky toward the corral, Bob said: "What do you suppose that was all about? I never seen Andy let one of the men talk to him like that."

Pinky spat in the dust and looked off toward the dairy barn. "Don't rightly know, but I've got some suspicions about that Cassidy fella. Seems a little rough around the edges, if you know what I mean."

"You think he's a hardcase?" Bob asked. Pinky shrugged. "Why would Mister Marshall hire someone like that?"

"Guess he figures if he gives him a job, maybe he won't be rustling his cattle. Most ranchers got to protect themselves like that now and then."

Bob pondered that for a while but soon lost himself in his work with the beautiful wild horse. Knowing that the animal did not belong to him, he had tried not to name it. Eventually someone in the Marshall family would give it a name, and the horse would have to learn to respond to it. But he talked to the animal so much that he couldn't keep calling it just "Horse" or "Boy." He found himself thinking of it as Blaze for the distinctive white markings on its face. *So Blaze you are and always will be to me,* he thought, *no matter what they finally name you.* By noon Blaze was letting him fit the hackamore in his mouth.

After dinner Bob itched to return to the corral, certain that Blaze was just about ready to be mounted, but he figured he'd better not press his luck with Barnes. Reluctantly he made his way to the dairy barn where Mike Cassidy was pounding shingles.

"Howdy," he called down. "Glad to see you. Your ma

makes a hell of a good meal, boy."

"So she fed you, eh? I wondered why you wasn't in the messhouse. Thought maybe you decided to high-tail it so you wouldn't have to work on the roof."

"Can't hardly complain about that, seeing as I asked to do it now, can I?"

"Why did you ask to do it?" Bob asked, cocking his head and squinting up into the sun.

Cassidy finished pounding a nail before he answered. "You've got quite a way with the horses, Bob . . . anybody can see that. Barnes is a fool to have you doing silly-assed chores, when you should be down in the corral or riding the range. Why, the way you handle a horse, I bet you can round up more cattle than any man here. Don't matter how old you are, if you can do a man's work. I just figured Barnes needed that brought to his attention." Cassidy grinned down at him, and Bob couldn't help but grin back. For whatever reason, this shady character had taken a liking to him, and Bob could see no reason to spurn his friendship. Unlike the other men, Cassidy recognized his talents and treated him as an equal. So what if Pinky suspected him of being a rustler—that wasn't the worse thing in the world to be. Bob knew that plenty of the big ranchers tried to force out their smaller counterparts by grabbing their strays and branding them with their own mark. So was it really a crime if someone rustled a few head from the big ranchers?

"Grab a hammer and climb on up here. Let's see if we can't finish this damn' roof today, so's we can do a man's work tomorrow!" Cassidy said. Bob joined him on the roof, as happy as he'd been since he started working at the ranch.

Late that afternoon, the patching job completed, they wandered over to the corral so Bob could demonstrate the progress he had made with Blaze. To his surprise, Cassidy offered him a few good tips on handling the horse. Bob prided himself on his horsemanship, but he had to admit Cassidy knew a thing or two that he didn't. Too, the cowboy had a way of offering advice that made it easy to accept. Bob went to bed that night determined to learn everything he could from his new friend.

In the following days it seemed as though Bob and Cassidy were assigned to work together more often than not. Whether by coincidence or because Cassidy had suggested to Andy Barnes his preference for working with the boy, Bob did not know, nor did he care. He was too busy reveling in the attention of this man who was rapidly becoming his mentor.

One day in late July they were riding the range together. Someone had spotted a few stray cattle in a small cañon west of the ranch, so Barnes had sent the two of them to round them up. They had ridden all day with no sign of the strays, so they decided to make an early camp and continue looking in the morning. It was still full light as they finished their supper of beans and biscuits.

Cassidy pulled out paper and tobacco and rolled a cigarette. "Want one?" he asked, offering it to the boy. Bob had sneaked a few of his father's cigarettes but had never really learned to enjoy them, partly because of his mother's lectures on the evils of smoking. But it looked harmless enough, and, besides, if both Maxi and Cassidy did it, why shouldn't he? He took the cigarette and lit it from a stick pulled from the fire. He inhaled the smoke and willed himself not to cough. By the third or fourth puff, a pleasant buzz started oozing through his brain. He settled back against his saddle, enjoying himself immensely.

"Ever done any shooting?" Cassidy asked, blowing out a smoke ring.

"Sure. I started hunting with Pa when I was just a kid . . . maybe eight years old."

"Nah, I don't mean hunting with a rifle. I mean shooting with one of these." Cassidy reached into his saddle holster and pulled out a Colt .45 revolver.

"Can't say as I have," Bob admitted. "Pa's got a Thirty-One caliber for shooting snakes and such, but I ain't never used it much."

"Well, we better fix that, pardner. Any man riding range with me ought to have himself one of these and know how to use it, too." Cassidy dumped the remains of his coffee in the fire and set his tin cup on a rock about ten yards away. "See if you can hit it," he said, handing the gun to Bob.

Bob checked the gun's chamber and saw that it was fully loaded with six cartridges. Nervously he pointed the heavy gun with his right hand and fired. The bullet missed. He aimed again, fired, and missed. Four more times he pulled the trigger—four more misses. He lowered the gun and stared in disbelief at the cup still sitting undisturbed on the rock.

"Ain't as easy as it looks, is it?" Cassidy said matter-of-factly. "What do you think you're doing wrong?"

"I don't know. Seems like I'm aiming right at that durn cup. I don't see how I could have missed it."

Cassidy took the gun and reloaded, then handed it back. "Don't aim right at the target. Aim a little below it 'cause the gun's naturally going to come up a tad when you fire. Also, don't stand there with your arm straight out and your elbow locked. Relax a little. That's right. Now stop squinting at the target. Look down the barrel and focus on the sight. There you go. Try it now."

Bob pulled the trigger, and the cup leaped off the rock. He let out a whoop, and Cassidy clapped him on the back.

"Damn, boy, you're one fast learner!"

They practiced until it got too dark to see the target. Cassidy promised him that tomorrow he could strap on a belt and practice drawing from a holster. Bob's hand ached from the weight and kick of the gun, yet the power of the weapon and the thrill of hitting the target left him feeling exhilarated. They rolled out their bedrolls, but Bob was too excited to sleep.

"Mike?" he threw out into the darkness.

"Yeah?"

"That was pretty good shooting, huh?"

"Damn' good shooting."

"Ever seen anybody learn any faster?"

"Don't believe so, kid. 'Specially not using such a small target. I mean, hell, anybody can hit a man at ten yards away, but it takes talent to hit a cup." Cassidy laughed softly, the sound fading away into the dark.

A chill went through Bob. All of a sudden he was aware of all the night sounds around him—the soft breeze rustling the sagebrush, the quiet movement of the horses hobbled nearby, a coyote howling somewhere far away.

Minutes passed before he asked: "Have you ever shot a man?"

Cassidy took his time answering. When he did, Bob had to strain to hear him. "It's a rough country out here, boy. A man's got to look out for himself. Gotta look out for his partner, too. Now if you was in some kind of danger, I wouldn't hesitate to shoot at whatever was threatening you. You'd do the same for me, wouldn't you?"

" 'Course, I would," Bob said.

"You and me is going to stick together, kid," Cassidy said. "You know, I'm going to give you that Forty-Five. Man's gonna live out here, he's got to have himself a decent gun."

Bob stared up at the sky, remembering the way the gun had felt in his hand—solid, smooth, cold, and comforting. "Thanks, Mike," he said. "I'll learn to be the best damn' shot you ever saw."

"I don't doubt it, kid," Cassidy said. "I don't doubt it."

Chapter Four

Two years passed, bringing little change to Circle Valley. The sun rose over the sage-covered hills, the wind blew through the long prairie grass, and Annie Parker birthed yet another baby. Maxi struggled to support his large brood—were it not for the wages brought in by himself and Annie and the older boys, they would not have survived.

Bob worked at the Marshall Ranch for all but a couple of months in the dead of winter. No longer a boy, he was treated by Andy Barnes and the other men as their equal and even deferred to on matters of horse care and training. Jim Marshall had overheard him calling the beautiful wild horse Blaze and agreed that the name seemed to fit; Bob and Blaze were a common sight, more often together than apart, throughout the valley. Many of the local girls took note of the blond, blue-eyed, square-jawed young man atop the high-spirited mount with the distinctive facial markings, but Bob kept aloof from female entanglements. Not that he was a recluse—far from it. A skilled dancer and harmonica player, Bob enjoyed the local barn dances as much as the next fellow. Yet, there was always some part of himself that he reserved in these social encounters. He was determined to remain free from any personal responsibilities that might keep him bound to Circle Valley.

Besides, although he liked female companionship well enough, it didn't hold a candle to the good times he shared with his friend Mike Cassidy. Cassidy worked intermittently at the Marshall Ranch throughout 1883, and showed up again for spring branding in 1884. Much to Annie Parker's consternation, he undertook to educate her oldest son in the ways of life on the range. She cried, argued, and pleaded with Bob to disassociate himself from this "bad apple," and prevailed upon Maxi to do the same, but Bob shrugged off their concern, pointing out that they had no firm proof of any illegal activity by his friend.

"Some things are so obvious a body don't need proof," grumbled Annie.

"Nothing's obvious to me, Ma," Bob said. "Mike's a loner and a bit of a drifter, I'll grant you that, but I never seen him do anything I wouldn't do with a clear conscience."

"Something just isn't right about the whole situation. How is it he was able to waltz right in here and get a job, and start bossing Andy around to boot? 'Cause Mister Marshall was afraid of what would happen if he didn't hire him, that's why. And how come he's taken such a shine to you . . . giving you an expensive gun and teaching you how to shoot? He came here looking for the greenest hand he could find so he could take advantage!"

"He ain't taken advantage of me," Bob said, trying to remain calm.

"Not yet, maybe. Give it time," Annie said sourly, rubbing her belly that swelled with yet another baby, soon due.

Summer came to Circle Valley in fits and starts. One day proclaimed itself with a glorious warmth that could make a body forget the storms of winter; the next arrived with a persistent wind that blew dust in one's face and loneliness in one's heart. Grateful to be busy after a winter of relative inactivity, the cowboys at the Marshall Ranch worked long hours, rounding up and branding the calves born in March and April.

Branding was hot, tiring, filthy work, but to Bob it was an excuse to demonstrate his superior horsemanship and dexterity with a rope. He and Mike Cassidy were responsible for cutting the unbranded calves from the herd, roping them, and dragging them to the fire. With single-minded concentration, Bob would maneuver his mount through the herd, signaling directions with his knees, his left hand holding the reins, while his right hand threw the loop around the unsuspecting calf's neck. It took skill and timing, and Bob rapidly became a master of both. He and Blaze, that he had trained to be a fine cutting horse, worked together as a perfectly tuned unit; often Bob experienced a thrill almost sensual in nature when Blaze responded in a split second to his command or even anticipated their next move. Man and horse were poetry in motion, and Bob often found himself so totally caught up in the cadence and rhythm of his work that he was unaware of the passage of time. The work on the ground—the branding with a hot iron, cutting off the testicles, and marking the ear—was smelly and bloody, but Bob and Cassidy, perched atop their mounts, rose above it all, temporary kings in the hierarchy of ranch work.

During a break one day the two of them strolled to the chuck wagon for a cup of the hideous brew the cook called coffee. It was one of those cloudy, blustery days that reminded the men that spring was a fleeting notion in the high country, a mere pause between the harshness of winter and the silkiness of summer. Bob shielded his cup with his hand to keep the wind-driven dust devils from dirtying his coffee.

"I've lived my whole god-damn' life out here, and I still ain't used to this fucking wind," growled Cassidy.

Bob glanced at him over the rim of his cup. Cassidy

wasn't usually much of a complainer. "It'll die down by to-morrow," Bob said. "To tell the truth, I'd be mighty hot doing this work without a breeze to cool me down."

"You beat everything, kid," Cassidy said, making a face as he tossed the contents of his cup on the ground. "Every-thing's just fine and dandy as far as you're concerned, ain't it? You going to spend the rest of your life busting your butt to put somebody else's brand on these god-damn' doggies?"

"What do you mean, Mike?" Bob asked.

"How much is Marshall paying you, son . . . thirty-five dollars a month? Hell, one of these steers is going to sell for maybe twice that. You're getting used, boy. We all are."

"I don't see it like that," Bob said.

"No? Well, maybe you should, kid, less'n you want to wind up like Manny over there, dishing up beans and pouring java in your old age." Cassidy nodded toward Manny, the cook, who, indeed, was stirring a pot of beans in preparation for dinner.

"What's got into you, Mike? I thought you liked working for Mister Marshall."

"Oh, I just lo-o-ove working for Mister Marshall. Why, I thank Mister Marshall in my prayers every night for his kindness and generosity."

Cassidy had never used this mocking tone with Bob be-fore. The boy glanced at him sideways, uncertain what it meant.

"Grow up, kid. It's every man for himself out here. You think all those calves we been branding actually belong to Marshall? Hell, no. Barnes and some of the others been out rustling mavericks."

"How do you know that?"

"Jesus, Bob, it's obvious to anyone with eyes and a brain. You'd see it, too, if you wasn't so busy humping that horse of yours. Not that it is yours, of course. Nothing belongs to you or me or any of the boys. It's all Marshall's, or at least it will be, if we don't do something about it."

"Like what?" Bob asked, although he wasn't certain he wanted to know the answer.

"Like rounding up some of those mavericks for ourselves. Hell, they're fair game as long as they been weaned. I say we get in on some of the action. What about you?" Cassidy fixed him with his beady eyes, and Bob had the feeling this was some kind of test. Cassidy was right; there was no law against fixing your own brand on a calf of unknown origin. But Bob knew it was a tricky business finding a calf that was weaned but not yet claimed by the mother cow's owner. There was a fine line between mavericking and rustling—one that Bob had a feeling Mike Cassidy wouldn't mind crossing.

But Mike was also correct that they would never get ahead just working as hired hands. Look at what had happened in his own family—father, mother, and as many children as possible all working for wages, and still they were barely scraping by. Maxi had always dreamed of starting his own cattle herd; maybe his son was the one who could make the dream a reality.

"I think you got something there, Mike," Bob said. "I'm in!"

"Put her there, pardner!" Cassidy cried, and they shook on it.

Spring was over as quickly as it had begun, and summer rushed in to fill the void. The summer of 1884 was one of the most beautiful anyone could remember in Circle Valley. The prairie grass grew tall and lush, columbine and paintbrush colored the hills, even the sagebrush seemed to emit more of its distinctive spicy scent than usual. Bob spent every waking and most sleeping moments outside, sometimes going for days without gracing a doorstep. He and Cassidy rode the range, mostly tending to Jim Marshall's cattle, but occasionally finding a maverick to claim as their own. They used a brand registered to one of the local ranchers, a friend of Cassidy's named Ike McCord. Bob had taken an instant dislike to McCord, a dirty, weasly-looking man with a scraggly, unkempt beard. But Cassidy assured him they would share the profit from their steers, regardless of who owned the brand.

They had been at this new venture for a few weeks, when one day they ran into Ike McCord on the banks of Panguitch Creek. As they rode up, Bob could see that McCord had roped a calf and was heating an iron in a makeshift fire.

"Howdy, boys. Just in time to lend a hand," McCord called. He raised the glowing iron from the fire, and a jolt raced through Bob. McCord was heating a running iron, not his own branding iron. There was only one reason for a man to use the straight, pencil-like running iron—to change an existing brand. Bob shot a quick glance at the calf McCord had roped. Its left flank sported a well-known mark belonging to a rancher west of the mountains, over near Parowan.

Bob looked over at Cassidy, expecting his friend to intervene, but Cassidy was already dismounting, getting ready to assist McCord. Cassidy expertly threw the calf to the ground and tied its front legs and one back leg with his piggin' string. As he held it down, McCord seared the animal's hide with the running iron, changing the bar in the brand to a half box.

McCord stepped back and surveyed his work. "I'm a hell

of an artist, ain't I?" he chuckled.

"A fuckin' Rembrandt!" laughed Cassidy, letting the bawling calf get to its feet.

"That's my second one today, and, let me tell you, it's a hell of a lot easier with two men. Glad you came by." McCord set the hot end of the iron in the creek and kicked out the fire. Bob carefully avoided looking at either of them. "I'm heading back to the home place for some grub. Whyn't you boys come along and fill yourselves up?" McCord said, packing up his equipment.

"Don't mind if I do. Ain't had any home cooking in a spell," said Cassidy, swinging into the saddle. He took off after McCord without a word or a backward glance at Bob.

"I'll be damned. Did you just see what I saw?" Bob whispered to Blaze. The horse's ears perked up, and its body shifted slightly. The young man watched his friends, confirmed rustlers he now knew, ride away. He turned and looked in the opposite direction, toward the plains and the Sunset Cliffs, purplish in the distance. The sun was high in the sky, and he could feel a drop of sweat meander down his back. The close-by sound of Panguitch Creek spilling over its rocks reminded him of the creek at home and Maxi, drunk, feverishly crying: "Make your own rules, son!" Clicking his tongue at Blaze, he straightened in the saddle, swung around, and followed after Mike Cassidy.

The McCord homestead was a sorry-looking place. The house itself, no more than a shanty, leaned precariously to one side. There was only one outbuilding, an all-purpose shed, and the small corral had several broken rails. As they rode up, several ragged-looking children spilled out of the cabin. Bob scrounged in his saddlebag for some hard candy which he passed out to each dirty little hand. It came to him that a stranger approaching the Parker homestead would be met with a similar, if not so poverty-stricken, scene. The thought made him shudder.

He joined Cassidy, and they went around back to wash up.

"You been awful quiet," Cassidy said, looking at him sidewise. "Something eating you?"

Bob wiped his face with his bandanna. "Ain't nothing to say."

"Right." The older man angrily jammed his sweat-stained hat on his head. "Look, kid, don't go getting all high and mighty, thinking you're better'n these folks. Ike's not a bad fella. He's just trying to feed his family."

"What about you, Mike? What's your excuse for rustling?"

Cassidy's eyes narrowed in anger. He moved in until he was right in Bob's face. "I don't need no excuse, kid. I'm just doing the same as everyone else, including the Jim Marshalls of this world. You ask me, them big ranchers are full of shit! They think they can graze their cattle wherever they god-damn please, but let a guy like me or Ike try to raise a few head, and guess who's at the head of the line bitching about us grazing on Public Domain. You fucking well know who. I'm going to rustle every last god-damn' cow I can from those fuckers 'cause, by God, they'd do it to me!"

Bob looked down at the smaller man, puzzled by the outburst. He had never thought much about the equities of cattle ranching, but now that his mentor had spelled it our for him, what he said made sense.

Cassidy backed away. Suddenly grinning, he put his hand on Bob's shoulder. "Hell, kid, I got a little worked up, but you see what I mean, don't you?"

Slowly Bob nodded his head. "Yeah. Yeah, Mike, I see

exactly what you mean." He smiled back, and, laughing, the two of them went in to partake of the McCords' paltry supper table.

A few days later Cassidy told Bob he would be gone for a couple of weeks, herding some cattle and "a horse or two" over into Colorado. The part about the horses worried Bob; rustling cattle was one thing, but horse thievery was another, an entirely more serious offense. But when Cassidy returned, he opened his wallet, took out three hundred dollar bills, and handed them to Bob. "Here you go, pardner. We did pretty good on them horses."

"What's this for? I didn't do nothing to help." Bob held the money gingerly. It was more than he had ever seen at once.

"We're partners, ain't we? I figure the time'll come when you do some trading on your own, and I'd expect you to divvy up with me. Next time I run a herd over to Colorado, you come with me, kid. You ain't seen nothing till you seen one of them mining towns. Yes, sir, kid, that Telluride . . . now that's one hell of an experience. I'm telling you, there's saloons and dance halls and girls and money, lots of money in that town. Time's coming when you and me is going to have to blow out of here and seek greener pastures . . . know what I mean?" He gave Bob a broad wink.

"You just name the day, Mike. I'd give anything to get out of this place," Bob said, eagerly pocketing his money.

Cassidy laughed softly and stared into the distance. "Won't be long now, son."

Annie Parker went back home for the birth of her ninth child in April of 1884. Little Lula was an easy enough baby, and her older sisters provided most of her care, but poor

Annie, who looked ten years older than her thirty-nine years, was completely exhausted from years of continuous childbearing combined with the back-breaking work of running a farm and working the dairy on the side. Her body ravaged from having given so much of itself and getting so little in return, she was forced to stay home, performing only minor chores, rather than return to the Marshall Ranch.

Maxi, as usual, was home for the summer, but, on this particular day in June he had gone to town on an errand. Annie churned butter on her doorstep and kept an eye on the younger children, playing in the yard. Her second oldest, Dan, was out working in the fields that looked, for once, as though they might yield a bumper crop. Annie had been through enough disappointments and disasters to know that the family's fortunes could turn on a dime, but still she hoped and prayed that this summer might be the beginning of some prosperity for the Parkers.

As she worked, little Eb and William played shoot-'em-up, using sticks as pretend guns. The boys' game made her think of the other day when Bob, on a rare visit home, had been showing off his expert marksmanship with that Colt .45 Cassidy had given him. While Dan looked on in awe, Bob rode Blaze at full speed around two trees, shooting at a target as he went. Every shot hit the mark.

Frowning, Annie looked up, her sharp ears catching a distant rumbling sound. Leaving her churn, she walked around the cabin and spotted some riders approaching from the south. They seemed to be kicking up an awful lot of dust. As they got nearer, she could see they were trailing a small herd of cattle. She squinted, trying to recognize the riders—finally, she made out Bob riding Blaze. Annie relaxed. *He must just be coming through with some of Mr. Mar-*

shall's herd, she thought. *But in that case, why is he heading north, instead of south?*

Puzzled, she watched Bob ride up and lean over to open the corral gate, then help the rest of the men—Cassidy and two others she didn't recognize—herd the cattle, maybe thirty in all, into the pen. Bob leaped down from Blaze and ran to the woodpile where he loaded up and headed back to the corral.

"What's going on here?" asked Annie.

"Got some branding to do," replied Bob, not stopping.

"Mister Marshall's cattle?" she called after him.

He didn't answer.

While Bob built a fire, the others sat their mounts, taking a quick breather. Cassidy rolled a cigarette and glanced over at her. "How do, Miz Parker," he drawled.

"I'll thank you not to smoke on this property," Annie said sharply. Cassidy gave her a long look, took a deep puff, and threw the cigarette to the ground. Annie looked closely at the milling cows. All but one or two were already branded, some with marks she knew, others with unfamiliar ones.

Bob removed a branding iron from where it was tucked behind the cinch strap of his saddle and placed it in the fire. Wordlessly, Cassidy untied his lariat and moved his horse into the herd while the two others dismounted to do the work on the ground. As each moved to his assigned spot, it became obvious to Annie that these men had worked a branding together before.

She grabbed Blaze's bridle as Bob mounted up. "Leroy," she cried, forgetting how he hated that name. "Whose cows are these? They're already branded."

Bob looked at her strangely. "Don't worry, Ma, they're our cattle." He touched Blaze's sides with his heels, and the horse moved expertly into the herd.

"Hot iron!" called the man tending the fire. Cassidy's horse dragged a cow over, and the man applied the iron that, as near as Annie could tell, was a simple U shape. When the bawling cow got to its feet, she could see that the new mark had been placed right next to an existing U brand, so that it now looked like a double-U brand.

The men worked without a break—within an hour the job was done. Hot, sweaty, and dirty, they gathered by the water pail for a cool drink.

"I don't know what you boys are up to, but it don't look quite right," Annie said, hands on her hips. None of them except Cassidy met her gaze. "Leroy, who are these men?" She nodded at the two strangers.

"Ike McCord and his cousin, Red," Bob answered. "You know Mike, of course."

"I surely do. Gentlemen, my son says these cows belong to you-all. That right?"

Ike and Red glanced at each other, then down at the ground. Bob seemed to find something of great interest in the branches of an old cottonwood tree. Only Cassidy seemed completely at ease. Smiling, he said: "Yes, ma'am. Bought and paid for. They just needed to be rebranded, ain't that right, boys?"

"That's right," the McCords said, nodding in unison.

Annie turned her gaze on Bob, waiting for him to confirm what Cassidy had told her. Her son gave her that same strange look he had earlier, defensive and a little sad. "Gotta be going, Ma," he mumbled.

"Can't you stay to supper, Son? We ain't seen you for weeks, and your Pa'd hate to miss you."

"Sorry, Ma. We got to get these critters back onto grazing land. Tell Pa . . . ," he hesitated and looked down.

"Tell Pa I'll be back soon."

With that, the men swung onto their mounts and herded the cattle back southwest. Biting her lip, Annie watched them go. Just before he disappeared into the swirling dust, Bob turned in the saddle and waved his hat. Taking a deep breath, Annie reached down for the toddler pulling at her skirts. *I can't worry about this now,* she thought. *I've got too much else to do.*

Two weeks passed with no sight of Bob at the Parker homestead. Then one evening around dusk, he galloped up on Blaze, leaped down, and started tearing at the straps that secured his saddlebag and bedroll. Annie and several of the children ran out of the house.

"Where's Pa?" Bob asked in greeting.

"Over to Beaver, attending to some business," Annie said, nervously clutching her hands in her apron.

"Shit!" Bob whispered.

"Leroy Parker! Kids, go inside," Annie ordered. By the time she had shepherded them all inside, Bob had led Blaze to the horse barn. She followed him there.

"Son, what is it?" she asked, her hand unconsciously splayed over her chest.

Bob slid the saddle off the sweating horse and leaned his head against Blaze's neck briefly before he turned to Annie. "Ma, there's a warrant out for my arrest. I've got to be leaving."

Annie's hand went to her mouth. She stared, uncomprehending, at her tall, strong son. Bob turned back to the horses, laying the saddle blanket over Babe's back.

"You stole those cattle, didn't you?" Her voice came out harsher than she intended.

"No, I didn't," he said, but he couldn't look at her. "It

weren't me. Ike and Red McCord rustled them . . . all I did was help brand them."

"But you knew they were stolen, didn't you?" She grabbed his arm to make him meet her steely gaze.

"Yeah," he said softly, dropping his eyes. "Yeah, I knew." He pulled away and fit the bridle over Babe's head.

"Why is the law after you, instead of the real thieves?"

"Well, see, the thing is . . . ," he paused. "See, I signed a bill of sale for those cattle and gave it to Ike. So it makes it look like I was the owner. But them altered brands didn't fool nobody, so now the real owners think I'm the one who rustled them and then sold them to McCord. It's just a misunderstanding, see, and I was thinking Pa could talk to the marshal and get it straightened out, but Pa ain't here." He lifted the saddle onto Babe and yanked on the cinch.

"Why in the Lord's name did you do a thing like that?" Annie cried, her voice breaking.

"Aw, hell, Ma, I don't know. Mike said. . . ."

"Mike! I knew that Cassidy would have something to do with this."

"It ain't his fault! I can think for myself. I didn't have to do nothing I didn't want to."

"But, Son, that's what I don't understand . . . why did you want to do this?" She grabbed the front of his shirt and held on tightly, knowing somewhere deep within herself that she might never hold her son again. Bob looked at her for one long, penetrating, sweet moment, and then pulled away. When he spoke, his voice was strong and steady.

"Mike's my friend, and he asked me to do it as a favor for him. The McCords have already had a couple of run-ins with the law, and they were afraid the marshal would come down hard on them this time. And Ma, you should see how Ike McCord and his family live. He's got a bunch of sickly looking kids, and they're barely scratching out a living. What would happen to those poor kids, if Ike got thrown in jail?"

"So Cassidy told you to take the fall for them?" Annie said, unmoved.

"He didn't tell me nothing . . . he asked. And I agreed to do it. Hell, I figured Pa could work out a deal with the marshal . . . maybe he still can. But I can't wait around to find out." Bob finished outfitting Babe and started bridling her colt, Cornish.

"Leroy, you don't have to go. Turn yourself in to the marshal, and let your father try to work something out. I'm sure he'll go light on you," Annie pleaded, although she knew it was in vain.

"I do have to go, Ma." Bob hugged her close and smelled her familiar scent of sweet milk. He held her away and looked at her—hair gone gray, dark circles under her eyes. "Even if the law wasn't after me, it's time I went. Mike's been telling me about Colorado, Ma. How there's gold and silver just falling out of the mountains at your feet, and big towns with lots of money. Before long, I'll be sending you and Pa some of that money. Soon as he can get things squared away here, Mike's going to join me in Telluride, and the two of us'll be partners."

Annie slowly shook her head. "You just can't see it, can you, Son? Cassidy's no friend of yours. He's used you to do his dirty work, that's all. He's tempted you with stories of gold and riches and made outlawing sound glamorous, but he's wrong, Son. There's no life worth living, except an honest one!"

Bob dropped his hands from her shoulders and stepped back. "Ma, there's people right here in Circle Valley, supposedly fine, upstanding citizens and leaders of the church, who don't think twice about cheating honest folks like us. I never cheated nobody who didn't have it coming." She started to cry, and he tenderly wiped a tear from her cheek.

"Tell Pa I'm sorry about having to take Babe and Cornish. I'll send money for new horses, when I can." He turned to Blaze and pressed his face against the horse's neck. "I'll miss you, boy. Wish you could go with me." Quickly he turned away and in a choked voice told Annie to see that Dan returned Blaze to Mr. Marshall. Then he was out the barn door, trotting away on Babe, leading the colt, Cornish. This time, he never looked back.

Maxi returned home the next day, and, when Annie told him what had happened, he went immediately to Circleville to talk to Marshal Wiley. He was back soon, tight-lipped and angry.

"That god-damn' Wiley's in on it," he told Annie, pacing the length of the tiny cabin. "He knows god-damn' well the McCords are the real thieves, but he won't go after them, because they're family men. You know what he had the gall to tell me? Told me, if I kept stirring up trouble about this, there'd be a bishop's trial, and we all know how the Parkers fare before the bishop!"

Annie stared at Maxi, her face like stone, something gone dead in her eyes. "Let it go, Maxi. He's not a boy any more, he's a man. He made his own bed, now let him lie in it."

Astonished, Maxi stared back at her, then clomped out the door. Annie went about her chores mechanically. She fed her family supper, put them to bed, and finished some long overdue mending. She slept soundly that night, waking only once at the sound of the old owl hooting down by the creek.

Chapter Five

1886

The mule train inched along a narrow road carved out of the side of the cliff. At the head of the line, Bob Parker held back on the reins, making sure his horse had secure footing before moving on. A half mile behind him was the Smuggler Mine. A few miles ahead, or rather below, lay Telluride. In between, switchbacking its way down the mountain past Bridal Veil Falls, was this treacherous stretch of road that had claimed more than one mule unfortunate enough to slip over the edge and fall to its death. Winter travel was the most dangerous when the path was covered with ice and packed snow, but the trip was precarious at any time of year.

After two years of running the mule trains loaded with ore from the mines to the mill down in the valley, Bob knew every bend and turn in the road by heart. Instinct told him when to slow down, when to let his horse take its lead, when to hug as tightly as possible the side of the cliff. This left his mind free to wander. Primarily he pondered the irony of the fact that for a town so full of money and as free spending as Telluride was, very little of that money seemed to be making its way into his pockets.

The problem wasn't lack of thrift on his part. He did everything he could think of, within reason, to conserve his money. He lived in the miners' boarding house, instead of renting rooms on his own; he didn't gamble or drink much; he stayed away from the cat houses. His only extravagance was Cornish, his horse, that he kept boarded with a rancher downriver. Horses were expensive to keep in this town where hay sold for ninety dollars a ton. Most miners did without, walking everywhere they needed to go. Bob had had to sell Babe shortly after he got here. But he couldn't bring himself to sell Cornish; why he wasn't sure, since he rarely saw the horse. Something in him was afraid the break would be final, if he let go of this last piece of home.

Ordinarily Bob delivered the ore to the stamp mill, then loaded up the mules with fresh supplies for a return trip to the mines. Today, however, the mine foreman told him a return trip was unnecessary, so, once the mules were unpacked and stabled, Bob headed into town.

His first stop was at the mine offices where he picked up his pay. He savored the feel of the thick wad of cash, knowing it would not last long. The lion's share of it would go to pay the board for Cornish that was a couple of months overdue. Ambling down Colorado Avenue's broad wooden sidewalk, he paused in front of the National Saloon, drawn to the sound of the animated crowd within. Resisting temptation, he turned away, deciding he had better take care of his horse's bill while the money was still in his pocket.

Whistling his favorite new tune—"Clementine"—he headed out of town, following the San Miguel River down the valley. Several people passed him in both directions, on horseback and afoot, for this was the only road leading to Telluride. The town sat in a box cañon, surrounded on three sides by nearly impassable mountains. Bob loved almost everything about Telluride—the natural beauty of its setting, its energy and vitality. He didn't even mind six days a week of hard work, although he felt lucky to be a mule train driver rather than one of the miners. He seriously doubted whether he could keep his sanity, if he had to spend ten hours a day underground.

His only regret was that Mike Cassidy had never joined him here. Bob had heard very little from his family since his hasty departure from Utah, but he had had a letter from Annie, telling him that Mike Cassidy had left Circle Valley for parts unknown. For a while, after receiving this news, Bob held out some hope that Cassidy was headed for Telluride, but months passed with no sign of him. Eventually, Bob realized that Cassidy was not going to show up. He was sorry about that, but not bitter. Cassidy had been a friend to him, he was convinced. The scruffy little cowboy had taught him to ride and rope and shoot—things he would never have learned as well, if at all, from poor Maxi. Most of all Cassidy had given him the confidence to leave home— never mind that it was under a cloud of suspicion. Bob shuddered to think what his life would have been like, if he were still living in Circle Valley. He would probably still be working for Mr. Marshall full-time, while lending Maxi a hand with their scrubby little homestead. Granted, he wasn't exactly making a fortune in Telluride, but here, at least, he was his own man, free from the restrictions of family responsibilities.

The Stanley place, a pitiful little cocklebur outfit, came into view. Bob went directly to the shabby cabin without first checking on Cornish. Abner Stanley's daughter answered the door.

"Afternoon, miss," Bob said, removing his hat. "Your pa around? I've come to pay for Cornish's board."

"He ain't here," the girl said, looking shyly at the ground. She appeared to be about sixteen and was plainfaced with limp brown hair that could have used a wash. Nevertheless, Bob grinned at her pleasantly, trying to remember his manners although it had been a while since he had talked to a female who wasn't the sporting type.

"Gosh, miss, I just walked all the way from town, and I'd sure hate to make another trip. Do you think you could give your pa the money for me?"

Her eyes briefly left the ground to look at him, and she blushed. "Yes, I guess so," she said, staring at the floor again.

Bob counted out the bills and held them out to her. When their hands touched slightly, her blush deepened. "That should even my account. Tell your pa it's from Bob Parker," he said. She nodded and quickly retreated back into the cabin.

Chuckling at the girl's shyness, Bob strolled down to the stable. Cornish, his pride and joy, had matured into a beautiful, long-legged animal. He was considering entering him in one of the local horse races, not just to win some money, but for the sheer thrill of flying over the ground on a fast horse. Bob watched the races whenever he had a chance, sometimes betting on them, if he had any extra cash, and he thought Cornish might prove to be a winner.

He circled the horse, talking gently. Cornish looked thin, he thought, and his mane was matted in places. "They taking care of you, boy?" Bob said, stroking his flank. The hay bin was empty. Frowning, he grabbed a pitchfork and filled it up. As Cornish munched hungrily, Bob curried the animal with slow, even strokes. When it had finished eating, he saddled up and rode out.

Halfway back to town, Cornish started favoring his right front foot. Bob hopped down to check it and was shocked to see that there was no shoe on the hoof. He checked the other hoofs and found those shoes to be almost completely worn down. "God damn that Stanley for a chiseler," he said, fiercely angry that someone would mistreat his horse. He resolved to get Cornish reshod, then ride back out to the Stanley place to have it out with the son-of-a-bitch.

He led the horse the rest of the way into town and left him with the blacksmith, who promised to have the job done by the morning. Still doing a slow burn over Cornish's treatment, he wandered down the street, at loose ends. He would have liked to get a drink, but paying for his horse's board and four new shoes had left him dangerously short of money. As it was, he would probably have to borrow from someone to get by until next payday.

"Hey, Bob, why the long face?" said a voice behind him. Bob swung around to see Eli Elder, red-haired and freckle-faced, grinning at him. When Bob told him about his bad luck with Cornish, Eli, an old friend from Utah, offered to buy him a drink. They ducked into the National and ordered whiskey.

"What would our mamas think . . . a couple of good Mormon boys drinking the devil's brew?" asked Eli, downing his drink in one gulp.

"There's a lot of things about this town my ma wouldn't care for, but she sure don't mind the money I send her," Bob said, sipping slowly.

"You still sending money home?"

"A little . . . when I can. Won't be sending any this month," Bob commented ruefully.

"I stopped doing that a long time ago. I knew Ma was tithing most of it to the church, and the last thing I want to do is support them fat sons-of-bitches." Eli was even more estranged from the church than Bob.

On the day of Bob's flight from Circleville, he had ridden northeast to Kingston, where he had stopped at the Elder place to rest Babe. Without going into detail about the reason for his departure, he had told the Elders of his plan to go to Colorado, and Eli had decided on the spot to go with him. Bob had never been sure why Eli had been so anxious to leave Kingston—there was a vague mention of some trouble with a girl—but he had been glad for the company.

The two of them had crossed the remote, desert-like plains of eastern Utah, occasionally becoming lost in the maze of cañons known as Robbers' Roost. *The perfect hideout,* Bob had thought. *Not even God could find a man here.* Doubtful that they were being followed, and sure that no could find them anyway, they had camped by the Dirty Devil River for a few days, exploring the many cañons that were offshoots of the river. Finally, they had moved on, although Bob had been sorry in a way to leave the utter solitude of the place. They had crossed the Grand River at Moab and had ridden southeast to Telluride, marveling at the craggy magnificence of the Uncompaghre Mountains, so raw and forbidding compared to the hills surrounding Circle Valley.

Both of them had been hired immediately by the mine companies, but, since then, their paths had diverged. Eli was captivated by the hustle-bustle bawdiness of Telluride; he seemed to spend all his free time in the gambling halls and saloons, and, when he could afford it, the whore's cribs. Bob could take only so much of the crowded town before he yearned to be out on the open range again. Periodically he would up and leave, hiring on at a ranch somewhere until the need for a more reliable source of income sent him back to the mines.

One day, just after returning from one of these sojourns to Wyoming, Bob, looking weary and bedraggled, ran into his friend outside the Pick and Gad, one of the local sporting houses. Feeling flush, Eli treated Bob to the specialty of the house—a bath and a shave topped off by an hour with one of the girls. Bob did not bother to tell Eli it was his first visit to a whorehouse. The experience was both more and less than he had expected. On the one hand, the marvelous, exploding release into the sweet warmth of a woman's body was like nothing he had ever felt before. Yet, aside from that climactic moment, when the whore wrapped her legs around him and called out—"Yes, yes, honey, do it to Rosie, do it to me."—the whole thing had seemed totally impersonal. Bob had not known what to expect, but he was taken off guard when he entered the whore's room and, without a how d'you do, she flicked the towel from his waist and checked him for disease. Other than the words that were wrenched from her in the heat of passion, she spoke only to tell him to leave the money on the dresser. He left feeling physically satisfied, but sad and lonely.

Bob declined Eli's offer of a second drink. "Damn, you are one straight arrow, brother," Eli said.

"It's easy to be virtuous, when you don't got any money to spend on vice," Bob replied with a grin, and walked back to his boarding house.

The next morning he picked up the newly shod Cornish and rode out of town, intending to confront Stanley about his poor treatment of the horse. The same mousy-looking girl answered his knock, peeking out from behind the barely opened door. Once again, Bob asked for her father. She reddened and stammered: "H-he ain't here."

"Well, miss, mind if I ask where he is?"

Her eyes seemed to cut to the side before resuming their perusal of the floor. "Don't know for sure," she mumbled.

Bob knew something fishy was going on. If he had had them, he would have bet a month's wages that Stanley was hiding behind his daughter's skirts. But he didn't feel he could take advantage of this poor girl by busting in the door. "Miss," he said, as reasonably as he could, "I ain't aiming to cause any trouble. I just need to talk to your pa. When will he be back?"

"He didn't say," she said, never meeting his eye.

Bob clapped his hat on his head and called out: "Listen up, Stanley. No one treats my horse like shit and gets away with it. You can't hide forever behind this pretty, young thing." The girl blushed furiously. Bob gave her his best devil-may-care smile and touched his finger to the brim of his hat. "Pardon my language, miss. Tell your pa I'll be back." He swung onto Cornish and trotted away, exasperated but also pleased with the way he had handled the situation.

Possessed of a rare day off and with no chores he really needed to do, he decided to ride down the valley a few miles to Placerville to check out the horse races. Sure enough, a crowd had gathered for several impromptu races, and, although he decided not to enter Cornish until the horse regained its strength, he spent the rest of the afternoon watching the others run. He even placed a few bets with the little bit of cash he had left and came up a winner.

Late in the afternoon, feeling pretty good after a successful day at the races, he sauntered back to where Cornish was tethered. A large man with a huge, walrus mustache was untying the reins.

"Hold on there, pardner," Bob said. "I don't take kindly to strangers fooling with my horse."

"Are you Robert Parker?" the man said gruffly, still holding Cornish's reins.

"Who's asking?" asked Bob, suddenly wary. Something about this scene seemed eerily familiar.

"Yes or no?" the man demanded.

"Yeah, I'm Bob Parker. Who are you?"

"You're under arrest, Parker," the man said, removing a pair of handcuffs from his belt.

"Says who?" Bob asked, grabbing the reins and putting his boot in the stirrup. But before he could hoist himself up, the man threw a quick punch to his kidneys. Grimacing in pain, he lost his grip on the pommel and fell backwards, his boot caught in the stirrup.

"The law says so, buster. Now I got you for resisting arrest, too. Come on, get up!" The marshal kicked him hard in the ribs. "I ain't got all day."

Slowly Bob extricated his boot and got to his feet, rubbing his sore back. "You got a warrant? What am I charged with?"

"Stealing this here horse." Before Bob could react, the marshal grabbed his arms roughly and slapped on the cuffs.

"What? This horse is mine!" Bob shouted.

"Prove it."

Bob stared at him, aghast. Of course, Cornish was his horse. How could anyone think otherwise? "I brought this horse with me all the way from Utah," was all he could think to say.

"Yeah? Show me the papers," the marshal sneered.

"I don't got no papers. Cornish ain't never been sold, so there ain't no bill of sale or nothing like that. Who says I stole him?"

"Abner Stanley. Get on up there," he pushed Bob toward Cornish.

"Stanley!" Suddenly Bob saw red. "That god-damn' cheat. I paid him good money to board Cornish, and he didn't even bother to feed him proper!"

"Tell it to the judge, boy." The marshal boosted Bob, hands cuffed behind his back, into the saddle, then climbed aboard his own horse, and led Bob to the local lock-up. The next day he was transferred to the jail in Montrose, sixty miles away.

No one believed that Cornish was, and always had been, his horse. Because he had so rarely ridden Cornish around town, there were no witnesses to testify they had seen Bob with the horse, at least none that came forward. Bob gave the marshal Eli Elder's name, but, if the marshal ever talked to Eli, Bob never heard about it. Stanley swore he had not received any of Bob's payments, and his daughter, eyes glued to the floor, backed him up. It was Bob's word against Stanley's, and no one was about to give the young, itinerant mule-train driver the benefit of the doubt.

Trial was set for the first week in January, which was the next time the circuit judge would be in town. That was four long months away, and Bob sweated every day of it. He had been released on bond—he put up his saddle, bridles, and gun as collateral—so at least he didn't have to sit in jail, but not a day went by that he didn't think about skipping town. His fundamental sense of fairness, though, prevented him from leaving. Unlike the trouble in Utah where, he had to admit, his hands had not been totally clean, this time he was completely innocent. It was one thing to high-tail it when the law was justified in looking for you, but he'd be damned if he was going to run when he had done nothing wrong.

In desperation he wrote Maxi, asking him to forward any solid evidence of Cornish's ownership. He heard nothing. Finally, the trial date arrived. It was a bitterly cold day, the sky so sharp and deep blue that it looked like you could cut your teeth on it. The hotel where Bob had stayed the night before did not waste much money on extra coal for its guests' rooms, so he had awakened when it was still dark, joints stiff with cold. Tired and bedraggled, he arrived early at the courthouse and met his attorney, a Mr. Tippitt, whose only recommendation was that he was the cheapest lawyer in town. They had only a few minutes to confer before the judge, an irascible-looking old man with finger tips stained brown from tobacco, called the courtroom to order. As they settled back in their seats, the courtroom door opened, letting in a blast of cold air. In walked Maxi Parker.

Bob's face lit up. He leaned over and whispered the news to his attorney who glanced back at Maxi and nodded. Maxi gave a half-hearted wave to Bob who smiled back broadly.

The prosecutor presented his case, which consisted solely of Abner Stanley's testimony. When it was the defense's turn, Bob took the stand and gave his side of the story. Coached by his lawyer, he did his best to keep to the facts and avoid getting angry, although he couldn't help casting a few dirty looks in the direction of that jackass, Stanley. When Bob finished, Tippitt asked for a recess so he could confer with a surprise witness. The judge coughed thickly and spat into an ashtray. "Who is this witness?"

"The defendant's father, Your Honor," Tippitt replied.

"He ain't going to say anything to hurt your client. Just put him up here. Let's keep this thing moving."

"But Your Honor, I've never spoken to him before," Tippitt argued.

"Well, neither has Davis." The judge gestured toward the prosecutor who was starting to look worried. "So you're even. Come on up here, Mister Parker. Let's get you sworn in."

Maxi recited the oath and sat down, nervously fingering his hat. Tippitt took him through the preliminaries: his name, occupation, family history. Then there was a pause. Not knowing what Maxi had come to say, Tippitt was not sure what to ask next. Leaning forward, the judge broke the silence. "Why are you here, Mister Parker?" he said, fixing the witness with a rheumy-eyed stare.

Maxi glanced at him, then turned his gaze on Bob.

My God, he looks old, thought his son. *Has it only been two years since I last seen him?*

"I'm here to stand up for my son, Robert Leroy Parker," Maxi said, his voice strong and proud. "He's a good boy, though I guess he isn't a boy any more. He was raised to be decent and honorable, and his mother did her best to make him God-fearing." *Don't tell them that part didn't take,* thought Bob.

"I saw with my own eyes the birth of the horse my son's accused of stealing. My mare Babe foaled Cornish in the spring of Eighty-Four in my horse barn in Circleville, Utah. When Bob left to come to Colorado, I gave him Cornish to bring with him." Maxi looked directly at Bob, seeming to send him a message that he would do even this—lie in a court of law—on behalf of his flesh and blood. Bob returned his gaze unflinchingly. Maxi swung around in his chair to face the judge. "I give you my word, sir, that my son owns that horse fair and square."

The judge nodded and looked at the prosecutor. "Any questions?"

"Do you have any proof of your prior ownership, sir?" asked Davis.

"Don't be an ass, Davis," the judge growled. "Mister Parker's obviously a fine man, an upstanding citizen in his community and a leader of his church."

Maxi ducked his head slightly.

"This man's word is good enough for me. Case dismissed!" The judge rapped his gavel, turned to shake Maxi's hand, and left by a back door.

Bob leaped to his feet and enveloped his father in a giant bear hug. "You did it, Pa! You did it!" he cried. "I would've been sunk without you!"

Maxi smiled sadly. "You got lucky. The judge was a fair man, after all. You don't find too many of that kind any more these days," he said, with a pointed glance at Abner Stanley who turned and slunk out of the room. "Where can we go to talk, Son?"

With Maxi's help, Bob settled up with his lawyer. Then they dashed through the cold into the nearest saloon, stomping their feet as they joined the crowd of men trying to warm their bones. They ordered coffee, and Bob asked for news of the family.

"They're well," Maxi said. "Dan's working for Mister Marshall, though the poor boy don't have nearly the way with horses that you do. He tries hard, but he knows he isn't as good at things as you are. All he talks about is coming to Colorado to work with you in the mines. The younger boys are working on the farm with me, and the girls are a help to your ma, but I won't kid you, Son, it's still a hand to mouth existence."

Bob stared into his coffee. "I'll try to send more money now that I don't have this trial hanging over my head any more, Pa. But I'm barely making enough, driving the mule train to pay my own keep. The only time I get a little ahead is when I win at the races."

Maxi snorted. "Your mother wouldn't be pleased to know the money you send is from gambling winnings, but I guess she don't need to know that." He paused and tentatively placed his lined, work-scarred hand over Bob's. "You know, Son, we're grateful for whatever money you send, but what we really want is for you to come home. Your ma hasn't been the same since you left. You know how she favored you, and something's gone out of her with you gone, though she'd never admit to it. And God knows we could use your help on the farm."

Bob pulled his hand away and sat back in his chair. He stared at the steam rising from his cup.

"All right, Son, I know you don't cotton to farming," Maxi sighed. "Truth be told, I never have, either, but I'd still rather be working my own land than calling some other man boss. You must feel the same way, Son. Wouldn't you rather be digging up your own dirt than hauling rocks up and down these mountains?"

"I ain't going to haul rocks no more, Pa. I've had enough of mine work. I'm a cowboy. I want to be out on the range, riding and roping. That's what I do best."

Maxi nodded, his mouth set in a grim line. Finally he said: "You're right, Son. A man should do what he likes best in life, if he can. Maybe the life of a cowboy is your calling. But that don't mean you have to roam around with no place to call home. I know, sure as I'm sitting here, that Jim Marshall would hire you . . . maybe even make you foreman . . . and then you could come see your mother every now and then. She misses you bad. She needs to see you."

"What about the warrant out for my arrest?" Bob asked.

"That's all blown over. Everybody knows that wasn't your fault . . . you just fell in with the wrong crowd."

All of a sudden a hard glint came into Bob's eyes. He cocked his head and dropped his voice a notch. "What if I told you that rustling them cattle was my idea? That I talked Mike and the McCords into going along with me?"

Slowly Maxi took a sip of coffee and swallowed hard. "I wouldn't believe you," he said, but his hand shook as he set down his cup.

Bob sighed, and his expression softened. "Pa, I can't

come back to Circle Valley. I appreciate what you done for me today, and, like I said, I'll try to send money. But I ain't coming back."

Maxi knew he was defeated. "It will kill your mother," he said glumly.

The steely look came back, and Bob leaned forward, speaking almost under his breath. "It's a wonder Ma ain't dead already after ten kids and a life of nothing but slaving away on that damn' farm. And that ain't my fault. You're the one forced her to have all them kids. You're the one who gave up a decent job in Beaver 'cause of some stupid notion you wanted to be a farmer. Well, you may have dragged down Ma, but you ain't going to drag me down, too! I ain't going to be tied down to any two-bit, scrubby dirt farm that's too poor to support a couple of damn' cows much less a dozen people!"

Maxi's face dropped, and a sadness such as Bob had never seen came into his eyes. Instantly Bob regretted speaking so harshly, yet he did not feel he needed to apologize for what he had said. He had spoken the truth, hurtful as that might be. Wearily Maxi put some coins on the table and rose to leave.

"Hold on, Pa," Bob said. Maxi appeared not to have heard. Bob caught up with him outside on the sidewalk. The older man headed toward the livery stable, his head hunched into his shoulders against the cold.

"Pa, wait. I'll ride with you as far as Moab . . . how's about that?"

Maxi stopped abruptly and swung around to face him. "No!" he roared, the word carrying on the thin, brittle air. "You want to be on your own now, that's fine. We want nothing more from you. All I ask is that you not disgrace the Parker name!" They stared at each other for a moment, close enough that their breaths, visible in the cold air, mingled around their heads. Then Maxi turned and hurried down the street.

Too proud to call him back, Bob watched his father go. Stuffing his hands in his pockets, he strode down the boardwalk in the opposite direction, collected his saddle and gun from the town marshal, and retrieved Cornish from the stables. With the last of his money, he bought supplies, then rode north out of town into a wind that bit like a sharp tongue.

Chapter Six

Payday was packing them into the National. The long, mahogany bar was nearly hidden beneath the elbows of the men standing shoulder to shoulder before it. Every table was filled, and a large number of men had no set spot but drifted around the room, watching a card game here, joining a conversation there, pushing through to the bar for a refill.

Payday was sure to bring the miners to the saloon, in their heavy boots and thick coats, their faces pasty white, and their fingers permanently stained black. Feeding off the mine workers was another set of men—the gamblers, confidence men, and pimps—easily identified by their fancy duds and clean, well-manicured fingernails. The third group of patrons was the cowboys with their sunburned, weather-beaten faces and their bandannas, spurs, and high-heeled boots. They kept mostly to themselves, partly out of choice and partly because the scam artists didn't figure them to have as much money to be conned out of.

One cowboy, though, seemed to be drawing quite a crowd. Short and stocky, with a round, open face and ruddy cheeks, he sat at a corner table, greeting people as they wandered over to him and frequently consulting a little, leather-bound ledger book he kept on the table in front of him. Most of his visitors pulled out their wallets and handed over cash, a few gave him I.O.U.s, and a smaller number collected money from him.

Engrossed in his business, the cowboy did not notice the saloon doors swing open, nor did he see the man who entered push his way through the crowd to his table. He didn't look up until several pieces of tack, a pair of chaps, and two sharp-pointed spurs crashed down on the table. Like a cat startling at a loud noise, he leaped to his feet and went for his gun, stopping in mid-draw, when he realized the man in front of him was empty-handed and smiling broadly.

"Whoa, buddy," he said, holstering his six-shooter, "you oughta be more careful where you're tossing your gear. I just about sent you to the bone orchard."

The blond, blue-eyed man chuckled and held out his hand. "It ain't my gear any more. It's yours. Assuming you might be Matt Warner."

"I not only might be, I am," said Warner, shaking his hand. "And who might you be?"

"Roy Parker. That's a name you probably savvy right well, seeing as how I lost big to you today. So big, in fact, I ain't got the cash to settle up with you, but I figure this stuff here plus my saddle ought to cover the debt."

Warner leafed through his ledger book. "Roy Parker, eh? Yeah, there you are. Dog-gone it, buddy, you're right. You went for broke, didn't you? I like your style! Have a seat, pardner. Least I can do is buy you a drink."

Nearly two years had passed since Bob Parker had beaten the horse-stealing rap in Montrose. As he had promised Maxi, he spent that time cowboying throughout the Rocky Mountains, drifting as far north as Miles City, Montana. Now, in the fall of 1888, he had returned to southwestern Colorado, not to work for the mine companies again, but to hire on at one of the area ranches. He came back sporting a new moniker, the name Bob Parker having brought him nothing but bad luck, and, otherwise, unchanged—still handsome, carefree, quick-witted, and with a confident air about him that seemed to make him the center of attention no matter where he went.

"That Betty's a hell of a mare," said Roy. "Never thought she'd beat the Mulcahy colt. Where'd you train her?"

"I got me a little place over in Utah, in the La Sal Mountains," said Warner, his sharp eyes appraising Roy.

"That right? I'm a Utah boy myself, come from Circle Valley over near Beaver."

"Well, hell, buddy, we practically grew up next to each other!" cried Warner. "Ever hear of Levan? That's my hometown. 'Course, you won't find any Warners there, 'cause that ain't my given name. Thought it politic to find me a new one." Matt winked broadly.

Roy grinned at him. "I hear you, friend. Being from that part of the country, I'm going to make a wild guess that you and the Latter-Day Saints have more than a passing acquaintance."

Warner reared back in his chair, laughing. "One of Brigham's babies, you bet! You might say I've lapsed some since my boyhood days, though. What about you, Roy? What brings a good Mormon boy like you to the sinning city of Telluride?"

"Trying to get rich, just like everybody else in this damn' town. Appears I'm headed in the wrong direction, though," said Roy, ruefully eyeing the gear still covering the table.

Matt chuckled and downed his whiskey. "Got a proposition for you, Mormon boy. I been looking for someone to go in with me on my next trip. Right now, it's just me and Johnny, my jockey. We're traveling with Betty and some other race horses, plus extra saddle horses and all our camping gear. It's a load of work for us two *hombres*. I could use a man who knows a thing or two about horses and who ain't going to swindle me, neither. I can tell you ain't one of them cheating, lily-fingered, fancy-pants types," he said, gesturing around the room. "How about it, Parker? Partners?"

"Holy shit, Matt, there's nothing I'd rather do than trail along with you, but you wiped me out . . . I ain't even got a saddle no more!" Roy grinned, knowing Warner had set this up.

Matt laughed. "No partner of mine is going to ride around bareback! Guess I'll just have to loan that outfit back to you."

The rest of that fall and winter they traveled all over southwestern Colorado, matching up Betty in as many races as possible. Confident they had a sure-fire winner, they bet everything but their saddles on each race. Roy had never had so much fun. After each race, they made the rounds of the saloons in town, treating all the locals who had just lost money to them. None of their winnings wound up in the bank, but they didn't care—they were having one hell of a good time.

In December, they made a killing matching Betty against the Cavanaugh stud at Mancos. Shortly after the race, a bout of cold weather set in, so they holed up for a while just outside of town. One afternoon, needing fresh supplies, Roy and Matt went into Mancos, leaving Johnny at the campsite. When they got to town, they split up; Matt went looking for a poker game, while Roy took his shopping list to the general store.

The streets were empty—it was too cold to be outside, if you didn't have to be. There was no snow on the ground, but it felt imminent—the air was heavy, and everything seemed dull and colorless. Roy stepped into the store, breathing deeply into the warmth that surrounded him. He pulled off his heavy gloves and held his hands in front of the stove.

"Be right with you, sir," called the storekeeper, who was with some customers in the back of the room.

"Take your time. Feels good just to warm myself a bit," Roy answered. The sudden heat made him a little sleepy. His mind wandered, first back to that bitterly cold day in Montrose when he had been acquitted and Maxi had left him standing in front of the saloon, then further back to a memory of Annie sitting in front of the fire at home, rocking a baby to sleep on her breast. He shook his head and came back to the present, aware that the voices at the back of the store had changed pitch, becoming not louder but more intense.

"Please, Mister Hicks, I got nothing left to feed my family. I ain't a beggar. I'll pay you back. You got my word."

"I've been taking your word for over a year now, man. It's no good any more," said the storekeeper, slamming shut a worn ledger book. "I'm sorry, but I can't give you any more credit. You owe me more now than you'll ever be able to pay."

Roy heard the sounds of muffled weeping. He edged around the stove to get a better look and saw a pitiful sight—a young couple and their two children in tattered clothing, their feet wrapped in muddy rags. The woman was sobbing into the top of her baby's head; the man had his arm around a little girl with dark circles under her eyes and pale cheeks.

"If not for me, for my children," the man pleaded. "We walked fifteen miles to get here. My daughter won't make it back without something to eat."

"Ain't you got a wagon?" asked Roy, his heart going out to these unfortunate settlers.

The man swung around and looked at him suspiciously. "No," he said, "we sold it six months ago to buy food." The little girl turned her big eyes on Roy. She wavered on her feet, near to collapsing.

She's about the age Lula would be now, he thought. He dipped his hand in a jar of peppermints and handed her one.

"Here you go, darlin'. Pick out some others, when you're done with that." He turned to the storekeeper. "Listen, Hicks, is it? Fix these people up with enough provisions to last the winter. Whatever the lady says they need."

The woman stared at him, too shocked to speak. "Can you pay for all this . . . cash, no credit?" Hicks muttered. Roy opened his wallet, showing the wad of bills inside. Hicks's eyes grew large, and he straightened up. "Yes, sir, whatever the lady wants."

Roy put his hand on the young farmer's back. "Friend, you come with me. We're going to set you up with a wagon and team. Now don't you start crying, too. I don't cotton to tears in a man. Oh, and Hicks, rustle up something for these folks to eat while you're filling their order."

An hour later Roy and his charge, still looking dazed, pulled up to the front of the store in a sturdy wagon. By this time word of Roy's generosity had gotten around, and a small crowd had gathered to eyeball the benevolent stranger with a pocket full of cash. Hicks and several others loaded boxes, crates, and barrels into the back of the wagon. As a final touch, Roy picked out a pair of woolen mittens for the little girl. Her mother, looking quite pretty now that the color was high in her cheeks, smiled shyly and put her hand on his arm.

"Sir, I'd be pleased to know who it is that's doing this kind deed," she murmured.

"It don't matter none, ma'am," he said, suddenly embarrassed.

"It does matter. It matters to God, but, then, He already knows your name." Impulsively she leaned over and kissed him on the cheek. When her husband looked about to do the same, Roy quickly grabbed his hand and shook it.

"Go on now," he said, "best get those kids under some warm blankets." Laughing gaily, they bundled up their children in the back of the wagon and clattered off down the street, waving and shouting thanks until they were out of sight.

As they pulled out, Matt Warner sauntered up. "Who are they?" he asked, squinting after them with bleary eyes.

"Just some folks needed a little help," Roy said, turning to go back to the store for his own order.

"A little help!" cried one of the bystanders. "Why, this man bought them supplies for the entire winter and the horse and wagon to haul them in! More than a little help, I'd say."

Warner grabbed Roy's arm and pulled him to the side. "What the hell you doing, spending our money on some fucking sodbusters? You lost your mind?"

Roy shook him loose. "They was starving, Matt. You'd've done the same thing."

"Like hell I would," Warner growled, wobbling on his feet.

Roy decided to jolly him out of his whiskey-induced irascibility. "Hell, Matt, you don't fool me. You're the biggest do-gooder around, always buying everyone drinks."

"That's different," Warner hissed. "It's one thing to buy drinks for the poor suckers you just beat in a race. Then maybe they won't feel so bad about losing and put up more money next time. But there ain't no percentage in charity giving, you idiot!" Disgusted, Warner placed the flat of his hand on Roy's chest and shoved him hard. Roy fell back a few steps but kept his balance. His fist shot out and caught Warner full on the jaw, cracking his head back. Matt fell in a heap on the frozen dirt. Groaning, he rose to his knees, rubbing his sore chin.

"I ain't some lackey you can push around, partner," said Roy, standing over him. "I suggest you get in here and help with these supplies before you freeze your sorry ass off." He held out his hand to Warner, who glared at him, but finally let himself be helped up.

"Jesus, Parker, what kind of man decks his own partner?" he asked, working his bruised jaw back and forth.

Roy laughed and clapped him on the back. "Hell, it's good for a man to get busted in the chops every now and then. Builds character." Matt grinned in spite of himself, and together they went about their business.

Chapter Seven

The winter of 1888–89 moved on, the days slowly lengthening while spring played hide-and-seek. Roy and Matt were able to get up a few races, but the spreading reputation of their mare, Betty, made it more and more difficult to match her up. Most of their winnings were gone, spent on whiskey and cards as well as the expenses of their operation. Roy didn't care—he was happy living from race to race, feeling flush today and never thinking about tomorrow.

April found them in Cortez, nearly broke, knocking back a few in one of the many saloons. The locals all wanted to hear about their exploits with Betty, but none was foolish enough to offer a challenge. Roy laughed and joked with the men, enjoying the camaraderie whether he ginned up a race or not. Matt worked the room more intently, his sharp eyes sizing up each new arrival for his potential as the next patsy.

The doors swung open, and Matt's round face lit up. "Tom!" he cried. "Dang it, bro, what the hell you doing here?" He bear-hugged the newcomer, a lean-looking cowboy with narrow, deep-set eyes and a thick, dark mustache flecked with gray. "Roy, lookit here! It's my brother-in-law, Tom McCarty. Married my older sister, Teenie, God rest her soul. What brings you to these parts, Tom?"

"Heard you were pirooting around down here, and I decided to check up on you." He threw his arm around Matt's shoulders and turned to Roy. "You must be Parker. Funny, you don't look stupid, but I can't figger out no other explanation for someone hooking up with this trouble-making son-of-a-bitch!"

"He's been tame as a dobbin on my watch," said Roy, pushing his hat back on his head in mock surprise.

McCarty laughed and gave Roy a hearty handshake. The three of them took a table and ordered whiskey. "Yes, sir," McCarty said, wiping his mouth with the back of his hand, "last time I seen this owlhoot here, we'd just given the slip to a bunch of federal officers that chased us some six hundred miles over the border, ain't that right, Matt?"

"Damn right," nodded Warner. "Whatever happened to poor old Josh? That's the fella was riding with us," he explained to Roy. "He caught a bullet, and we had to leave him in Kanab to find a doctor."

"You ain't going to believe this," chuckled Tom. "Josh mended up just dandy and decided to find himself another occupation. Guess he didn't like getting shot at."

"Why were the feds after you?" asked Roy innocently.

"We was raiding cattle over in Mexico, and a border patrol ambushed us. We killed four of them before we got away . . . that's when old Josh got hit. It was a damn' close call," McCarty stated matter-of-factly.

Roy nodded, trying to conceal his dismay. Matt had been involved in the killing of four United States officers? He had had some inkling that his partner occasionally walked on the shady side of the law, but this was different. This was murder. He pushed his hat low on his forehead and swallowed his drink.

"Hear you two been winning a lot lately. Guess the drinks are on you today," Tom said, signaling the bartender for another round.

"We won a shitload of money, but ain't none of it left," laughed Matt. "Easy come, easy go. We can't get any of these plow-chasers to put up a bet no more . . . they all heard about Betty, and they don't want none of it."

"Whyn't you get up a race against an Injun?" suggested McCarty. "They're just dumb enough to do it."

"I don't cotton to racing Injuns much," said Matt. "They can't never pay you when you win."

"They ain't got regular cash, maybe, but they'll give you some of them Injun blankets that are easy enough to sell. Or hell, make them put up their race horse. It'll go for a pretty penny, even if it's one of them damn' paint ponies!"

"Maybe so," mused Matt. "What do you think, pardner?"

Roy looked up from his drink. He was still struggling with the fact that Matt, happy-go-lucky, friendly Matt, had murdered four people. But then it wasn't really murder, if you were acting in self-defense, was it? After all, the feds had just shot their friend. What choice did they have but to shoot back? What was it Mike Cassidy always used to tell him? It's every man for himself out here—the only rules are the ones you make up as you go along.

"I think we ought to race any and all comers, be they red or white or purple polky-dotted!" he declared.

"There's a man with some sense," laughed Tom. "You boys come stay with me. We'll see if we can't win us an Injun pony."

McCarty's cabin was hidden in the nearby foothills. Matt and Roy moved their outfit up and started scouting around Indian country for a match for Betty. It didn't take long to discover that the Utes were accomplished horsemen and avid gamblers. Within a week they had set up a race against an Indian horse named White Face.

The race course was near the Indian village, nestled in a

pretty little cañon west of town. Roy, Tom, and Matt rode out on horseback, and Johnny, their jockey, drove an empty buckboard that they hoped would be filled with Indian blankets and trinkets on their return trip. Betty was tied to the back of the wagon. As they crested the hill overlooking the village, Roy gave a long, low whistle.

"Looks like every last Injun in the territory turned out to watch. Wonder if they know something about White Face we don't."

"You know as well as I do there ain't a horse in three states can beat Betty," scoffed Matt.

"Roy's right, though," said Tom. "I see plenty of Injuns, but nary a white man. Seems like word of this race would've gotten around town enough to bring some lookers."

"Hell, Tom," said Matt, "no respectable white man is going to bet on an Injun pony, and no one'll bet on Betty 'cause they know she's going to win. Why bother to show up for a race, if you can't bet on it?"

"Maybe you're right. Just keep your piece handy in case of trouble," Tom replied, loosening his Winchester in his saddle scabbard.

Their arrival in the village caused quite a stir. Women and children came running for a close look at the white man's famous race mare. Roy entertained the little ones with rope tricks while Tom and Matt made the final arrangements with the village leaders. When all was set, the three of them gathered around Betty while Johnny prepared to mount.

"Ain't nothing dumber than a red-face with a chip on his shoulder," muttered Tom. "These damn' Injuns think they're racing for the honor of the entire Ute nation. They put up every last thing they own, including White Face."

"Hell, one of them wanted to wager his squaw, but I told him she was too ugly to be worth anything," joked Matt.

Roy laughed with the rest of them, then turned serious. "The Utes are a proud people, boys. We got to handle this real careful. Johnny, see if you can't bring in Betty less than a length ahead. We want to avoid trouble, if you get my meaning."

"No problem, boss." Johnny nodded as Roy boosted him in the saddle. He brought Betty around to the starting line, prancing and pawing from the noise and excitement of the crowd lining both sides of the course. The Indian jockey, a boy of about sixteen wearing nothing but a loincloth, led White Face to the line. Even from a distance, Roy could tell that the Indians' horse was no match for Betty. For a pinto, it was a fine piece of horseflesh, but it couldn't compete with Betty's long withers and strong chest. Johnny would have to struggle to keep less than a length ahead.

The starting gun sounded. As instructed, Johnny held Betty back, letting White Face take the lead. With ten yards to go, Roy started to get nervous, but then Johnny crouched low over Betty's neck and let her go. She won by a nose.

There was a stunned silence. Then murmurs of disbelief rippled through the crowd. Johnny quickly walked Betty back to the buckboard, while the others, sensing trouble brewing, started loading up the blankets they had won. The Indian chief and two warriors marched up, their dark faces stony with anger.

"Not good race," announced the chief. "Race again."

"Race again, my ass," Tom snorted. "We beat you fair and square, old-timer. Now back off."

The chief's eyes flashed, and his warriors moved forward threateningly.

Roy stepped up and calmly addressed the crowd. "White man be happy to race again. What else do Indians have to put up?"

The old chief hesitated, well aware the village had just lost everything of value it owned.

Roy looked him in the eye. "I know chief understands honor of keeping his word."

The chief stared at Roy for a long moment, taking the measure of the self-assured white man. Lifting his head proudly, he turned to go. Roy watched him retreat, feeling unaccountably sad, while the others resumed loading their booty. Suddenly one of the young warriors leaped forward and grabbed a pile of blankets right out of McCarty's arms. Startled, McCarty reached for his quirt and began fiercely whipping the Indian, boxing the boy's ears until the blood ran. The furious crowd erupted, surging forward to surround the outsider. In the midst of the screaming women and whooping braves, McCarty finally realized what he was doing. He dropped his quirt and went for his six-shooter. But the gun wasn't in its customary place on his hip. Too late, he remembered he had left it and his rifle holstered to his saddle. He picked up the quirt again as the injured brave dropped into a crouch and circled him, murder in his black eyes. The Indians' screeching cries rent the air, sending shivers up Roy's spine, but they held their place, allowing the embarrassed brave the dignity of fighting to regain his honor.

McCarty, eyes locked on the approaching Indian, sensed movement behind him. Praying for a rescue, he called out in a thin voice: "That you, boys?"

"Right behind you, Tom," came Matt's voice, tense but controlled. Pushing through the crowd, Matt and Roy rode up on either side of Tom, their Winchesters cocked and aimed. "Anybody moves, this Injun here's drawn his last breath," Matt warned, pointing the rifle at Tom's would-be attacker.

"And he'd only be the first one to go," added Roy, staring straight at the old chief.

"Now, we're going to back out of here nice and slow," said Matt. "Tom, find your mount, and, while you're at it, grab that damn' Injun pony."

"My pleasure," grinned Tom, his bravado restored. He yanked his rifle from his scabbard and swung up on his horse, then trotted over to where White Face stood, still breathing heavily from the exertion of the race. A big, fierce-looking buck held the horse's reins. Tom held out his hand, but the man stood like a statue, refusing to turn them over. Slowly Tom raised the rifle in his other hand, cocked it, and pointed it at the man's heart. Their gaze met and held—the Indian's telegraphing murderous hate, Tom's grim but confident for he knew he held the trump card in the form of his trusty Winchester.

Finally the Indian dropped the reins and took a step back, his eyes never leaving Tom's. McCarty leaned over to grab the reins. As he straightened up, he spat, the wad landing in the dust right at the Indian's feet. The big brave stood rock still, his only reaction a narrowing of the eyes.

Laughing, Tom swung his horse around, and, leading White Face, called out: "Let's go, boys. I've had enough of this stinking place!"

Roy and Matt waited long enough for Johnny to get a head start in the buckboard, then put the spurs to their mounts, sending a few warning shots behind them as they high-tailed it back over the hill.

They reached Tom's cabin in the dead of night, put up the horses, and unloaded the wagon. Exhausted, Matt and Tom fell into their bunks, but Roy, too exhilarated to sleep, posted himself at the window, convinced they had not seen the last of the raging Indians.

After a couple of hours Matt woke up and saw Roy still sitting guard. "Relax, pardner," he said, swinging his legs off the bunk. "We ain't going to see no more of them yellow-bellied Injuns."

"I ain't so sure about that," said Roy. He picked up his Winchester and checked its load.

"If they was going to jump us, they'd've done it right then, when they had us cornered. They ain't got the guts to follow us here."

"No? You must know something about Injuns I don't. The ones I know are too proud to let a white man quirt them without fighting back. Or spit at them." Roy shook his head in disgust. "What the hell was McCarty thinking? Is he always so damn' reckless?"

Matt glanced at his brother-in-law, snoring fitfully on his bunk. In sleep, his face aged considerably—the sharp lines became slack, and the gray in his hair stood out. "Yeah, I reckon so. Tom's got a dandy mean streak to him. Sometimes he gets so riled up he don't know what he's doing. Drove my sister into an early grave, he did. But, hell, he's a loyal son-of-a-bitch, and, like it or not, he's family, so we stick together. You can savvy that, can't you?"

Roy turned away from his look-out and took in the scene—Tom noisily sleeping, Johnny curled up in his bedroll in the corner, Matt looking cross and rumpled, the smell of stale sweat and sour breath in the air. For a brief moment the desire to be home, back in Annie's cabin in Circle Valley, swept over him like a strong wave, leaving him feeling disoriented. He sighed and removed his gun belt. "Take over the watch for a while. I got to get some sleep."

He woke at daylight, eyes flying open, instantly alert. Raising up on one elbow, he made out Matt's figure in shadow across the room, slumped in the chair, his chin on his chest. An empty whiskey bottle sat on the floor next to him. *Jesus Christ,* Roy thought, *what am I doing hooked up with a lousy drunk and his crazy brother-in-law?*

He hauled himself out of bed and slammed out the door to relieve himself. Shivering in the cold, half light of dawn, he surveyed the line of trees that rimmed the clearing. He saw nothing unusual, but something didn't feel right. His skin crawled, and it was too damn quiet. Yes, that was it. Where was the morning time chatter of birds and chipmunks?

Casually he buttoned up and shuffled back inside the cabin. "They're here, boys," he announced, kicking Matt's chair and grinning when Matt nearly fell on the floor. "Nice job at look-out, pardner," he added, strapping on his gun belt.

"Shit," muttered Matt, fumbling around behind him. "Where's my fucking rifle?"

Tom and Johnny roused themselves and quickly the four men checked their ammunition and prepared for a fight. Five minutes passed in silence. "You're full of shit, Parker. There ain't no Injuns out there," Tom grumbled, peering out the window.

"You willing to make a little wager on that?"

"Fuck you, Roy, this ain't no game."

"I'm having a hell of a good time, Tom. Why ain't you?"

"Shut up, you two, here they come," whispered Matt, settling his Winchester on the window sill.

Out from the cover of the trees rode about fifteen Indians, their brightly painted faces eerie in the half light. Roy recognized the chief and the two braves Tom had so injudiciously insulted. "Looks like a party, Tom . . . all your buddies showed up."

The Indian chief advanced a few feet ahead of the others and raised his hand. "We no come to fight," he called.

"Come to make deal with white man."

The four men inside the cabin looked at each other in surprise. "Deal, my ass," muttered Tom. "It's a trick."

"Maybe, but I think we better hear them out," said Roy, " 'cause I'm looking at the numbers, and I don't much like our odds."

"Are you crazy? Four white men against fifteen Injuns? It ain't no contest. Hell, I can take out two or three of them before old Geronimo there says 'How'!"

"Shut up, Tom," Matt hissed. "Roy's right. We ain't got nothing to lose by hearing them out."

"Johnny, you stay behind and cover us," instructed Roy, handing the little jockey some extra cartridges.

"G-gosh, Roy," Johnny stammered, staring fearfully at the rifle he held. "I ain't much of a shot with one of these."

"That's OK, just point it out the window and pull the trigger. You're bound to hit something," said Roy, clapping him on the shoulder. "Now, Tom, try and remember we're going out there to parley . . . you don't got to prove your dick's longer than theirs. Not yet, anyway."

"Fuck you, Parker," growled Tom.

With a broad smile, Roy threw open the door and led the way, his hands held out to his sides. "White man ready to talk." He spoke directly to the chief, but out of the corner of his eye he could see the Indian Tom had whipped, casting a murderous look behind him where McCarty stood. The brave's ear looked raw and swollen.

The chief nodded and pulled himself up tall. He regarded the blond, blue-eyed white man down the length of his straight nose. "White man's horse beat Indian pony in fair race. But white man not treat Indian fair." His gaze shifted to Tom who stared back sullenly. "Indians want White Face back."

"What the . . . ?" Matt angrily started forward, but Roy held out his arm to stop him.

"Hold on, now," said Roy. "Indians bet White Face, and white man's horse won the race, fair and square. You said it yourself, Chief."

"We take White Face," the chief stubbornly repeated.

"Over my dead body," yelled Tom, and before anyone could move, he drew his .45 and fired. For a split second everything was still. Then, very slowly, the young brave who had looked at McCarty with hate in his eyes and vengeance in his heart slid off his horse and lay on the ground, blood spurting from a black hole in his chest. Several of the warriors leaped from their mounts and drew their weapons, but, by this time, Roy and Matt had the drop on them. The chief made a sound the likes of which Roy had never heard before, half groan, half keening cry, and held up his hand to forestall further bloodshed. Looking from one to the other, his anguished gaze settled on Roy, whom he took to be the white man's leader.

"Indians cannot fight white man's guns," he stated solemnly, sorrow and resignation etching deep lines in his face.

"Chief very wise to know this. Chief save many lives," Roy said, returning the old man's gaze with as much dignity as he could muster. The chief's expression did not change, but somehow the tension went out of the air—the fight was over, and everybody knew it. Moving slowly and deliberately, the Indians lifted the dead warrior over his horse and disappeared into the trees.

Lowering their guns, they watched the Indians retreat. Roy thought he would punch whoever spoke first. He felt dirty somehow, although he could not fault his own actions. The cabin door creaked open, and Johnny peeked around the corner, still awkwardly gripping the Winchester.

McCarty chuckled, first to himself, then more and more loudly until Matt caught the fever and joined in. Roy stared at them, waiting for their laughter to play out.

"What's the matter with you, Parker?" asked Tom, trying to catch his breath. "You sorry you didn't get to pick one off, too?"

Roy lifted his eyes to the flat buttes that lined the horizon, pondering his next move. Tom was a murderous hothead, no doubt about it, but he was also Matt's brother-in-law, and, for better or worse, Matt seemed determined to stick with him. That meant Roy was wedded to McCarty, too, at least until he was ready to split with Warner. But Tom was a wanderer; Matt had said he'd been known to disappear for months and even years at a stretch. Sooner or later he would take himself off to other parts. Until then, Roy could bide his time. Hoisting his rifle over his shoulder, he grinned sardonically at McCarty. "Better watch that temper, friend. Next time, it might be a fair fight."

Chapter Eight

The young cowboy backed up slowly, one hand holding a bulging flour sack, the other waving a six-shooter from side to side. Pivoting on his heel, he jammed the gun into his holster and whistled for his mount. At his master's signal, the horse approached and stood ready for action—feet braced, head up, ears pricked. In one smooth motion, the cowboy leaped into the saddle without touching the stirrups and spurred the horse into a dead run. Crouched low over his mount's neck, the cowboy let out an excited whoop as they flew over the ground. The road took a sharp turn to the left. The cowboy rounded it at full speed and nearly collided with a man on foot. At the last minute, the man leaped out of the way. Reining in, the cowboy stared at the familiar figure standing in the middle of the road.

"Holy cow, Bob," the man called out. "You like to run me over! There a posse chasing you?"

"Dan!" cried Roy in delight, leaping down from Cornish and hugging his younger brother. "What are you doing here, you little squirt?" He stepped back to take a look and realized the young man in front of him was no squirt. Dan had grown at least eight inches in the five years since Roy had left home and now topped six feet by a good two inches. He was solidly built, too—a regular bear of a man.

"I came to find you, of course," Dan replied, flashing the famous Parker grin. "Weren't easy, either, but I done it."

"You sure did! How'd you track me down?"

"I was up toward Kingston one day, and I ran into Eli

103

Elder's father. He told me he'd had a letter from Eli that mentioned you. Said Eli'd heard you were down around Cortez racing horses. So I went home and told Ma and Pa I was going to come find you. They tried to talk me out of it, but I told them I'd had enough of farm life . . . I want to be where the action is, just like you, Bob!" Dan's broad face lit up with excitement. "Anyway, I got to Cortez and started asking around for you, but no one knew of a Bob Parker. One fella, though, said he thought there was a cowboy name of Parker, living out in the mountains this direction, but he didn't think his first name was Bob. But I rode on out here just in case it was you, and, by dang, here you are!"

"In the flesh!" grinned Roy. "Listen, Dan, people don't know me as Bob around here. Call me Roy, OK?"

Dan shrugged. "OK. Short for Leroy, right? Say, why was you riding hellbent for leather just now? If I hadn't heard you war-whooping and got out of the way, you'd've mashed me flat as a pancake!"

"Just practicing," said Roy offhandedly.

"Practicing for what?"

"Aw hell, I don't know, just for fun. Come on now, I want you to meet my partners."

The brothers returned to McCarty's cabin, Dan catching up Roy on the family news. Nothing much had changed. Two of their sisters had married local boys and moved out, but the rest of them were still scratching out a living on the farm.

"I hope you didn't leave Ma and Pa short-handed by leaving," said Roy. "I know they count on you around there."

"They counted on you, too, but that didn't stop you from leaving," bristled Dan.

"That was different," said Roy sharply. "I had to leave."

"Maybe so, but you could go back now anytime you wanted to without there being no trouble."

Roy gazed into the distance at the peaks of the San Juans, snow-capped even in early June. "I don't know about that," he murmured. "I ain't sure you can ever go home."

They alighted at the cabin, and Roy introduced his brother to Matt and Tom. Johnny was no longer part of their band—they had had to let him go, when they couldn't find any more challengers for Betty. Their match against the Indian pony White Face had been their last.

Matt and Tom enthusiastically welcomed Dan. "Whyn't you tell us you sent for your brother?" asked Tom. "Damn' smart move."

Roy caught Tom's eye and telegraphed a warning. "I didn't send for him. He just showed up."

Matt, who was already halfway through a bottle of whiskey despite the early hour, put a beefy hand on Dan's shoulder. "Can you beat that?" he drawled. "You showed up just in time to help with the biggest job ever pulled in southwestern Colorado! You must be living under a lucky star, kid!"

Confused, Dan looked to his brother. "He's just passing through," Roy said quickly. "He ain't going to be here long enough to get involved."

"Hey, wait a minute," protested Dan. "I aim to stick around for a while, especially if you guys need me to help out."

"We don't need your help," Roy insisted.

"The hell we don't," countered McCarty, fixing Roy with a beady stare. "You know damn' well we're going to need at least two, maybe three extra men for this job. Here's one just dropped into our laps. Why the hell are you trying to get rid of him?"

"Because he's my brother," shouted Roy, clenching his fists. "I don't want him involved."

"Looks to me like he's free, white, and twenty-one. Whyn't you let him make up his own mind," said Matt, pulling a swig from the bottle.

"What are you guys talking about?" asked Dan uncomfortably.

"Tell him, Parker," said Tom.

Roy sighed and raised his eyes to the heavens in a why-me-Lord look. "Come on, Dan, I'll fill you in. Let's go where these two pikers ain't going to be breathing down our necks." Shooting an exasperated look at his partners, he led Dan down to the corral. He often came here to cogitate on a difficult problem, finding it cleared his head to be around horses.

Stepping on the bottom rail and leaning over the top of the fence, the two men watched the animals in the pen, carefully avoiding eye contact. A stranger would have been struck by their similarities—both square-jawed and big-boned—but might have missed their differences. Dan's broad, open face conveyed a certain doggedness coupled with a total lack of guile, while Roy's features, on the surface so like his brother's, gave one the impression of quick-thinking intelligence, humor, and strength.

Dan broke the silence. "So what's up, Roy. What's the big secret?"

"See that filly yonder . . . the sorrel with the long legs? That's Betty, Matt's best race horse. We've won a hell of a lot of money with that horse . . . thousands of dollars. I still can't believe Matt dealt me in on that. He didn't owe me nothing, but he made me a full partner. I owe him a lot." He paused to consider for a moment, then went on. "It's been a great ride . . . I ain't never had so much fun in my life. But it's over. We can't get up a race for Betty no more. Everybody's heard about her, even the Injuns, and ain't nobody going to challenge her again."

"Why don't you go to a different part of the country where they ain't never heard of her?" asked Dan.

"We thought about that. Problem is, it takes money to move around an outfit as big as ours. We got ten, twelve horses to feed, and we'd have to hire our jockey back. We just ain't got the money to do that. Fact is, we're plumb broke. We're living on the last of our winnings right now, and that'll be gone in two, three weeks."

"Broke!" cried Dan in disbelief. "You just told me you made thousands of dollars on that horse. Where'd it all go?"

Roy shrugged. "I wish I knew. One minute we'd be so flush we felt like we owned a gold mine. The next we'd be counting our spare change just to buy a cup of coffee. It just never seemed to last."

They were silent a moment as Dan digested the fact that his brother had let thousands of dollars trickle through his fingers. Finally he asked: "So what's the job your partners are talking about? I get the feeling it ain't exactly on the up and up."

Roy turned on the fence rail and looked at his brother earnestly. "Danny, you don't want to get mixed up in this. If you was smart, you'd ride right back to Circle Valley."

A stubborn expression came over Dan's face. "I ain't going nowhere. I followed you here 'cause I was sick and tired of chasing a plow, day after day, the same old grind. You always got to do the fun stuff . . . cowboying for Mister Marshall and pulling hi-jinx with that Cassidy fella. Now I get out here, just when you're about to do something really big, and you try and send me away. Well, I ain't going!"

Roy saw it was no use. "Have it your way. Here's the deal

. . . we're going to rob the bank in Telluride." He announced it so matter-of-factly that Dan wasn't sure he'd heard right.

"Come again?"

"The San Miguel County bank in Telluride . . . we're going to hold it up."

Dan swallowed hard. "Holy cow, Bob, why?"

Roy shrugged. "We need the money."

Slowly, Dan's look of incredulity turned to excitement. By God, he'd been right—his brother was living a life of adventure, and now he could, too! "Holy cow," he repeated, "how you going to do it?"

Roy smiled to himself. Dan hadn't wasted much time wrestling with the moral question involved. "We've been casing the place. About noon most days, the cashier leaves to run errands or what not. That leaves just one clerk minding the store. We're going to march in there and suggest ever so politely that he hand over the cash. That's about all there is to it."

"How you going to get away?" asked Dan, hanging on every word.

"Well, that's where you come in, that is, if you ain't got the good sense to make tracks right about now." Dan shook his head emphatically, so Roy continued. "You and a couple of other boys are going to stake our relays . . . have fresh horses ready for us at a couple of pre-arranged places."

"Is that all?" Dan sounded disappointed.

"Is that all? That's maybe the most important job. No way in hell we're going to get away without fresh mounts. Everybody's got to do their part for the whole thing to work." Talking about the job made Roy get excited about it, too. Somewhere along the way, he'd gone from trying to dissuade Dan from participating to encouraging his involvement. *What the hell,* he thought. *He's bound and determined to stay, so I might as well let him in on it, long as he steers clear of the really dangerous stuff.*

"Count me in!" Dan cried, pounding Roy's shoulder vigorously. "I can see it now . . . 'Wanted: Dead or Alive, the Parker Brothers, Meanest Sons-of-Bitches West of the Rockies'!"

Roy shook his head and laughed. "The whole idea is to do it without anybody knowing who done it. I don't want my picture on no wanted poster."

"Right, right," Dan agreed. "I can't believe you're going to rob a bank! Ma always said you'd do big things."

Roy rolled his eyes and stepped off the rail. "It ain't done yet, kid. Come on, let's grab some grub, and we'll fill you in on the rest of the plan."

Three weeks later, on June 24, 1889, a trio of duded-up cowboys rode down the main street of Telluride. They were a sight to behold in their colorful shirts, bright bandannas, and shiny spurs. Even their horses' tack was top-notch, the silver-studded bridles and fancy saddles creaking with a brand-new leather sound. Many a passerby took notice of the handsome group, and a few of the bolder young ladies sent inviting looks their way.

"You sure getting all done up like this was a good idea?" muttered McCarty out of the side of his mouth. "Seems like all we're doing is attracting attention to ourselves."

"Relax, pale face," replied Matt, tipping his hat at a particularly pretty girl. "Cowboys always dress up when they go to town. This way we look like just a bunch of cowpunchers here to kick up our heels."

They dismounted in front of a saloon across the street from the bank. Casually Roy surveyed Colorado Avenue from one end to the other. Not surprisingly, it bustled with activity on this weekday morning. Even the saloon hosted a fair-size crowd despite the early hour, as miners who had just gotten off shift sought to chase their fears with a little red-eye. They took a table by the window to keep an eye on the comings and goings at the bank. Roy and Matt appeared to be at ease, laughing, joking, playing a game of two-card monte. Tom tried to act natural, but his eyes kept darting around, and he found it nearly impossible to sit still.

At ten minutes to twelve, a quiet settled over the three of them. "Any time now," Matt whispered.

Roy had never felt so alert in his life. It seemed as though he noticed everything—the ticking of a clock behind the bar, the soft slap of cards hitting the tables, the constant ebb and flow of traffic on the street. His brain expertly processed this jumble of sights and sounds—he felt that at any given second he could assess where he was in the universe in relation to everything around him. He was ready.

The door of the bank opened. A middle-aged, chubby man, wearing a bowler hat and carrying a leather case, emerged. "That's him," Matt said. "That's the cashier." Wordlessly, they rose from the table and sauntered out to their horses for a final confab.

"This is it, boys," said Roy. "Once we do this, there ain't no going back." He locked eyes with Matt, half hoping his partner would get cold feet.

But Matt grinned and winked. "Let's show these city bastards a thing or two!"

Roy nodded once, quickly. Leading his horse across the street, he handed the reins to McCarty. "Now, Tom," Roy said easily, "I know you got a eye for the ladies, but don't you go running off with some purty gal while Matt and me is doing our banking!"

"Shut up, Parker," snapped Tom.

"Well, you seem a bit jumpy is all, which, it occurred to me, might be due to a lack of female companionship, if you get my meaning." Roy lazily checked his saddle rigging. He couldn't explain why it was he loved to bait Tom. He knew it was dangerous, given Tom's explosive nature, but he found the man's nervous intensity annoying.

"Come on, Roy," urged Matt. "Now ain't the time."

Roy shrugged and stepped up to the board sidewalk. "I believe a man ought to enjoy his work, don't you?"

They entered the bank and gave it a quick once-over. Incredibly, there were no other customers, only the clerk sitting behind his cage, reading a newspaper. He looked up and squinted at them from underneath a green eyeshade. "Can I help you?" he squeaked, then cleared his throat, and repeated his offer in a deeper voice. *Christ,* thought Roy, *he's just a kid.*

Matt stepped to the window and handed him a check. "Like to cash that," he mumbled, as Roy sidled over to the wooden rail that separated the cage from the lobby portion of the bank. The near-sighted young clerk bent low over the check to examine it. In a flash, Matt had his gun out of his holster. With his other hand, he grabbed the clerk's hair and smashed his head down on the counter. The young man screamed and moaned in pain. "Keep quiet, kid, and you won't get hurt," warned Matt, putting the barrel of his six-shooter to the clerk's temple.

"What do you mean, he won't get hurt? You already broke his nose," complained Roy, vaulting over the rail and cleaning out the clerk's cash drawer. "That weren't necessary now, was it? Hey, lookit here! The vault's open. That was mighty considerate of you, kid." He ducked into the vault and came out a minute later lugging two bulging

111

sacks. "Jackpot!" he grinned. "Let's go!"

Matt released the clerk who fell to the floor, quivering and crying. The gunman shook his head in disgust. "I got a notion to shoot you for being such a damn' coward!"

"Forget it! We gotta go!" Roy shoved one of the money bags at Matt.

As if they had all the time in the world, they left the bank and strolled to their horses. Tom's eyes widened at the sight of their heavy load. "Christ, boys, we ain't going to be able to carry all this," he said under his breath.

"We'll split it up more evenly when we get out of town," replied Roy, securing the bag to his saddle. Matt did the same, and they swung onto their mounts, and put them into a leisurely pace. They rode like that for two blocks, then, at a signal from Roy, dug their heels into their horses' sides and galloped the rest of the way out of town, whooping and yelling and firing their guns in the air. The townspeople turned to watch, but there was curiously little reaction to the fleeing bandits. Telluride was a jaded town—it had seen almost everything, or at least thought it had.

Roy felt the strength of Cornish beneath him and settled into a rhythm with the galloping horse. "Burn the breeze, boys!" he yelled, his words lost in the rushing wind. They pounded down the road, headed for Keystone Hill where Bert Charter, one of McCarty's recruits, would be waiting with fresh horses.

Just ahead lay a junction in the road, the only one between Telluride and their first relay. So far, their luck had held—the stick-up itself had gone like clockwork, and they had made it out of town with no trouble. But their luck was about to change. Crossing the road in front of them rode two men on horseback, and one of them was well known to both Roy and Matt.

"Hey, boys," the man greeted them as they raced past, faces averted, "what's your hurry?"

They knew they had been recognized.

Meanwhile, in town, the bank cashier, a man by the name of Painter, returned from his errands. His brow furrowed in irritation when he failed to see Shee, the clerk, at his post. *Young people these days,* he thought to himself, *can't be counted on for anything.*

"Shee?" he called out. "Shee!"

A pitiful mewling sound came from the teller's cage. Painter lumbered over the gate and found the clerk curled up on the floor, his hands pressed to his bloody nose.

"My God, Shee, what happened?" Painter cried, holding his handkerchief to the lad's face. Shee took several gasping breaths and moaned softly, unable to answer. Painter looked up and saw the empty cash drawer, hanging open. He stared at it stupidly for a moment, then bent back over the prostrate clerk.

"Shee, listen to me, boy. How long ago did it happen? Who was it? How many were there? You've got to tell me what the hell happened!"

Slowly Shee's eyes focused on the cashier. He mumbled something that Painter could not make out. "I can't hear you, boy," he said, and leaned closer.

"It's gone, all gone," Shee groaned.

Painter sprinted from the bank to sound the alarm.

Roy had nearly gained the summit of Keystone Hill when he realized he would have to stop to redistribute the stolen money. The bag tied to his saddle was so heavy with gold coins that its weight actually threw Cornish off balance. He signaled Matt and Tom and pulled up. Leaping down, he started to transfer the coins and greenbacks to his saddlebags. Matt followed his example, and both of them filled Tom's bags as well. They worked quickly, the only sound that of their own and their horses' ragged breathing.

As they resecured the bags, Matt paused and cocked his head. "I hear something," he warned. They all froze and listened to the unmistakable sound of galloping hoofs.

"Shit!" cried McCarty, as they rapidly mounted and urged their horses up the mountain. The redistributed bags helped matters, but the rocky terrain and steep slope of the hill slowed them down. "How close is the relay?"

"Not close enough," panted Roy, looking over his shoulder. At that moment a lone horseman came into view, enthusiastically putting the spurs to his mount. "How do you like that! They only sent one posseman after us," said Roy, feigning wounded pride.

"I'll learn him some respect," Matt cried, getting off a couple of shots.

The man abruptly reined in his horse, causing the animal to rear and dance around in circles. He looked at the bandits in shocked surprise, then glanced back in the direction he had come. They could tell by his panicked expression that he had not intended to get so far ahead of his fellow possemen. Matt squeezed off another shot, propelling the man out of his saddle. In desperation, the frightened pursuer unbuttoned his fly and pretended to take a leak, although he was literally too scared to piss. Laughing uproariously, Roy, Matt, and Tom scooted over the hill, just as the sound of more men on horseback reached their ears.

Bert was waiting for them at the appointed spot, in a thick growth of trees by the shore of Trout Lake. "They're right behind us," shouted Matt, as they leaped down and began transferring their saddlebags to the fresh mounts.

Bert tied a swatch of mesquite to the tail of one of the used horses. "This windfall oughta spook them," he said, slapping the horse hard on its flank. As the animal jerked forward, the prickly shrub tickled its legs, sending it into a wild frenzy. It careened down the slope, bucking and kicking and throwing the approaching posse into a complete state of disarray. The four outlaws raced off, headed south toward the Mancos Mountains, leaving the confused posse far behind.

The second relay was manned by Bill Madden, a Texan whom they had met tending bar in Mancos, and Dan Parker. Roy had purposely given Dan an assignment at a remote outpost to keep his brother as far removed from trouble as possible. Once again they switched mounts smoothly, although just as Roy was preparing to ride out, he noticed McCarty hanging back, counting money out of his saddlebags. "Holy Christ, Tom, we ain't got time to count it now!"

"I ain't counting it all," Tom replied, taking a handful of bills and wrapping them in his kerchief. He stuffed the bundle into a hollowed-out log by the side of the trail. He built a small cairn of rocks by the log, and then joined the rest of them.

"What the hell you doing?" asked Matt.

"Didn't you fellas wonder why that posse gave up on us so easy?" said Tom. When nobody answered, he went on. " 'Cause weren't nobody in charge, that's why. They was all just a bunch of greenhorns who thought it'd be fun to chase some bad guys, long as they didn't get too close to get shot at. There weren't a real lawman in the bunch. You know how I know that?" Again his partners were too stunned to reply. " 'Cause I just happen to be buddies with Jim Clark, the town marshal, who was tickled pink to be away on official business today."

"How much did it cost you?" asked Roy, surprised at Tom's foresight.

"Ten percent of the take. I figger we got twenty thousand dollars, so I left about two grand in that log."

"Good thinking," said Matt.

It took them two and a half hours to cover the thirty-five miles to Matt's horse camp in the Mancos Mountains. Without fresh horses and lacking any leadership, they figured the posse was far behind, if it was still in pursuit at all. The outlaws planned to hole up for the night and strike out again in the morning.

Matt had asked his old jockey, Johnny, and a couple of other friends to meet him at the camp. He then proceeded to hand over to them his entire horse herd and ranch outfit, no strings attached. When they protested his generosity, he waved them off. "I'd rather you boys had it than the government, and once they find out it's mine, they'll confiscate it for sure. Here, I'll write you out a bill of sale, so they won't think I gave it to you."

Having finished that piece of business, the three ringleaders sat down to divvy up their haul. Tom's estimate turned out to be surprisingly accurate—they had stolen $20,750. Subtracting the $2,000 payoff to Marshal Clark and the small cuts for the three relay men, Roy, Tom, and Matt each netted slightly under six thousand dollars.

Roy and McCarty were satisfied with their take, but Matt just stared at the pile of dough in front of him, shaking his head.

"What's the matter?" asked Tom, taking a swig of whiskey and passing the bottle to his brother-in-law. "Don't you think six grand is decent pay for five minutes' work?"

Matt drank the bottle half down. "I just traded a twenty thousand dollar ranch for six thousand measly bucks. I figured this job would make me rich, but I'm worse off than before."

"Hell, Matt, you've probably had fourteen thousand dollars' worth of fun today, so you're even," said Roy philosophically.

Matt chewed on that for a while as he polished off the whiskey. He tossed the empty bottle into a corner and started to chuckle. "Reckon you're right, Roy. Jesus, can you believe that guy pretending he had to take a piss, so he wouldn't catch up to us!"

Soon, the whole gang was laughing and slapping knees as they recounted the day's exploits.

When dark fell, they rode several miles into the trees and pitched a fireless camp. They mapped out their escape route—over into Utah at the nearest point, and then north to Brown's Hole, that no-man's-land at the intersection of Utah, Colorado, and Wyoming. Roy took Dan aside to tell him he could not go with them in the morning. "No one knows you're mixed up in this, Danny, and I want to keep it that way. If you ride with us, sooner or later, they'll figure out you're part of the gang, and then there'll be a price on your head, too. You can't do that to Ma. There's no going back for me, but you still got a chance. Go home, kid."

Dan argued and then sulked, but finally agreed to let Roy go off on his own, with the promise that he keep in touch so that Dan could join him again someday. Of course, Roy knew that his days as a Parker were numbered. Having committed a serious crime, he would have to disappear for a while, and, when he reëmerged, it would not be as Leroy, Bob, or Roy Parker, but under an assumed name. The likelihood that he would be able to maintain contact with his family was nil. That fact did not make him happy, but he accepted it as the price he had to pay for the kind of life he wanted to lead. He wanted to live out in the open, wild and free, beholden to no man and with no responsibilities to tie him down. It wasn't enough just being a cowboy. When you got right down to it, cowboying was miserable work and boring to boot. Besides, ranch hands were nothing but pawns to the big cattle barons, and those were precisely the men Roy wanted to destroy.

He intended to lay low for a while, work legitimate jobs, maybe use his stake to do some ranching of his own. He would not go looking for trouble, but he would do whatever was necessary to live life on his terms.

He lay on his bedroll and stared heavenward. The tall pines obscured his view of the stars. The night was so dark it was like being in a windowless cell. They had timed the robbery to coincide with the new moon, of course, just in case some ambitious posse tried to track them at night. So far, their planning and preparation had paid off. The only piece of bad luck was getting recognized as they sped out of town. But that one coincidence was enough to make him a wanted man. *Funny,* he thought, *how small twists of fate can change a man's life. The key is to control what you can and hope the rest don't do you in.*

As he drifted off, he thought he heard the mournful cry of a hoot owl, exulting in the perfect darkness of the night.

Chapter Nine

"I'll see you and raise you a hundred."

Roy peered over the top of his cards, trying to determine if Matt was bluffing. Warner's poker face revealed nothing. Tom passed. Roy fanned his cards again—three queens stared back at him. Chances were good his queens would win the pot—Matt had had lousy cards for the entire three days they had been playing. Still, his luck could have changed. But what the hell. Nothing ventured, as the saying went. He laid his cards face down and started unbuttoning his shirt.

"I ain't interested in taking the shirt off your back," joked Matt.

Smiling, Roy pulled the shirt apart and undid the thick money belt secured around his waist. It contained nearly six thousand dollars, his share of the Telluride heist. He winced as he slid the belt off; it had chafed his skin to the point of leaving raw, red sores, but he had not dared to take it off until now. Even though he felt relatively safe in this isolated hide-out on Diamond Mountain in Brown's Hole, one never knew when one would have to made a quick getaway.

He threw the belt on the table. "See you and raise you six thousand dollars," he said, staring steadily at Matt.

Tom whistled long and low. Matt tipped his chair back. "You must got one hell of a hand," he mused. Roy gave him a lop-sided grin. "OK, partner, I'll call you." Matt tossed his money belt on the pile. "Turn 'em up!"

Roy laid his queens on the table. Matt let out a whoop

and threw his hand down—four jacks! Roy smiled and shrugged his shoulders, taking his loss with good humor. "Easy come, easy go," he laughed.

"Aw, hell, partner, keep your god-damned six thousand dollars. If I took it, I'd have to wear another damn' money belt, and my belly can't take it." Matt said, gingerly rubbing his sore midriff.

"A bet's a bet," insisted Roy.

"God dammit, Roy, I'll shoot you, if you make me carry another damn' dollar of this stuff!"

"All right, all right," Roy gave in. "I won't forget I owe you a favor, though."

Suddenly the door to the cabin burst open. All three men crouched and drew, then relaxed when they recognized Charley Crouse, the man who was letting them hide here on his property.

"You bastards is nothing but a bunch of nervous Nellies," Charley growled, kicking the door shut. "They ain't nobody going to find you here, and, even if they did, it'd take them a week to figger out who had jurisdiction over you. You might as well come on out and live like the rest of the hardcases around here."

What Charley said made a certain amount of sense. Tucked into the secluded Green River valley and inaccessible except by hard to find trails, Brown's Hole was a haven for all kinds of misfits, from outlaws like the three of them to regular cowboys who merely did a little rustling on the side. Lawmen rarely ventured into the Hole, and those who did faced a bureaucratic nightmare trying to extradite their prisoner back over state lines.

Charley owned a cattle ranch in the Hole, but his main interest was horseflesh. He raised and raced fine horses which, as Matt and Roy could testify, was a feast or famine proposition. If he happened to be down on his luck, he was not above rustling a few cattle from his neighbors to help get back on his feet. Nobody begrudged him a few strays here and there, particularly since his wife, Mary, a fine Mormon woman, was one of the mainstays of the community. Before showing up in Telluride, Matt, too, had ranched on Diamond Mountain, becoming fast friends with the Crouses.

"Charley's right," Tom said, going to gaze out the cabin's one tiny window. "I'm sick and tired of sitting around here with nothing to do but play cards with you shysters. I'm moving on."

"Where to?" asked Matt, thinking that he, too, had a good case of cabin fever.

"Lander, maybe, or Rock Springs. Anywhere there's a little action. This money's burning a hole around my waist!"

"I wouldn't do that, I was you," said Roy lightly. "The trail ain't gone cold yet. You start throwing around big chunks of dough, somebody's bound to notice."

"Let 'em. I don't aim to hide out the rest of my life, dodging idiot sheriffs," McCarty spat and folded his arms across his chest.

"Suit yourself," Roy shrugged. "I kind of like it right here myself. Charley, you need a hand with those horses of yours?"

Charley rubbed the back of his neck in embarrassment. " 'Fraid not, Roy. I lost big at a race in Nebraska couple of months ago and the wife'd tar me, if I brought in an extra mouth to feed right now. You might try the Bassetts . . . they got a pretty big operation."

"I heard about them Bassetts," Matt said. "Husband's a real Nancy, I guess, so the wife pretty much runs things."

Charley chuckled and took Tom's seat at the table. "The

whole damn' family puts on airs, you ask me, always reading books and playing music and whatnot. Mary likes it, though. Says she feels civilized, after visiting over there. Aw, hell, you get right down to it, Herb's a good man, even if he is a bit of a pantywaist. But Matt's right, you're better off talking to the missus about a job."

"How about it, Matt?" Roy asked, his mind made up.

Warner hesitated. "I don't know, partner. Reckon I'm with Tom on this one. I got a hankering to go to town, live it up a little. Maybe it's too soon, like you said, but Tom and me can take care of ourselves."

"Fair enough. If you're ever looking to partner up again, you come find me," Roy said, and they shook on it.

The next day, the trio split up, Matt and Tom riding north to the wild frontier towns of southwestern Wyoming, Roy heading down the mountain to the Bassett Ranch. He would miss Matt's jovial companionship, and he would never forget how the round little cowboy had taken him in as a partner when he was down on his luck and penniless, but, all in all, it was time to go their separate ways. Roy had never been completely comfortable around Tom McCarty, whose dark moods and explosive nature spelled trouble, yet Matt was devoted to his brother-in-law, and Roy knew better than to make a man choose between family and friends. McCarty wasn't the only wild card in their band, either. Lately, Matt's drinking had gotten out of hand, and Roy feared it was only a matter of time before that, too, caused problems.

So he was on his own again, and it felt pretty damned good. He had bought a horse from Charley Crouse, a beautiful bay named Banner, and, as he rode down the valley toward the Bassett Ranch, he breathed in the fresh air, pungent with the smell of sage and piñon pine, and drank in the cloudless blue sky, and decided that at this particular moment in time there was nowhere else on earth he would rather be.

The Bassett place lay just past the point where the Green River turned south through the spectacular Cañon of Lodore. The mighty waterway cut a wide swath through sandstone cliffs dotted with greasewood and juniper bushes. It was rough country—beautiful in its own way but not for the weak or timid.

As Roy rode up to the main house, a girl, who looked to be about ten or eleven years old, dashed around the corner, clutching some kind of wooden toy to her chest. Following close behind was a boy, slightly younger, whose face was red with fury.

"Give it back, Ann, it's mine!" the boy cried, near tears.

"Come and get it, you big baby," she taunted, holding the toy out and then snatching it away as the boy lunged for it. She giggled and started to run away, but the boy managed to grab the back of her dress and throw her off balance. She fell to the ground, and the boy jumped on top of her, wrestling for the toy. They rolled over and over in the dust, the boy crying with frustration, Ann laughing uncontrollably. Roy observed it all from his perch atop Banner, enjoying the antics. It reminded him of the Parker household, although this girl was a mite rougher than any of his sisters.

A door slammed, and he looked up to see a handsome young woman standing on the porch, wiping her hands on her apron. "Ann, Eb, stop that this instant!" she ordered. "Can't you see we have a visitor?"

"Oh, shut up, Josie!" Ann retorted, extricating herself from Eb's clutches. "Here's your stupid toy. Who wants it, anyway!" She flung the toy down and stomped off.

Josie glanced at Roy in embarrassment. "Please excuse her. She's a bit high-spirited." She brushed back a strand of copper-colored hair, leaving a smudge of flour on her freckled cheek. Roy smiled at her, taken with the girl's pleasant looks and manner. "Are you here to see Mother?" she asked, flushing prettily.

"I don't rightly know," Roy said. "I'd like to talk to somebody about hiring on here."

"That would be Mother," Josie stated flatly. "She isn't here, but . . . oh wait, here she comes now."

Twisting around, Roy saw a woman, riding sidesaddle, coming up the road. She sat ramrod straight on her mount which, Roy couldn't help noticing, was of Thoroughbred quality. He tipped his hat as she came abreast of him.

"Are you Missus Bassett, ma'am?"

"I am. What can I do for you?" In contrast to her stiff carriage, her voice was warm and friendly with a slight Southern lilt. She looked young, too young to have a daughter as old as Josie. Her hair was vibrant and dark, her skin taut, her complexion fair under the broad brim of her hat.

"I was wondering if you might need another hand around here. I've done a fair share of cowboying, and I ain't afraid of hard work."

"Who might I be speaking to?" she asked pleasantly.

The question brought him up short. Who, indeed? He had known ever since that night hiding out in the Mancos Mountains that he would have to take an alias, but that's as far as his thinking had gone. Now the moment was here, and he had to decide quickly.

"Cassidy!" he blurted out. He smiled at the appropriateness of his choice. His old mentor would be proud to share his name, he thought.

Elizabeth Bassett cocked her head and hesitated, as though waiting for more, but, when Roy did not offer a first name, she smiled graciously and held out her gloved hand. "Welcome, Mister Cassidy. As it happens, we are in need of additional help. Whereabouts do you hail from?"

"Here and there," he replied vaguely.

She raised her eyebrows almost imperceptibly, looking at him with amusement. "I see. Well, Mister Cassidy, we don't ask too many questions around here. All I expect from my men is their hard and honest labor, and, in return, you shall be treated fairly and with respect. I do not object to you keeping your own herd of cattle, if you are so inclined, as long as that does not interfere with my operation."

"Yes, ma'am, that's mighty generous of you," said Roy, warming to this charming, yet authoritative, frontier woman.

"Take your things to the bunkhouse and join us in the main house for dinner." She touched the reins to her horse's neck and trotted off.

When he showed up for the noontime meal, he was surprised at the number of people in the large formal dining room. He had assumed that his invitation to eat with the family was merely for the purpose of introducing him to Mr. Bassett and would not be repeated on a regular basis, but here were all four of the other ranch hands, seated comfortably around the huge table as though they took every meal here which, it turned out, they did. There were several children about, too, and, except for the plusher surroundings, Roy felt as though he could be sitting down to eat at Annie's crowded table.

"Have a seat, Mister Cassidy," Elizabeth said, directing him to a chair next to her husband. "Herbert, this is our new man. Mister Cassidy, my husband, Herbert Bassett."

"Pleased to meet you," said Roy, extending his hand. Bassett shook it limply. He was a small man and considerably older than his wife. A full, gray beard covered his face, and he wore wire-framed eyeglasses.

"Likewise," Bassett murmured, and turned to his dinner. The presence of a new ranch hand did not seem to arouse much interest in him.

"Let me introduce you to the rest of my family," Elizabeth went on, unperturbed. "You've met my oldest, Josie, I believe"—Josie gave him a shy nod—"and I hear Ann and Eb put on quite a show for you." She looked at Ann sternly, but the girl merely stared back insolently.

"I've got a younger brother named Eb, about your age, too," said Roy, smiling at the boy.

"This is my son, Sam," she gestured to a boy of about thirteen, "and last, but not least, is George." A boy of around five gave him a big grin, revealing two missing front teeth.

"Hey, buddy, did you lose those teeth fighting b'ars?" joked Roy. The boy giggled and covered his mouth.

"We don't stand on formality around here, Mister Cassidy," Elizabeth said. "With your permission, I'd like to call you by your Christian name, if you would be so kind as to share it with us."

This time he was prepared. He winked across the table at her youngest child. "It's George, ma'am." His namesake giggled again.

"Indeed? Your mother and I must have much in common to have chosen two of the same names for our children," said Elizabeth.

You sure as hell don't remind me of my mother, thought Roy, but all he said was: "Yes, ma'am, I reckon you both got mighty good taste."

She went on to introduce the hired men, including one Isom Dart, a black man whom Roy had admittedly been surprised to see at the supper table. He soon discovered that Dart was not just another hired man, but a trusted confidante to the Bassett family. Apparently, Herbert and Elizabeth Bassett had left their Southern prejudices behind when they emigrated from Arkansas. Roy had occasionally come across a Negro cowboy, although he had never worked closely with one and certainly never taken orders from one, but he was game. After all, if this dainty Southern belle respected Isom Dart, so could he.

After dinner, Herbert Bassett, who had hardly spoken two words during the meal, invited George to attend church services the following morning, which he would be conducting in the library.

"I ain't much for church-going, sir, but maybe I'll give it a try," Roy said, wondering if attendance was mandatory.

Elizabeth came to his rescue. "Some of the men choose to attend, some do not. It's up to you, though we'd be pleased to have you."

"Thank you, ma'am."

"Oh, by the way, George," she continued, "there's a barn dance at our neighbor's place this evening. We'll all be going over, and you're welcome to come, too."

He hesitated, thinking how pleasant it would be to squire this woman around a dance floor, but decided it would be best to lay low for a little longer. "I'm much obliged, ma'am, but I think I'll just get settled in tonight."

She gazed at him with that penetrating look she had, as though she could read his every thought. "I understand." She laid a small but sturdy-looking hand on his sleeve. "There will be plenty of other opportunities. Barn dances are about the only socializing we have here in Brown's

Park"—he noticed she referred to the Hole by its less threatening name—"so somebody hosts one every couple of weeks or so. You come to the next one, George." She squeezed his arm ever so softly, then turned and marched from the room in what seemed to Roy to be a curt dismissal delivered with an intimate touch. A confusing woman, but her allure was undeniable.

George, as he was now known, slipped easily into the ranch routine. Dart and the others quickly recognized his skills as a cowboy, and he rapidly became a prized hand. The men were friendly with him, but not overly inquisitive, and an easy camaraderie soon developed. George had that rare ability to fit in with any group—to become integral to it so that, whether they realized it or not, people began looking to him for leadership. Even Isom Dart, the *de facto,* if unnamed, foreman, often unconsciously deferred to the new man, although George, recognizing Dart's special status with the Bassett family, was careful never to question his authority.

George's relationship with the family was cordial as well. He rarely saw Herbert Bassett—he had attended one church service just to be polite, but, after that, reverted to his childhood trick of busying himself with chores on Sunday morning—but Bassett had graciously allowed him the run of his library. Despite his lack of formal schooling, George used this opportunity to his advantage. He had never had access to good books, his mother's copy of the Book of Mormon being the only one available in the Parker home, and it came as a revelation to him that it was possible to string together words and sentences in a way that made a story leap off the page and live in his imagination. Although he frequently struggled with some of the more difficult language, he kept at it, and soon took to carrying a volume with him to pull out whenever he had a private moment.

The Bassett children were immediately won over by George's good nature and fun-loving ways. He and Isom Dart, who also loved children, were always willing to climb rocks to their secret cave hide-out, or help them braid a lariat rope, or conduct mock pony races for them. Even Ann Bassett, with her bossy and impudent ways, was won over by the genial new ranch hand. For his part, George thought someone ought to take a strong hand to little Miss Ann's backside, but Herbert was too disengaged and Elizabeth too distracted to pay much mind to the disciplining of their unruly daughter. Poor Josie, who did most of the household chores while Elizabeth tended to the ranch, did her best to keep Ann in line, but it was a hopeless task.

Although the eldest Bassett daughter was stuck in the house most of the time, she did not fail to notice the good looks and jovial nature of the newest hired man. At mealtimes, he knew how to mind his manners; he held chairs for the ladies, passed dishes politely, never shoveled in his food. He participated in the conversation without being overbearing, and offered humorous commentary that was never bawdy or raucous. Before long, Josie was counting the minutes until the next meal, the memory of wide, blue eyes, lanky blond hair, and a smiling, strong face putting a spring in her step.

Only Elizabeth Bassett seemed immune to George's charms. While she acted friendly enough, the intimacy she had shown him that first day had never been repeated. She treated him with the same business-like formality she treated the other men, with the exception of Isom Dart who was a clear favorite. That suited George just fine. The last thing he needed right now was to draw attention to himself by getting entangled with the mistress of the house. Although he could not help stealing glances, now and then, when she would reach her arms up to grab the pommel of her saddle, drawing the bodice of her dress tight across her curving figure, or when the sunlight would touch her hair just so and bring out the auburn tints in it. But these were just natural male reactions to a handsome woman, he told himself. Mostly, he was able to view her as what she was—his boss.

As Elizabeth had promised, some three weeks after George's arrival, another community barn dance was announced, this time at their neighbors, the Hoys. Josie made a point of mentioning it to him, and he told her he did, indeed, plan to attend. He figured it was safe now, five weeks after the robbery, to show himself a little. There had been no signs of pursuit since he had ditched the posse outside of Telluride, and he doubted anyone in Brown's Hole would associate George Cassidy with the infamous bank bandits.

On Saturday night, he rode over to the Hoy place with Jim McKnight, one of the other Bassett hands. Trotting up to the large, brightly lit barn, the first person he saw was Charley Crouse. Luckily, George had had the foresight to warn Charley in advance about his new name.

"Howdy, George," Charley greeted him, winking broadly.

"Charley, nice to see you. You know Jim, I reckon." Charley nodded. "Did you bring the missus?"

"More like she brung me," Crouse grumbled. "I ain't much for these fandangos. Listen, later on some of the fellas are gonna get up a poker game at my cabin in the woods. You know where that is, don't you?" He shot the outlaw a sly glance. "Come and join us, when you've had enough of this damn' shindig."

George laughed. "We'll see, Charley. Been so long since I enjoyed myself, I may want to stay for a while, kick up my heels with some of these pretty ladies."

"Just keep clear of my girls, Cassidy."

"Why, Charley, I'm a perfect gentleman!"

"See that you are," Crouse warned, stalking off grumpily.

Jim McKnight watched him go with a grin. "Ain't hard to be a gentleman around Crouse's daughters . . . they're so damn' ugly a man's scared to get near 'em! Truth to tell, I wouldn't be getting my hopes up too much, I was you. There ain't exactly heaps of girls, good-looking or otherwise, in Brown's Hole."

"What about Missus Bassett and Josie?"

Jim looked at him sideways. "They're the cream of the crop, no doubt about it. Don't go getting ideas, though. Missus Bassett, she don't dance with no one, less'n old Herb shows up. And Josie, well, she's just a kid. Only fifteen."

"Ripe for plucking! Hell, Jim, I'm just kidding. All's I'm looking for is a little fun. Come on."

They entered through the barn's huge doors to a dance in full swing. Two fiddlers sawed away on a raised platform at one end of the barn, and a table full of pies, cakes, and sweet cider anchored the other end. Josie had been keeping a close eye on the door. Her face lit up when she saw George Cassidy enter. She had dressed with particular care tonight, wearing her best calico with the frilly collar and arranging her hair in a fancy way. She was too young to wear it up so she had left it long and flowing, not in its usual braid, and had fastened a pretty bow amid the strawberry tresses. If only she could hide those awful freckles spattering her nose and cheeks. She started to make her way toward George, when young Tom Jarvie intercepted her to ask for a dance. She hesitated, but then accepted, hoping George would notice her as she twirled on the dance floor.

George, indeed, noticed her right away, just as he had noticed all of the details of the barn's large space. Although he was determined to relax this evening, he had no intention of letting down his guard. Thus, he sized up the barn and combed the crowd carefully. He observed how lively and pretty Josie looked, but his eyes did not linger. They swept on until they alighted on Elizabeth, and there they paused. She stood in profile to him, laughing and talking animatedly with a group of women. Her dark hair was piled on top of her head, little wisps and tendrils softening the edges of her face. Her dress was a shade of emerald green designed to complement her hazel eyes, and the bodice molded to her shape perfectly, accentuating her small waist and firm breasts.

He took in all this in less than a second—long enough to leave no doubt in his mind as to who was the belle of this ball. The sight of Elizabeth set something stirring in him, but with a supreme act of will he tamped it down. This woman was unattainable, and, even if he could have her, he didn't want her. That is, he did not want the mess that came with romantic involvement. He had vowed long ago to steer clear of such things, and his decision still made good sense. For some reason he found himself hunting for Herbert Bassett in the crowd. He spotted him off in a corner with some other old-timers.

"Watch out," warned Jim McKnight, "here come the Crouse girls."

Following Jim's gaze, George saw two young women heading his way, giggling and whispering into each other's ears. Unfortunately for the poor creatures, they were the spitting image of their rapscallion father. Jim expertly disappeared into the crowd, leaving George to fend for himself. He didn't care. He had come to dance a jig or two, and it might as well be with the Misses Crouse. Turning on the charm as fully as if they were beautiful leading ladies, he squired them both around the dance floor before making his escape, leaving them to swoon and speculate over the handsome new cowboy.

As he made his way to the food table, Jim caught up with him. "Didn't mean to leave you all alone there, hoss, but I had to answer a call of nature right quick."

"Your loss," said George, grabbing a piece of pound cake.

"That right?" laughed Jim. "I've heard those homely girls can be mighty accommodating to a man. I mean, it don't matter what they look like in the dark, now does it?"

"You wouldn't be speaking about any of the fair flowers of Brown's Park, would you?" A tall, dark-complexioned man with a handlebar mustache shouldered his way between Jim and George.

"Why, hello, Val," said Jim. "You met George Cassidy yet, the new man at the Bassett place? George, this is Valentine Hoy, the owner of this dump he calls a barn."

"It's good enough for the likes of you, McKnight. I heard about you, Cassidy." Hoy clasped George's hand. His grip was firm, and he held on for a long time, perusing the outlaw's face through narrowed eyes.

George was instantly on guard, although his expression remained friendly. "Ain't been here long enough to get a reputation," he said easily.

"Word gets around quick here in the Park," Hoy said. "Elizabeth Bassett seems to think you're one hell of a good hand. Where you from?"

George poured himself a cup of cider and sipped at it

slowly before answering. "Born in Utah, but I've wandered around some."

"Ever been southwest, down near Ute country?"

Hoy's eyes bored into him. The noise and pandemonium of the dance melted away as George concentrated on this man who was asking too many questions. Did he know something? Probably not, but he couldn't be sure. Best to answer by keeping close to the truth.

"I been through there. Worked a mule train for one of the mining outfits for a while."

Hoy nodded and continued to stare, another question seeming to lurk behind his hooded eyes. Finally, he looked away and muttered: "Pretty country down there."

"Listen, Val, George and I were heading outside for a smoke. Care to join us?" Jim McKnight had not missed the tension between the two men, which he chalked up to jealousy on Hoy's part. Everyone knew Val Hoy carried a torch for Elizabeth Bassett.

"Nah. Enjoy yourselves, boys." Hoy favored Cassidy with one final inspection and then moved off.

George set his cup down and turned to go, intending to have a smoke with Jim and then high-tail it out of there when he felt a tug on his sleeve. Josie Bassett stood at his side, eyes cast down, the color high in her cheeks. Having finally gotten up the nerve to approach him, she was suddenly and unaccountably struck shy. To her complete dismay, she couldn't think of a thing to say.

" 'Evening, Miss Josie. Ain't you a sight for sore eyes." George desperately wanted to leave before Hoy, or somebody else, could ask him more unwanted questions, but he could not be rude to sweet young Josie.

"Y-you don't have to call me miss," Josie stammered.

"All right then. Say, Jim, I'll catch up with you later."

George smiled down at the blushing girl, unaware of the effect it had on her. She gazed at him, tongue-tied.

"Right nice party, ain't it? You having a good time?"

"I am now." She turned red with embarrassment. Ducking her head, she caught her lip between even, white teeth. "I mean, I was glad to see you decided to come."

The fiddlers struck up a reel. George took her hand and pulled her toward the clearing in the center of the barn. Josie laughed with excitement, her eyes sparkling. Sensing danger in this place, George planned to dance one dance and then beat a speedy retreat. But they were not long into the reel before he found himself enjoying the feel of her in his arms, light as a feather and responsive to his lead, and, when the music ended, they stayed on the floor for a second dance. The fiddlers ended with a flourish, and he spun her in a circle, her skirts slapping his knees. He caught her by the waist and pulled her close.

"Again?" he asked, smiling down at her flushed face with the girlish freckles. She was a cute little thing, no doubt about it.

"Yes," she breathed, as the fiddlers launched into another tune. Out of nowhere, suddenly Elizabeth was there, her hand on Josie's shoulder, her expression pleasant but determined.

"Josie, dear, you're so flushed. Perhaps you should go have a cup of cider." Her tone was that of a concerned mother, but there was something else in it that suggested she would brook no argument.

Josie tried nonetheless. "I'm fine, Mother, really." She took a step toward George, who had dropped her hand the moment Elizabeth had appeared.

"I insist, dear. Missus Hoy could use some help with the pies, too."

Josie appeared ready to protest, but apparently thought better of it. Gathering her skirts around her, she flounced off. Elizabeth turned to face her ranch hand. Wordlessly, she lifted her arms, inviting him to dance with her. He stepped into her embrace, and they glided over the floor in a slow waltz. She felt different from Josie, more substantial, although she certainly was light of step. She was not afraid to touch him—her right hand grasped his firmly while her left exerted solid pressure on his shoulder. Her eyes never left his, although they remained inscrutable. When the music ended, she leaned into him ever so slightly and whispered in his ear: "Now you may return to my daughter, if you care to."

Aware of the stares around them, George backed up quickly. "I best be leaving now," he said, silently cursing her for having focused attention on him, but undeniably aroused by this sensuous woman.

"As you wish." She turned and left, dismissing him in her abrupt way.

He lingered for a few more minutes, afraid that a sudden departure would look suspicious. He tried to seek out Josie to thank her for the dances, but she turned her back to him when she saw him coming. Finally, he made it out the door. Jim McKnight came scurrying up behind him.

"How'd you do that?" he asked in awe.

"Do what?"

"Get Elizabeth Bassett to dance with you."

"Weren't none of my doing." George untied and mounted Banner.

"You mean she asked you?"

"Drop it, McKnight. It don't mean nothing." George wheeled Banner around and trotted off. For the first time since the robbery, he felt uncomfortable with the choice he had made. Was this what being an outlaw meant—that he couldn't go out in a crowd, couldn't dance with a pretty woman, for fear of drawing attention to himself? It was true he did not want to be tied down, did not want any romances, but, by God, he didn't want to live like a hermit the rest of his life, either.

He rode a couple of miles, letting the warm night air cloak him in comfort. As always, the calming rhythm of his horse moving beneath him helped to settle his thoughts. Things were all right. No need to go off half-cocked. This Hoy fellow probably knew nothing, and, even if he suspected something, ranchers in Brown's Hole knew better than to call in the law. Hell, half of the hired hands in the valley were hiding from something or other. As for the situation with Josie and Elizabeth, well, he could handle that. He would simply ignore Josie, and Elizabeth was too smart to let anything happen between them. She was toying with him, he knew, but he sensed it was harmless. *Just don't rise to the bait,* he thought. *Stay in control.*

He thought about the money he had stashed away up on Diamond Mountain. Soon, before winter came, he would leave this place and use the money to buy a small ranch somewhere. He would start slowly, rounding up a few horses, trading for more, until he had built a respectable outfit. He had no illusions about himself. He knew he would never be happy staying in one place for too long. But he also knew that he needed to be his own boss, and now, with the Telluride money, he had the means to do that.

Whistling softly, he let Banner set the pace back to the Bassett Ranch. The air was balmy, a rare occurrence in the Park, even in the middle of summer. Another couple of months and the nights would be cold again, frost tipping the sagebrush in the mornings. The sun would be low in the sky, and the light would have a transient quality about it. Then he would know it was time to leave.

Somewhere in the distance a coyote howled, its double-noted cry rolling over the hills. He smiled to himself. That sound had never seemed mournful to him. It was the sound of wildness and freedom, of independence and self-reliance. It was all the things he was and wanted to be. But it was so god-damned lonely.

Chapter Ten

By mid-August, Charley Crouse was back on his feet. Over the summer he had managed to build up his cattle herd and ship it off to Rawlins for sale; nobody asked how. With new stake money in his pocket he was ready to race again, and, knowing something of George Cassidy's previous experience, he called upon his friend to ride jockey for his best new race mare. George considered himself too big to be a really top-notch jockey, but what he lacked in proper size, he made up for in skill and general horse sense. He knew how to bring his mount in first over the finish line, and that was all that counted.

Along toward September Charley arranged a match with a hot new filly out of Green River. Word of the race spread quickly throughout Brown's Park, and a larger than usual crowd turned out to watch. It was a close finish, but George managed to win by outsmarting his opponent. He guessed that the inexperienced jockey would come out of the blocks at top speed in an attempt to take and keep an early lead, and that's just what happened. George held his mount back until he sensed the other horse tiring, then poured it on to come from behind and win by a nose.

The Brown's Park crowd loved it. Taking his cool-down lap, he waved and doffed his hat to several friends—people whose acquaintance he had made over the summer and who were naturally drawn to the outgoing young cowboy. It occurred to him that he was not trying too hard to stay anonymous, but by now he figured he had been in the Park long enough that anyone who wanted to turn him in would have already done so. He was confident that no one, not even Valentine Hoy, suspected that the smiling, good-looking cowboy who had a way with horses was also a bank robber on the run from the law.

As he finished his victory lap, he noticed Elizabeth Bassett off to one side, sitting gracefully atop her Thoroughbred. A large-brimmed hat covered most of her face, but he could tell she was watching him. Still in the saddle, he raised his hat and bowed slightly in her direction. The casual observer would have thought she missed the gesture, for she did not appear to react, but George was certain he saw a tiny smile tug at her lips and perhaps she just barely inclined her head at him.

Since the night of the barn dance, their relationship had not changed, at least not visibly. Elizabeth still rode right alongside the men, directing the work of the ranch. For their part, the men treated her with a free and easy respect, much as they would a male colleague, although they were mindful of their manners a bit more in her presence. On the surface she treated George no differently from the others, but he sensed a certain tension about her that had not been there before, a way of drawing herself up when he was near as though she was afraid they might accidentally touch.

As for Josie, he was well aware of the moon eyes she threw at him every mealtime, but he carefully kept his distance. What she felt for him, he realized, was merely youthful infatuation that, given time and lack of encouragement, would disappear.

George threw the reins to Charley Crouse and hopped down. "Hell of a race, pardner," crowed Charley. "You had me a mite worried there, till the end."

"I figgered that hoss'd be quick on the draw but would

run out of ammo before it was all over."

"You had it figgered right. Just next time, don't make it so close. You like to give me a heart attack!" Charley clutched his chest in mock distress.

"You ain't the only one suffering, Charley Crouse. I just lost my god-damned shirt on that race."

George turned at the sound of the unfamiliar voice. A tall, dark-haired man sauntered up, pulling off a pair of riding gloves. He had a long face with a high forehead and wide-set, dark eyes that twinkled with good humor.

"Elzy! Holy shit, man, where'd you come from?" Charley cried, pumping the man's hand.

"Just rode in. I should know by now not to bet against one of your ponies, but, hell, I saw this big lug of a jockey you're using and figgered there weren't no way you'd win this one."

"That's my angle now, don't you see . . . try and fool tenderfeet like you who don't savvy what a fine horseman I got here." Charley cackled and clapped George on the back. "George Cassidy, meet Elzy Lay. Elzy and me go back a ways, ain't that right, Elz?"

Lay gave George's hand a firm shake. "Pleased to meet you. That was a hell of a ride."

"Thanks. Elzy, is it? Ain't heard that name before."

"Nor will again, most likely. Short for Ellsworth, my middle name."

"You going to stay for a while, Elz?" asked Charley. "Mary and me'd be glad to put you up."

"I may hang around for a while, but you know me . . . can't never stay in one place too long."

"Listen, boys, I got to settle up with some folks here," said Charley. "George, why don't you take Elzy on back to my place. Tell Mary you're both staying to supper. She'll be tickled pink . . . she always did take a shine to this no-account drifter."

"And why wouldn't she, when all she's got to look forward to is this crooked bag of bones parking his boots under the bed?" Elzy teased back.

"Go on, get out of here. And mind your Ps and Qs around my girls," huffed Charley.

Laughing, George and Elzy pointed their mounts in the direction of Diamond Mountain. George gave one last glance around but did not see Elizabeth anywhere. No matter—they would scarcely notice one less mouth to feed at the Bassett table tonight. All except Josie, of course.

"So, how long you been riding for Charley?" asked Elzy amiably.

"Not long. I only been in the Hole a couple of months."

"Like it here?" George noted that Elzy did not ask where he had come from or what had brought him here. He liked that sense of reservation in a man—knowing that certain information would come out, if at all, in due time.

George shrugged. "Well enough. I'm working over at the Bassett Ranch. It's a pretty decent set-up. Reckon I'll be moving on soon though."

Elzy nodded. He did not ask why, if George had a good job with the Bassetts, he would leave. He seemed to understand that it was just in the nature of things to keep moving.

"I know the Bassetts." Elzy scanned the horizon thoughtfully. "Worked for them a while myself last time I was through. Hell of a woman."

George did not have to ask whom he meant, nor did he read any untoward meaning into Elzy's comment. It was a fact—Elizabeth Bassett was a hell of a woman.

"That she is. Her old man ain't bad, either, once you get to know him."

142

Elzy laughed. "Guess that's right, though I had a hell of a time trying to get out of his church services. Didn't seem to bother the old guy, though, when I stopped showing up. He'd still invite me in to his library, show me the latest magazines. How about that girl of theirs, what was her name . . . Ann? Christ, I never heard such a sassy mouth on a kid."

"That ain't changed none," George chuckled. "She's still bossing everyone in sight. Say, was Isom Dart there when you were?"

"Sure enough. Good man."

George nodded, glad that Elzy shared his assessment of the quiet, capable black cowboy. They rode on, chatting of this and that, mostly about horses, a subject on which Elzy Lay proved to be as passionate as George. When they showed up at Crouse's place, Mary Crouse welcomed Elzy with a friendly hug and asked them to stay for supper before they could tell her Charley had already issued an invitation.

Later that night, after finishing Mary's delicious stew and sweet potato pie, the three men sat on the porch smoking and drinking. Talk turned to old times, and, after some urging, Elzy offered up his story. He had been born in Iowa but moved to eastern Colorado as a young child. Much like George, he left home in his late teens, although his motive had been merely to seek adventure in the Wild West. He got as far as Denver where he took a job driving a horse car. One day, a drunk tried to molest one of his female passengers; Elzy threw him off the car, and the man hit the pavement so hard he thought he had killed him. He fled to Brown's Hole, worked for various ranchers, including the Bassetts and Charley Crouse, and had been drifting here and there ever since.

George listened easily as this friendly, engaging man

talked. They seemed to have a lot in common. It had been a long time since he had connected with somebody like this. There had been Matt, of course, before his drinking got too bad, but that friendship had been partly based on George's sense of obligation for Matt's having taken him in as a partner. Then there had been Mike Cassidy, George's unknowing namesake. He had not seen or heard from Cassidy in five years, although he still thought of him now and then. He had been just a kid then, and Mike had been like a big brother and teacher all in one. He had idolized the man, but now that he was older and wiser, he could see that the friendship had meant more to him than it had to Cassidy.

It was a little after midnight when George got up, a bit unsteadily, to leave. So determined was he always to stay in complete control of himself, that he could count on one hand the number of times he had been drunk in his life. But he had enjoyed the company and the conversation, and was so delighted at having made the acquaintance of Elzy Lay, that he had lost track of the amount of whiskey he had consumed. He caught himself on the porch rail and shook his head to clear it.

"Where you think you're going, you dang fool?" a bleary-eyed Charley said. "Stay here tonight."

" 'Preciate it, but I gotta be going."

"In this dark? There ain't even no moon tonight."

"Hell, Banner knows the way blindfolded. Tell Mary thanks for the supper."

He saddled up Banner, something he could have done sound asleep, much less drunk, and headed out, wondering at his decision to go back to the Bassetts tonight. Ordinarily, he would not think twice about staying over, when it got to be late. The smart thing would have been to sleep off the whiskey, eat one of Mary's hearty breakfasts, and head back in the full light of morning.

But now that he was on his way, he was glad he had come. Despite the blackness of the night, Banner had no trouble finding his way along the well-worn path down the mountain and through the valley. George threw back his head and inhaled deeply, letting the oxygen clear out the buzzing in his head. By the time he reached the Bassett place, he was completely sober.

All was dark at the ranch. He sneaked into the bunkhouse for his bedroll, then led Banner toward Vermilion Creek. About a mile up, he found a good spot to camp. He let Banner drink from the creek, then hobbled him close by. Spreading his blankets, he removed his hat and gun belt and settled down, hands clasped behind his head, staring up at the stars. He had no need of a fire on this warm night, so he lay in total darkness. He could make out shapes around him not so much by sight as by simply sensing their presence—a density that took up space.

Slowly he relaxed, and sleep had almost overtaken him when something jolted him awake. His eyes flew open, and he rolled to his side, grasping for his gun belt.

"I guess a woman ought to know better than to sneak up on a man with a gun." Her vibrant, musical voice came to him from only a few feet away, but she might have been invisible for all he could see of her.

He lowered his six-shooter and propped himself up on one elbow. "Come closer, Elizabeth. I can't see you."

For the longest time nothing moved. Then he could see her approaching, a black shape outlined against lesser blackness. She was close enough to touch before he could make out any details, and what he saw sent his pulse racing. She wore only a chemise covered by a fringed shawl that she clasped about her tightly. Her hair fell loose to her waist in a thick, dark mass. She stared down at him where he lay at her feet.

Neither of them spoke. Finally, she knelt beside him, still holding the shawl tightly around her.

"I couldn't sleep tonight," she whispered. "I was sitting on the verandah, when I heard you ride up and stop at the bunkhouse. It was too dark to see anything, but I knew it was you. Banner has that off-kilter stride I'd recognize anywhere. When you came back out and left again, I wondered where you were going, so I followed you." She paused, but he kept silent—this was her tale, and he wanted to hear her tell it. Looking away, over his head, she continued in a dreamy voice.

"There's been a lot of hired men come and go here. Some of them have been right nice, like that Elzy Lay I saw you talking to today. He was a real gentleman and a good horseman. Seemed like he had some book learning, too. And Isom's so devoted to us, of course. And then there's George Cassidy who hails from here and there. Quite the man of mystery. Something makes him different from all the others, though I can't put my finger on it. He's always laughing and joking . . . even when he's being serious, there seems to be a smile lurking behind those blue eyes. But there's something beneath all that good humor, isn't there? Something he's hiding. I don't mean something bad he's done, necessarily. It's more something about himself, the way he thinks about things, that he tries to hide with all his funning around."

She looked down at him, but still he said nothing. Abruptly, she asked: "Do you know how old I am?"

He blanched at the unexpected question. "No, ma'am."

"I'm thirty-four. Does that seem old to you, George?"

"No."

"You're lying. You're far more interested in my daughter than you are in me!"

"I ain't never. . . ."

"Yes, you have! I saw you dancing with her. You might as well have been making love to her there on the dance floor, the way you held her." Elizabeth's voice broke. She took a deep breath before continuing. "Then when you danced with me, you seemed so indifferent, so . . . cold. I tried to let you know I wanted you to hold me like you'd held Josie, but you seemed far away."

Slowly George reached out a hand and fingered the silky fringe of her shawl. His hand moved up her arm and grabbed the folds of cloth where she held it tight to her chest. He pulled her forward until her face was inches from his. He could smell the clean, woodsy scent of her hair and could feel the heat of her skin beneath the flimsy chemise. Every warning system he possessed screamed at him not to do this, that here was danger, but the nearness of her and the heat rising in his own body overrode good sense.

"I ain't far away now," he breathed, and pulled her to him until their lips met in a gentle kiss. She fell against him, pushing him back on his bedroll. Her hair cascaded over his face, tickling his nose, as she nuzzled his neck and nipped at his ear. Laughing, he shook his head free of her dark locks and rolled over on top of her. "Why Missus Bassett, you're a regular wildcat!" he said, his fingers fumbling with the buttons of her nightdress.

She grabbed his hand and pressed it tightly to her breast. Gravely she gazed up at him. "Only with you, George. I've never been like this with anyone before."

Her solemn tone jarred him back to his senses. My God, he had thought all along she was merely flirting with him, that she was interested only in a harmless dalliance. Could it be she felt more than that for him, that she was serious about him?

Instinctively, he rolled off her and drew his hand away. Although his blood pounded and desire rose in him thick and heavy, he had to get things straight with her. He could not allow her to trap him.

"What is it, darling?" She pressed herself to him again, but he put his hand on her shoulder and gently pushed her back.

"Elizabeth," he said, his voice low and determined, "this is only for tonight. You got to be clear on that. I can love you tonight, but I'll be gone tomorrow."

In the dark, he could not read her expression, but her voice came out sounding hurt. "I don't expect promises from you, George. But why must it be only one night? Nothing needs to change. I'll make no demands on you."

"That's just the way it is, darlin'." Gently he brushed the hair away from her forehead. "I'm trying to be straight with you. I'll stop, if you tell me to." Pushing the chemise off her shoulder, his lips caressed her soft, white skin. "Say stop and I'll stop," he whispered. "Say stop, Elizabeth."

"Don't stop!" she breathed, moving beneath him in a rhythm that reminded him of a wild horse bucking between his legs. "Never stop!"

The next morning, George awoke at daylight. He stretched lazily and looked around. The only evidence of the previous night's activity was the smell of her, and of them together, that clung to his blankets. He saddled up Banner, made a quick stop at the bunkhouse to pick up his few possessions, and headed up Diamond Mountain where he retrieved his cache of money and found Elzy Lay. That afternoon the two of them rode out of Brown's Hole, heading north.

Chapter Eleven

"Set me up, Frank."

The bartender traveled the length of the bar, sloshing cheap whiskey as he went, hardly bothering to raise the bottle between glasses. The men were packed so tightly into the bar that very little whiskey spilled onto the polished surface. George Cassidy downed his drink with one practiced flip of his wrist and closed his eyes, savoring the warmth as it slid down his throat. He had been out riding range for the U-Bar outfit, and this was his first visit to town in two months. As it happened, just about every cowpuncher within a hundred miles of Green River was also in town for the fall shipment of cattle to points east.

Cassidy signaled for a refill. As he raised it to his lips, the man next to him suddenly bumped his arm, spilling whiskey over Cassidy's hand and sleeve. The man, who was really no more than a boy, gave him a wary look, uncertain whether the rough, unshaved stranger would take offense. Slowly George set down his glass and dried his hand with his bandanna. His eyes narrowed into a steely stare. The boy backed up a step, color draining from his thin face. Aware of the sudden tension, the men close by stopped talking, although the din in the rest of the bar continued. Moving slowly and deliberately, Cassidy tucked his kerchief back in his pocket and turned to face the boy, leaning his elbows on the bar behind him. He gave him a penetrating look from head to foot, then suddenly winked and grinned. "I'd offer to buy you some of this red-eye, kid, but you don't look old enough to drink it. So I reckon you better buy me one!"

The onlookers burst out laughing as the boy expelled his breath and tentatively smiled back, a little unhappy about being the butt of a joke, but glad to have avoided trouble.

Later, with the smell of stale whiskey, unwashed bodies, and cigar smoke mingling in a stagnant haze throughout the room, George stepped outside for a breath of fresh air. Several cowboys lollygagged on the steps of the saloon, smoking and jawing about the just completed roundup.

"Howdy, George. You come up for air?" greeted John Burns, a friend from the U-Bar outfit.

"Trying to, but it ain't much better out here." Cassidy wrinkled his nose at the odor of cow shit which hung over the town like a ubiquitous bank of fog. Most cowboys got so used to the smell they didn't even notice it, but not him. A few days of cow-town smell were all he could take before he had to escape to the clear air of a remote campsite.

"You got something against the company here, Cassidy?" snarled Pete Brennen, misinterpreting George's remark.

George laughed as he seated himself on the railing. "Hell no, except maybe for yours, Pete."

Brennen, a surly fellow who was universally disliked but tolerated because he was the nephew of a big local rancher, drew himself up to his full height, which was considerable. "Explain yourself!" he scowled.

Cassidy folded his arms across his chest and gave Brennen a bored look. "Pete," he said, "your fly's unbuttoned." All the men burst into howls of laughter as Brennen instinctively checked his pants which were, indeed, hanging open. Red-faced, he turned away to button up, muttering to himself.

"Hey, look at that!" said Jim Patterson, nodding toward an approaching paint pony ridden bareback by a young half-breed boy. One of the pony's eyes was milk-white all over. "Kid, come here. What's wrong with that horse's eye?"

The boy ambled over and looked at the men shyly. "He was born that way."

"Shit, Jim, I bet that one-eyed horse sees better than you do with two eyes, especially when you're as pickled as you are now," joked John Burns.

"Oh yeah? I bet you can't even get aboard that wall-eyed excuse for horseflesh," said Jim, good-naturedly rising to the bait.

"Are you kidding me? Hop down off that horse, son. Get ready, boys, drinks are on Jim!" Burns lunged for the pony, but the minute it felt the unfamiliar weight on its back, it scooted out from under, leaving the gangly cowboy in a pile on the ground. Burns's failure was met with hoots and yells of derision. Several others, including Cassidy, tried their luck, but all suffered the same fate. Even burly Pete Brennen tried, but the frightened little pony threw him the hardest of all. Picking himself up from the dust, a fuming Brennen faced the rowdy crowd.

"God dammit! Ain't nobody can ride that piece of shit horse 'cept for a damn' half-breed kid!"

"That ain't true," broke in Cassidy. "I know who can ride him." The men hushed and turned to look at him. He lounged in a chair with the two front legs tipped up, the back resting against the wall.

"You think you're so damn' smart, but you got throwed like everybody else," Brennen said, slapping dust from the seat of his pants.

"I didn't say I could ride him, I said I know who can." Cassidy grinned mischievously.

"You talking about a white man?" asked Jim.

"Sure." Cassidy let the chair legs fall, then got up and casually perused the crowd that had grown considerably since the entertainment with the pony began. "You there," he called to the thin-faced boy who had accidentally knocked his arm at the bar. "This here is my good buddy . . . bought me a drink earlier, didn't you, kid? What's your name?"

"Justin Flint," the boy replied uneasily. He didn't relish being in the spotlight yet again.

"Justin here can ride that horse," Cassidy announced.

"What makes him different from the rest of us?" asked Burns. "He may be just a kid, but he's the size of a man."

"You're damned right he's a man." Cassidy clapped him on the back. "And I'm telling you he can get aboard that horse."

Justin drew himself up, starting to enjoy the attention.

"What the hell. Go ahead, kid, give it a try," urged Jim Patterson.

Justin looked at Cassidy who gave him a nod of encouragement. Purposefully, he strode toward the horse and, like the others, leaped from the steps onto the pony's back. The animal snorted and half-heartedly kicked its back legs out, but a few soothing words from Justin calmed it down, and soon it allowed the boy to hold onto its mane and parade up and down the street to the cheers of the surprised gathering.

"I'll be damned," said an amazed John Burns. "What's the secret, George?"

"Chaps," said Cassidy, tossing a coin to the little Indian boy who anxiously retrieved his pony and trotted off.

"Come again?"

"Injun ponies ain't used to the feel of chaps. All of us are wearing them, except Justin here. That's why I figured he had a chance of staying on. Come on, kid," he put his arm around Justin's shoulders. "My turn to buy you a drink!"

"Just a god-damned minute, Cassidy." Pete Brennen, an ugly look on his face, planted himself in George's path. "You think you're pretty damn' smart, don't you?"

"Stow it, Brennen," said Jim. "It was all in fun."

"Stay out of this, Patterson. This is between him and me." Brennen's hand hovered near his six-shooter, and he flexed his fingers in the classic gunfighter's stance.

George looked at him quizzically and held out his hands in mock confusion. "I'm at a loss here, pardner. Did I do something to offend you?"

"You made us all look like fools, and I don't like looking like a fool."

Cassidy chuckled. "Well, then, Pete, if I was you, I'd keep my mouth shut and my fly buttoned."

Brennen turned beet red, his eyes bulged, and he snorted like an angry bull. Bellowing with rage, he went for his gun, but too late realized he was looking down the barrel of Cassidy's six-shooter. He hadn't even seen him draw it out of the holster, but there it was, pointing steadily at him.

"Listen, pardner, I ain't got any beef with you, but if you want to fight, I'll fight. Not with these, though. Lay down your piece." Cassidy gestured toward Brennen's gun which was still filling his holster. Brennen hesitated, but with Cassidy's having the drop on him, he had no choice. He slowly removed his revolver and set it down. Cassidy twirled his piece a couple of times and handed it to John Burns. The crowd drew back, forming a circle around the two men.

"Ready when you are, Petey boy," said Cassidy, striking a casual pose despite the fact his opponent was at least three inches taller and forty pounds heavier. Growling, Brennen lunged forward clumsily. Cassidy nimbly ducked and side-stepped, coming up with his right fist planted solidly in Brennen's gut. Everyone could hear the air whoosh out of the big man. Cassidy threw a right to his jaw. Brennen crashed to the ground, dazed and wheezing. The fight was over, before it had really begun.

Burns, Patterson, and the others crowded around George, offering congratulations, but he pushed through to offer a hand to the prostrate Brennen.

"Come on, Pete. No hard feelings. Drinks are on me."

Brennen meekly accepted the hand up, and they retired to the bar for a raucous session of drinking and general carousing.

Later that night George wandered by himself down the sidewalk, uncharacteristically at loose ends. Most of the other cowpunchers had gravitated to the whorehouses, and he supposed that's where he was headed, too. It had been two months since he had left Elizabeth, but he still remembered the smell and feel of her on his scratchy blankets. Whatever comfort he found tonight would pale in comparison to that glorious night of love. Still, he did not regret his decision to leave Brown's Hole. He was a free man, unencumbered with ties to any person or place, and that's how he wanted it.

He passed a square of light emanating from the window of one of the higher-class brothels. He kept going, but paused several feet beyond. Did he really want to go back to the U-Bar campsite where nothing waited for him but a cold bedroll and the smell of cow shit? He jammed his hands deeply into the pockets of his duster. It was late October now, the days already nippy and the nights downright cold. He had been putting off finding a place to winter, largely because of his disappointment that Elzy Lay was not interested in being his partner in the little horse ranch he dreamed of owning. Elzy had joined him at the U-Bar for a brief time, but then announced he was moving on. George had asked no questions—he understood how it was when a man decided to hit the trail—but he missed the easy-going friendship he and Elzy had shared. He knew that sometime down the road he and Elzy Lay would hook up again.

The brothel doors banged open, and a couple of satisfied customers careened down the street. *What the hell*, George thought. *Maybe there's a sweet little thing in there with long brown hair and hazel eyes and a touch of a Southern lilt in her voice*. He sighed and reversed his steps. Just as he reached the door, another man came out, adjusting his hat on his head. The man glanced at him, then did a double-take.

"Bob? Bob Parker?" The man peered at him closely.

George froze, staring hard at this man who recognized him from his long-ago past, racking his brain to place him. Was he friend or foe?

"It's Al Hainer, remember? From the Marshall Ranch." The man smiled uncertainly and held out his hand.

"Al! Sure, sure, I remember you. I just didn't recognize you with all that hair on your face! Guess when you and I worked together we was both too young to grow anything but fuzz!" George shook hands enthusiastically, glad to see this reminder of home.

"Looks like you was just going in, but how about meeting me for a drink afterwards?" said Hainer.

George nudged Hainer in the ribs. "They got anything special in there?"

"Couple of 'em ain't bad looking, but you know how it is . . . you seen one hooker, you seen 'em all!"

George laughed. "Don't mind if I skip the honors then. Come on, first round's on me!"

They found the nearest saloon and spent the next few

hours catching up. Although not a Circle Valley boy, Al Hainer had worked at Jim Marshall's ranch in the summer of 1883, hence his acquaintance with Bob Parker, who now asked to be called George Cassidy. Hainer noted, without comment, his friend's adoption of Mike Cassidy's name.

Like so many young men of the time, Hainer had drifted around, working for various outfits throughout the West. For the most part, he had kept his hands clean, combining rustling and ranching no more nor less than the next fellow. Unlike many of his colleagues, however, he had managed to save a few dollars, so, when George mentioned his desire to start his own small outfit for the winter, Hainer quickly offered himself as a partner. Cassidy readily agreed, and the two fell to discussing potential sites for their new venture, finally deciding to head north to check out the Wind River area.

Within the week, the two adventurers settled their affairs in Green River and were on the road, crossing South Pass and following the Popo Agie River into Lander. Perched at the foot of the Wind River range, not far from the Indian reservation, Lander was a busy place, its streets packed with ranchers, soldiers, cowboys, and gamblers. George was so taken with the pretty little town and its friendly inhabitants that he was tempted to spend the winter right there, but, when he and Al got a tip about a place farther north in the upper Wind River area, they packed up and headed out. Sure enough, the ranch they had heard about was perfect. Situated on the banks of Horse Creek in a land of rolling hills and sagebrush-covered plains, the ranch was quite remote, which suited George just fine. Better yet, the previous owners had already built a cabin on the site, so the two partners were able to move right in and concentrate on raising horses.

And none too soon, for, by the end of November, winter had come to northwestern Wyoming. Although both men were accustomed to long and severe high-country winters, this one seemed particularly harsh, with temperatures dropping below zero and staying there for days at a time.

Needing a social outlet besides his partner, who turned out to be a rather taciturn man, George sought out his neighbors and was greatly pleased to find them a stimulating and friendly group of people. His closest neighbor was Eugene Amoretti, Jr., who owned the E A Ranch just south of George's property. Of noble Italian heritage, the Amorettis, father and son, were involved in banking as well as ranching, and George took advantage of this connection by depositing what remained of his Telluride haul in their bank in Lander. As the harsh winter took its toll on his savings, he also borrowed occasionally from the Amorettis.

Not too far away, on Jakey's Fork of the Wind River, lived the Simpson family—John and Margaret, and their grown son Will and his family. Well-educated and interesting people, the Simpsons welcomed George into their home, and he spent many an entertaining hour there while the wind whistled and the snow drifted outside. George also got to know the French Canadian Andrew Manseau, and Bub Meeks, a happy-go-lucky young man who liked cutting up almost as much as George himself.

As Christmas Day approached, with no let-up to the bitter weather in sight, Margaret Simpson decided to treat her neighbors to a warm, convivial Christmas dinner. Grateful for the invitation and for the friendship that had spawned it, George determined to make a trip to town, despite the deep snow and frigid cold, to buy presents for the Simpson children. He enlisted Manseau and Meeks, and, together, they rode the seventy-five miles into Lander. The chill winds had not managed to dampen the little town's festive spirit, and it was not long before the three good-looking bachelors found themselves invited to every social event in town.

"I'm telling you, George, you ain't seen nothing till you've seen some of these half-breed girls they got around here," Bub said as he combed his hair in front of the tiny mirror in their room at the Cottage Home Hotel.

"I ain't particular. I like them white, red, or somewheres in between," grinned George, shouldering Meeks aside as he tried to smooth down his stubborn cowlick.

"Well, for my money," Bub went on, "I'll take one of the Injun gals any time. Not that they're easy or anything like that. They just seem friendlier is all, not so stuck up like some of the la-di-da white girls."

George knew that the proximity of Lander to the Wind River Indian Reservation and Fort Washakie, the Army outpost that served as agency to the reservation, made the town a melting pot of sorts. For instance, there was a sizable French Canadian population, and Andrew Manseau had promised to introduce his friends to all those exotic young women. Indeed, they had only just arrived at the dance, when Manseau's countryman, Emery Burnaugh, wandered over with his pretty half-breed fiancée, Alice.

" 'Allo, boys!" said Burnaugh in his distinctive accent, half French, half Texan. " 'Ave you met my girl, Alice?"

The three men tipped their hats to the young lady. "Ain't seen you much lately, Emery," said Meeks. "Ain't nobody sending any mail up our way?"

Burnaugh was employed as the freighter, running mail from Lander to points north, including the Wind River region. "Not much, but what there is I cannot deliver in this bad weather. Maybe you take it back for me, eh?"

"Make you a deal," broke in Cassidy. "We'll carry your mail for you, if this pretty young gal wouldn't mind introducing us to her lady friends."

Alice blushed, but Emery readily agreed, and it was not long before George made the acquaintance of Dora Lamorreaux, a pretty French-Cheyenne girl. Bub's observation regarding the half-breed girls proved to be correct, for Dora was a most engaging companion, laughing merrily at all George's jokes and never tiring on the dance floor. As the evening progressed, they became exclusive dance partners, but George did not feel the least bit threatened, as he might have under other circumstances. Dora was a vivacious young lady whose only interest seemed to be in having a good time, and, that being the case, George was more than happy to show it to her. When the party ended, he asked if he might take her to the next night's dance, and she happily said yes.

Two days later George and his friends left Lander full of the holiday spirit. They had received much generosity there, and they were returning to Wind River with many gifts of their own.

On Christmas Day George and Al rushed through their daily chores before riding through yet another snowstorm to the Simpson Ranch. They stumbled in the door, their cheeks and noses red from the cold.

"Come in, come in, boys!" Margaret Simpson handed them each a cup of hot coffee to ward off the chill. "My Lord, this winter seems like it's gone on forever, and it's only December. But it's Christmas . . . so no complaining! Merry Christmas, George. Merry Christmas, Al." She gave each man a hug. Al accepted her attention stoically, while George swooped her up and twirled her around.

"Merry Christmas, Margaret! I brought you something from town!"

"Good heavens, George," she replied, somewhat flustered. "You shouldn't have done that."

"Why not? It's Christmas, ain't it?" George grinned, removing a small package from his pocket. Margaret unwrapped the tissue, revealing a little, beaded Indian purse.

"Oh George, it's lovely. What intricate beadwork! How did you know I just love these Indian things?"

Little Ella toddled up and tugged on George's pant leg. "What did you bring me?"

"Now, Ella . . . ," Margaret warned.

"It's OK, ma'am. Ella knows I wouldn't forget her." George picked up the little girl and settled her on his knee. He pawed through his saddlebags, pretending to have difficulty finding her present. "Now where is it? I know it's in here somewhere. Can't seem to find it." He waited until the child squirmed in suspense, then triumphantly pulled it out. "Here it is! What do you think, sweetheart?" He handed her a little doll dressed as an Indian maiden with a beaded dress and tiny moccasins. Ella's eyes grew large.

"Oh, George, she's wonderful. Just what I wanted!"

"Here's some sweets for my sweetheart, too, and for all the rest of you kids." The Simpson children crowded around as he passed out gifts—material for a new dress for Ida, a leather-handled knife for sixteen-year-old Jim.

The rest of the neighbors arrived, and the party was soon in full swing, with George the unrivaled center of attention. Will Simpson passed around the eggnog and his wife organized games for the children. Before long George and Bub Meeks were down on the floor with the kids, keeping the crowd in stitches with their antics. Only Al Hainer refused to share in the merriment. He sat by himself and looked on with a half-smile but couldn't be enticed to join the fun.

As they dined on Margaret's wonderful meal of roasted

chicken, cornbread stuffing, mashed potatoes, canned peaches, and several kinds of pie, talk turned to Cassidy's, Meeks's, and Manseau's trip to Lander. They filled everyone in on all the latest news from town and provided a few juicy tidbits of gossip.

Twelve-year-old Ida piped up: "I hear George has got a girlfriend now. Heard he took her to all the dances!"

"Do tell!" said Ida's mother, Caroline, cocking her head at George coquettishly. "Who's the lucky lady, George?"

"Why, I don't know what you're talking about, ma'am. I just had me a good time with all the ladies." His blue eyes flashed around the table, causing all the females, from six-year-old Ella to Grandmother Margaret to catch their breath and flutter their eyelashes.

"Don't let him fool you," Andrew Manseau said, laughing. "He had a special good time with Dora Lamorreaux!"

"I know the Lamorreaux family," said Gene Amoretti, who as the local banker knew just about everybody within a hundred miles. "Nice girl, Dora is."

Lucky girl, Caroline thought to herself.

George reddened under the attention. He would have to have a talk with Bub and Andrew to find out who was spreading gossip about him.

Sensing his discomfort, Margaret broke in to steer the discussion in a different direction. "I've got a letter for you, George, postmarked from Beaver, Utah, I believe it was. It was in the packet you boys delivered for Emery. Do you have family in Utah?" As the local postmistress, Margaret kept track of all her neighbors' correspondence. Her question had been asked innocently enough, but George's face darkened, and he hesitated briefly before answering.

"No, ma'am. Must be from a friend. I come from New

161

York City." He had instinctively named a place as far away from Wyoming as he could think of, but he realized even as he said it that New York City would seem an unlikely hometown for someone like him. Sure enough, Margaret raised her eyebrows, and several others cast skeptical glances his way. He shrugged and attempted to explain. "I came West, when I was real young. Can't even remember nothing about the East."

"Does your family still live in New York?" asked Will Simpson.

"Uh, no. My parents are dead, and my brothers and sisters kind of moved around a lot. Margaret, I don't believe I've ever had a finer meal," he complimented his hostess, hoping to forestall further questions. Everyone voiced their agreement, and the conversation moved on. Only Al Hainer, who knew George's story for the lie it was, kept quiet, every now and then casting an inscrutable look at his partner.

The winter of 1889–90 refused to go away quietly. The snow fell and the wind blew until even good-natured George, frequently forced to spend long periods of time alone with the increasingly uncommunicative Hainer, began to be cross and irritable. There was a brief break in the weather toward the end of January during which George returned to Lander. He looked up Dora, who was greatly pleased to see him, and they spent a pleasant afternoon riding horses along Squaw Creek. Dora was quite taken with the handsome young cowboy, but something told her to keep things on the light side, so she laughed and frolicked and kept her serious thoughts to herself. The Cheyenne girl's instincts were well-founded, for Cassidy was interested only in carefree female companionship. Not for him, a steamy romance or any amorous declarations. He was even careful to offer only chaste kisses on the cheek lest Dora begin to think she had some claim on him.

He returned to Horse Creek where a surly Al Hainer awaited him with unwelcome news. The unusually harsh winter had forced them to use up their stores of hay, and now they did not have enough left to keep the horses fed until spring. George dipped into his already depleted savings to buy hay from Andrew Manseau, but he knew it was a hopeless cause. His money gone, his stock barely hanging on, it appeared that his dream of operating his own ranch was going up in smoke. He would hang on until spring and then see what happened.

To make matters worse, a flu epidemic struck the Wind River area. One of the few people not affected by the illness, George did what he could to help, picking up home remedies from the Simpson Ranch and distributing them to his neighbors. On more than one occasion he fell asleep in his saddle as he made his rounds, but he pushed on, knowing people were counting on him.

Then, little Ella Simpson came down with a bad case. None of Margaret's remedies offered any relief, and the child lay for days on her bed, alternating between feverish sweats and joint-quivering chills. In desperation, the family decided to seek treatment from the doctor at Fort Washakie, sixty miles away. Will Simpson was saddled up and ready to go, when George rode in and insisted on going himself, pointing out that in all likelihood he could make the trip faster and that Will was needed at home. The situation was too serious to waste time arguing; Will simply nodded and sent George on his way, praying that this strong, capable, and determined man would return with a miracle for his daughter.

The skies were clear when George left Jakey's Fork that

morning, but, by noon, a familiar, sullen whiteness had descended, and the air was heavy with moisture. George pushed his horse on, knowing he must get as far as possible before the snow started. He could see the flat-topped Crowheart Butte rising in the distance when the first flakes fell. He was making good time, but already darkness was settling in, and he had no desire to camp overnight in a blizzard. He could not afford to stop anyway; every minute counted for little Ella.

The wind picked up. Snow stung his face and soaked his woolen coat. Night fell, and it became harder to tell in which direction he was headed. Somehow, he and his horse intuitively kept on the right path. He lost whole periods of time when he knew he must have fallen asleep in the saddle, but the difference between sleeping and waking was minimal—his mind wandered so that he didn't know if he were dreaming or merely lost in thought.

An image of Annie, rocking in front of a warm fire in their Circle Valley cabin came to him. Then he pictured her on the day he left home, worry lining her face as she begged him not to go. Suddenly a vision of Mike Cassidy floated before him, first on the roof of his mother's dairy barn and then around a campfire, smoking a cigarette and telling a young boy that sometimes you had to kill to survive. Mike Cassidy melted into Elzy Lay, grinning and tipping his hat, and, finally, Elizabeth Bassett swam into view, all tousled hair and hazel eyes and beguiling smile. He jerked awake, and his horse shied beneath him.

"Easy boy. Not far to go now."

To his left, dawn was breaking. The wind had died down, but the snow still fell in big cottony puffs. Although it was too overcast to see the sun rise, lightness slowly overtook the dark. He rode into Fort Washakie at what he thought was about seven in the morning, not too early, he hoped, to find someone awake.

Although his mission was to find the post's doctor, he stopped first at J. K. Moore's General Store to get warm and regroup. He slid off his mount, gritting his teeth against the ache in his muscles. Accustomed as he was to spending long hours in the saddle, his legs had practically frozen in place, and he walked stiffly and in pain to the store's entrance. Praying that the store would be open, he tried the door. A little bell attached to the door jingled as he entered, and he thought he had never heard a cheerier sound. The room he entered was large and stocked from floor to ceiling with goods of all kinds. It was dark, the wall lanterns not having been lit yet, and the outside light too gloomy to penetrate into the room. He smelled coffee brewing.

"Hello?" he called, his voice hoarse from the cold. "Anybody here?"

From the rear of the store came the clanking sound of somebody closing the door of a pot-bellied stove. A woman emerged from behind a curtain.

"I've only just opened, sir. Would you care for a cup of coffee while I get things ready?"

Even in his exhausted state, the girl's voice captivated him. It was low to the point of being husky, and it had a musical timbre to it that vibrated like a cello.

He walked stiffly to the back and laid his hat on the counter. Her eyes widened at the sight of him, clothes wet and dripping melted snow, face chapped, and eyes red-rimmed and bleary with fatigue.

"Miss," he croaked, "I've ridden sixty-some miles, all the way from Horse Creek, in less than twenty-four hours. Yes, I surely would like some of that coffee I smell cooking."

She sprang into action, stepping around the counter with

concern in her large, brown eyes. "Of course, Mister Cassidy. Here, give me your coat. Come sit by the stove."

She led him into the back room, and he sank wearily into a chair. He closed his eyes and let his head fall back as the heat started to work its way into his chilled bones. He could hear her preparing the coffee, but she said nothing, and he was grateful for her silence, wanting only to sit by the fire and let the warmth soak in. She touched his hand to let him know his coffee was ready and smiled softly at him as he took the steaming cup. After a few minutes the hot liquid rejuvenated him, and it slowly came back to him what she had said.

"How do you know my name?" he asked.

She smiled again and spoke in her husky voice. "My friend, Dora, told me about you. She described you, and then, when you said you came from Horse Creek, I knew who you were . . . George Cassidy."

George looked at her more closely. She was obviously a half-breed with those deep-set, dark eyes and high cheekbones. Her long, straight nose, too, was more Indian than white. Her complexion, though, was fair, her forehead high, and her lips lush and full. Her dark hair glowed with a healthy sheen.

"What's your name, Miss?" he asked.

"Mary Boyd."

"You're a friend of Dora's, you say? Why ain't I ever met you before? Don't you go socializing in Lander like the other girls?"

Mary stood to fetch the coffee pot. She refilled his cup before answering. "I live on the reservation with my family. What with working here at the store and my chores at home, I don't get to Lander much."

George would have liked to ask her more, but he suddenly realized he was wasting precious time. He had to find the doctor and hurry back to little Ella before it was too late. "Miss Boyd, I need your help."

She set the pot back on the stove and turned to him, her dark eyes full of concern.

"There's a little girl who's very sick. I came to fetch the doctor for her. First off, I need you to tell me where to find him. Second, I need to borrow a horse. The one I got ain't going to make it all the way back in this weather. While I'm hunting up the doctor, I wonder if you could get me the loan of a horse." He paused and rubbed his eyes. They felt as scratchy as his day-old growth of beard.

"Of course, I'll help you, Mister Cassidy," Mary said calmly. "But you'll be no good to anyone without something to eat and some rest. You can't go back out in this weather the way you are now."

"I got to. They're counting on me." George started to rise, but she placed a firm hand on his shoulder.

"Of course, they're counting on you. That's why you must see that you get there. You must take care of yourself so that you can return to them as quickly as possible. I'll fix you something to eat and then you rest here for a while." She nodded toward a cot in the corner of the room. "While you sleep, I'll fetch the doctor and find you a new horse. Doesn't that make sense?"

George just wanted her to go on talking forever. Her lovely voice was so soothing, and, while part of him thought he should not let this half-breed girl tell him what to do, it was comforting to let someone else take charge. Relaxing back into his chair, he folded his arms over his chest and gave her a tired smile. "Yes, ma'am. You're the boss."

Nodding briskly, she began to prepare a quick meal for him. As she worked, George filled her in on the nature of Ella's illness. She set his food down and watched him eat.

His uncombed hair, flattened by his hat, fell over his fore-head, making him appear younger than he probably was. Dora had made him sound like such a man of the world, but to Mary he seemed a little vulnerable. He finished and straightened up, giving her another small smile. She noticed how, even in his exhaustion, his smile reached all the way to his eyes. No wonder Dora was so crazy for him.

She cleared the dishes and wiped her hands. "I'll go find Doc Wilson now. Try to get some rest. I'll close up the store so you won't be bothered." He stumbled to the cot, the warm food and cozy room already lulling him to sleep.

When he woke, she was sitting in the chair, her hands folded in her lap. He blinked and sat up, holding his head in his hands. The rest had not really refreshed him—his head felt like it weighed a ton.

"How long have I been sleeping?" he asked.

"Only a couple of hours," she said. "I was about to wake you. I know you want to get back on the road."

"Where's the doc?"

"He's not coming. I described Ella's symptoms to him. He said it's just a bad case of the flu and gave me some medicine for you to take to her. Said there wasn't any point in going himself."

"God dammit! Sorry, Miss, but I promised Will I'd bring the doctor with me. I can't go back without him."

"You can talk to Doctor Wilson yourself, if you like, but I doubt you'll have any better luck. Anyway, he's gone out on a call, and by the time you track him down, a lot of time will have wasted. He seemed quite confident the medicine would do some good."

Once again, Mary's reassuring voice swayed George. She was right, he needed to take the medicine and go, now, be-fore it was too late.

"What about a horse?" he asked, slipping on his coat that had dried by the fire.

"Everything's ready," she said.

Outside, the snow still fell, although the sun was trying valiantly to break through. Just as Mary had said, a fresh horse, outfitted with George's saddle and gear, stood tied to the hitching post.

"This is Indigo," Mary said, gently patting the animal.

"Your pa's?" asked George.

"No." A troubled look crossed her face. "A friend's. He'll take care of your horse until you return with Indigo."

George tucked the medicine bottle into his saddlebags and turned to look at her. Flakes of snow clung to her dark hair and shoulders like a pearly shawl. She smiled and held out her hand, palm up. In it rested a shiny piece of translucent moonstone, no bigger than her thumbnail.

"Give this to Ella for me, please. Little girls like shiny things, and maybe it will bring her good luck."

He took the stone and studied it for a moment, too moved to speak. Who was this girl who had taken such good care of him and now offered a gift to a child she had never met?

"I don't know how to thank you, Miss Boyd," he began. She shook her head and reached out to close his hand around the stone.

He mounted up and put his horse into a quick walk. He had been at the fort only a few hours and faced another twenty-four hours in the saddle before his ordeal ended, but he felt good. His head was clear, his heart was light, and Mary's food had warmed his insides. He looked down at the milky moonstone still clutched in his hand. *Maybe it's my good luck charm, too,* he thought.

Chapter Twelve

Finally, after five months of constant assault, winter began to loosen its hold on the Wind River basin, but it left sad reminders of its long reign. Many families had lost loved ones to the flu, although Ella Simpson had survived, thanks to George Cassidy's valiant efforts. But even those who escaped that tragedy were faced with other disasters—dead or starving livestock, heifers too weak to calve, savings that had been wiped out to pay for extra hay.

Cassidy's and Hainer's herd had dwindled to just a few horses. They struggled to supplement it, riding the open range for days at a time in search of wild horses, but it was not enough. George knew they would have to move on, finding other work, to sustain them at least temporarily before they could make a go of their ranch. George joined the other Wind River ranchers in the spring roundup, then made a deal with Gene Amoretti to board what remained of his herd until he and Al could return. Packing most of their belongings with them, they rode south to town for extra supplies before heading east toward Hole-in-the-Wall.

Cassidy was mounted on Indigo, to which he had become quite attached since his perilous journey from Fort Washakie. Indigo was a reliable, if not flashy, horse, and George hated having to trade him back for his own stove-up mount. He would not think of keeping him, especially after Mary Boyd had treated him so kindly, and in the back of his mind he was grateful for this opportunity to see her again.

Although he would not admit it, he had spent much of

the last two months thinking about the pretty half-breed girl. When he had pressed Mary's moonstone into Ella's little hand, the child's feverish eyes had lit up, and he was half convinced that the tiny gem had done as much to cure her as the doctor's medicine. He could not forget Mary's beautiful voice, or the way she had calmly come to his aid, taking control of the situation in her no-nonsense way. He looked forward to seeing her, even if it were for the last time.

At Fort Washakie George sent Al on to Lander, promising to catch up with him later. Then he pointed Indigo toward J. K. Moore's General Store. The Army fort looked quite different on this sunny spring day than it had only two months earlier. Blue-jacketed soldiers mingled with Shoshone Indians from the reservation, some in native attire, some dressed Western-style, as Mary had been. People picked their way through muddy streets, happy to be out and about after enduring the harsh winter.

Moore's emporium was crowded. It took several minutes of searching for George to determine that Mary was not there. He introduced himself to the man behind the counter who turned out to be J. K. Moore himself.

"Oh, yes, Mary told me about you, Cassidy. Heard the whole story about your trip from Horse Creek and back. Mighty fine thing for you to do, son. Hope the little girl was OK."

George assured him of Ella's recovery and inquired after Mary.

"She ain't working today. Most likely you can find her at home. Just ride on out to the reservation and ask for the Boyd place . . . everyone knows where they live."

Moore was right. George had no trouble locating the Boyd home, a small cabin no bigger than the one in which he had grown up. As he rode up to it, he saw her sitting on the front stoop, churning butter. His heart lifted, and a smile broke across his face. "Afternoon, Miss Boyd."

She stopped her work and looked up, shielding her eyes from the sun. "Mister Cassidy! I'm so glad to see you. How is little Ella? I've thought so much about her."

She was just as he remembered—a husky-voiced beauty whose first thought was for others.

"She's fine, thanks to you. Keeps that moonstone with her everywhere she goes."

"Thank goodness. I had a feeling she'd make it, though. I just didn't see how God could let her die after you'd done such a brave thing to try and save her."

George reddened a bit under her praise. "I don't know if it was brave or just plain stupid. Anyway, I brought Indigo back. He's a fine horse. Your friend done me a real favor loaning him to me."

"I told him you needed a good, strong horse . . . that it was a matter of life and death."

"How did you know I'd bring him back?" George stroked Indigo's neck, unable to meet Mary's eyes as he waited for her answer.

"I just knew you would," she said softly. "I knew it would be a matter of honor for you."

George looked at her closely. It had been a long time since anybody had called him honorable. He caught himself wondering what it would be like to stick around for a few days, then brought himself up short. Damn if he would change his plans to go mooning after some girl, even if she did have a voice that sent chills up and down a man's spine.

"Where's my old horse?" he asked, eager to be on his way now that he realized he was in danger of feeling something for this girl.

"My friend Jake is boarding him. I'll take you there." She

rose from her stool and wiped her hands on her apron.

"I hate to bother you, miss. Can't you just tell me where to go?"

"Yes, I could. But the sun is shining for what seems like the first time in months, and I'd like to go for a ride. Just let me get my sister to finish this churning. I'll be right back."

Before George could offer any protest, she ducked into the cabin, emerging a minute later with a young girl and a teen-aged boy. All three shared the same deep-set eyes and high cheekbones of their Indian heritage.

"I'd like you to meet my brother, Bill, and my sister, Susan," said Mary.

Bill Boyd stepped forward and gave George's hand a firm shake. "Mary told us about what you did for that little girl. I told her we'd never see Indigo again, but I guess I was wrong. I apologize for thinking badly of you."

"No need for that. I got to admit I took a shine to this here horse. Maybe his owner will sell him to me."

"I'm going to take Mister Cassidy to see Jake," Mary said. "Tell Ma and Pa I'll be back for supper."

Bill looked troubled. "You sure about that, Mary?"

"I'm sure. It'll be fine." She hesitated, then added: "Just tell Pa I had to go in to the store for the afternoon."

Cassidy helped her into the saddle, then mounted up behind her. Her braided hair brushed his face as she arranged herself, and he was briefly reminded of Elizabeth Bassett although this girl's hair was really nothing the same. It was thick and straight and almost coal black, where Elizabeth's had been curlier and shot through with streaks of red. She was like Elizabeth in some ways, though—direct, assertive, comfortable around men. Yet she seemed less complicated and lacked the haughtiness that had sometimes character-ized the older woman.

They set a leisurely pace, neither of them in a hurry to reach their destination. George was acutely aware of her closeness; with every step Indigo took, Mary's thighs brushed against his. They rode in silence for a ways, trying to hold their bodies apart, but after a while they settled into the horse's rhythm and became less embarrassed by the incidental contact.

Finally, George said: "You didn't want your folks to know you'd gone with me. Why not?"

She gave a slight shrug. "Pa doesn't much like me being around men. I told Bill to say I'd gone to the store just so Pa wouldn't take it out on Bill. But I'll tell him where I was when I get back. I'm a grown woman. He can't tell me what to do."

"Is that why I ain't never seen you at any of the parties in Lander?"

"Yes. Pa's funny about that, but I do go into town now and then, just the same. We must have missed each other, is all, or maybe you just didn't notice me."

"I would have noticed you," said George. Mary did not reply. In a moment she adjusted herself in the saddle so that her back occasionally brushed against his chest. A tightness started to form in the pit of his stomach that he tried to ignore, but the feel of her strong, straight back and the sunshiny smell of her hair almost overwhelmed him.

He swallowed hard. "Who's this friend of yours we're going to see?" he asked, trying to find a safe topic of conversation.

"His name is Jake Two Feathers. He runs a little ranch between the reservation and the fort. He's a wonderful man. I know you'll like him." George found himself feeling almost jealous of Jake Two Feathers for having earned Mary's affection.

"Tell me about yourself, Mister Cassidy," she said lightly. "You look like you've led an interesting life."

George laughed. "Depends on what you call interesting. I've been around some, but there's a lot more I aim to see."

"Me, too," Mary said enthusiastically. "I've lived my whole life on the reservation, but I'm going to move on one of these days. Maybe to California."

"California!" George exclaimed. "Why there?"

"Oh, I've read all about it. It sounds so beautiful! It's got everything . . . ocean, mountains, desert. And it's never cold there. After this winter, I don't think I ever want to be cold again." She gave an involuntary shiver, and it was all George could do not to wrap his arms around her and pull her close.

"How are you going to get there?" he asked.

"I don't know," she said, suddenly subdued. "It's just a dream. Maybe that's all it will ever be." They were silent for a moment, then Mary said softly: "What about you, George? Where do your dreams take you?"

He did not answer right away. For the first time she had called him George, and she had asked about his dreams, and he knew whatever he said next would matter to both of them. Mary turned around to look at him with her clear, kind eyes, and suddenly he wasn't afraid to tell her.

"Somewhere where there ain't nobody to tell me where to go or what to do, where you can see a hundred miles in every direction, except there ain't nothing to see but mountains one way and plains the other and maybe some rivers and cañons in between."

"I believe you're living your dream right now then, Mister Cassidy," she said, smiling.

He shook his head. "It don't ever seem to last, though."

She turned back around and thought a moment, then said: "That kind of life seems too lonely for someone like you. Wouldn't you miss being around people?"

"Oh, sure. I like company as much as the next fella. Everybody needs entertainment now and then. But the real living goes on out here, out in the open, where there ain't no walls boxing you in. Don't you love sleeping around a campfire, Mary, with the breeze blowing and the coyotes howling and nothing at all between you and the stars?"

"Yes," she said in her low, throaty voice. "That would be heaven."

George's heart leaped up. He wanted to grab her shoulders, turn her around, and kiss her long and hard, for she knew now what he craved in life and had said she wanted it, too. But he couldn't, for, if what he wanted was freedom, he would not find it by falling in love with a woman like Mary. If he started in with Mary Boyd, it would be for forever, and forever was not in his vocabulary. He settled for affectionately pulling at her hair. She let her head fall back on his chest for just a second, and he wondered if she could feel the sweet ache inside him.

They reached Jake Two Feathers's small ranch, and found Jake in the barn, brushing down one of his dozen or so horses. Short and bowlegged, with a paunch that rode well over the top of his worn Levi's, Jake was not the rival for Mary's affections that George had feared. He was, however, as kind and generous as Mary had described, refusing George's offer to pay for the board of his horse for the last two months. He was pleased to see Indigo again, and asked George how the horse had fared on the arduous journey back to Horse Creek.

"This here horse has got a hell of lot of bottom to him," said George. "He ain't going to win no races, but, you can be damn sure, he'll get you where you want to go. How about that old plug of mine? You think he's good for anything but the glue factory?"

"Oh, yes," said Jake, patting George's horse protectively. "He's fine for short distances. He's so good-tempered and gentle. My children love to ride him."

"Say, Jake, what say we do a little swap? I could use a good, reliable horse like Indigo, and your kids could keep old Willy there. 'Course, I'll throw in some cash, too, to make it even."

Jake was amenable to the trade, and, after some brief bartering, the two men struck a deal. Soon George and Mary were back aboard Indigo, retracing their steps. As they rode, Mary told him a little about her family. Her father, Bill Boyd, had married her Shoshone mother in his home state of Missouri, but had lived for the past twenty-five years on the Wind River reservation where he made his living by ranching and trading with the Indians. He had come to love his wife's people, choosing to live among them, instead of with white society in Lander. Mary thought his gruff ways and over-protectiveness toward his six children stemmed from his conflicting desires for them; while he wanted them to follow in his footsteps by staying on the reservation, he realized the lack of opportunities that existed there. Sooner or later, he knew, he would lose his children to the white world, but he fought against it every step of the way. Mary's brother, Bill, whom George had met back at their cabin, had already struck out on his own at seventeen, and Mary, too, was chafing at the bit. As an unmarried woman, however, she was not as free to declare her independence. Her father had agreed to let her work in Mr. Moore's store, but he, otherwise, kept a tight rein on her, or at least tried to. As Mary had asserted earlier, she was twenty-one years old and her own woman, and not inclined to abide by her father's strict rules, although for her mother's sake she had so far kept her rebellion to a minimum.

George let Indigo meander down to the banks of a brush-lined creek. He dismounted and helped Mary down, careful not to hold on to her waist any longer than necessary. As he had with Dora, he acted the perfect gentleman, but for very different reasons. In Dora's case, he had not wanted the girl to get any ideas. With Mary, he was fighting to keep his own head.

He squatted and picked a stalk of cheat grass, slowly peeling its layers. "Why is it parents always fight against their kids going out on their own?" he mused. "You'd think they'd want them to get out of the rut they made of their own lives."

"Did your father try to keep you from leaving?"

"More my ma than my pa. I think Pa knew I'd leave soonest chance I got, but Ma . . . well, she didn't want me to go."

Mary sat beside him, her long, black braid falling over one shoulder. "She must have loved you very much."

George stared past her, lost in thought. "I was her oldest boy. She thought I'd really make something of myself."

Mary smiled. "I think Missus Cassidy's son has made something of himself. She would be proud of you, George."

Mary's use of his adopted name to refer to his mother startled him. *A lie*, he thought. *Everything about me is a lie. If they only knew, Mary and my mother, what kind of life I've really led, they would be ashamed, not proud.*

"Better be going, if we're going to get you back by supper time." He got to his feet quickly, suddenly all business. How had this girl gotten him to talk like that anyway? He had told her things he had never told anyone, things he had not even thought about in years.

Mary noticed the change in him, the way he suddenly shut her out after beginning to open up to her. She grinned and poked him in the ribs. "Watch this, paleface," she said, and, grabbing Indigo's reins, she mounted the horse from its right side, Indian-style.

"What do you know about that . . . a half-breed horse!" laughed George. "You got any more tricks up your sleeve?"

"Just might," said Mary, tossing her head.

When they neared the Boyd property, Mary stopped him a good hundred yards from the cabin. "Let me off here," she said. "I'll walk the rest of the way."

He frowned. "I ain't afraid to see your pa, if that's what's bothering you."

"Please, George. It's easier this way."

He started to help her down, but she ignored him, swinging her leg over Indigo's back and sliding to the ground unassisted. He chuckled, pushing his hat back on his head. "You beat everything, Mary Boyd!"

She held out her hand. "Good bye, George. Good luck." He clasped her hand and held on even as she made to leave, forcing her to meet his gaze. She waited, but he said nothing, just stood there, jaw clenched, eyes snapping. Then he let go. With a final smile, she turned and walked briskly down the road. After a bit, without checking to see if he still watched, she thrust her arm into the air and waved. As he pointed Indigo in the opposite direction, he waved back, but she never noticed.

Chapter Thirteen

"Where'd they go?"

Cassidy followed Al Hainer into the narrow cleft in the rock wall. Pinkish-red, sandstone cliffs surrounded them on three sides—a dead-end. Yet, George was certain the men they had been following had ridden directly into this narrow opening. "Damned if I know, Al. Any tracks?"

Both men dismounted and searched the ground. "Nothing but rock. Can't tell a damn' thing." Hainer kicked at some loose pebbles, spraying them against the side of the rock wall.

George wandered out the way they had come in, his head bent low. "See this?" He pointed to a small red stone imbedded in the earth; one corner of it showed a telltale scrape. "They came this way, all right. Question is, how'd they go through solid rock?" He started to laugh. "Looks like they pulled a fast one on us, partner."

Hainer spat in disgust. "Come on. I ain't going to waste any more time hunting those assholes."

The sound of scraping rock caught their attention. A shaft of sunlight broke through at the far end of the cleft in the wall. It slowly widened as the two men George and Al had been following, Nate Champion and Tom O'Day, muscled aside a large boulder. "I'll be damned. So that's how you did it!" said George.

Nate grinned and motioned them through. "Come have a look."

Cassidy and Hainer stepped through the narrow opening and stopped short, awestruck. "Welcome to Hole-in-the-

180

Wall," Nate said. Below them, sandwiched between the sandstone precipice where they stood and the Big Horn range to the west, lay a beautiful, green valley, covered with Wyoming shortgrass. Hundreds of cattle grazed lazily as the summer breeze ruffled the meadow. It was a rancher's paradise, tucked away in this unknown and virtually undiscoverable rent in the cliffs.

"God Almighty, look at all them beefs," breathed Al. "No wonder Carey and Nolan hate your guts."

"Fuck Carey and Nolan," said Nate, annoyed at Al for bringing up his bitter foes, two of the largest cattle ranchers in central Wyoming. "Believe me, they'd fuck you, if you don't keep your ass covered."

"You trailed all those cattle through this one notch in the wall?" asked George, amazed.

"Not all at once. But yeah, me and Tom, Flat-Nose, Walt, we been running 'em through here a few at a time. Drives those fucking ranchers crazy. They don't have a clue where we're taking 'em."

"Do they know who's rustling their cattle?" asked Al.

Nate gave him a dark look. "Yeah, I reckon. Who gives a shit?" He spurred his horse down the side of the hill, along a well-worn trail. George, Al, and Tom followed him to his camp by Buffalo Creek where he had constructed a small cabin and corral. The Hole-in-the-Wall valley was riddled with small streams and creeks, off-shoots of the Powder River. They were the reason for the valley's comparative lushness.

Nate hopped down and began unsaddling his mount. "You boys stay here tonight. Tomorrow, I'll take you up north a ways. There's a pretty piece of land by Blue Creek ain't nobody claimed yet. You fellas might as well take it, if you want."

"A squatter's claim?" asked Hainer uncertainly.

"Yeah, I guess you could call it that. It's legal, if that's what you're worried about."

"Sounds good to me," said George. "Hell, this is as pretty a valley as I've ever seen. Think I'll stay a while."

Nate nodded in agreement. "It's a damn' good set-up. Cassidy, I hear you got quite an eye for horseflesh. Come check out my herd."

The two men ambled down to the corral. Leaning on the top rail, George surveyed the half dozen horses inside the pen. He immediately picked out a good-looking horse with wild eyes and a skittish manner that probably had just come in off the range.

"Just brought that chestnut filly in a couple of days ago," said Nate, confirming George's guess. "Figger she's going to be a bitch to train."

"I'll work on her, if it's OK with you," George said. "I kind of got me a system for dealing with bronc's like that."

"Hey, I don't mind you busting your tail to break my horse," Nate grinned. He had taken an immediate liking to Cassidy when they had met just west of here at Tom Osborne's ranch. Cassidy was fresh from the Wind River area, and Champion had been out scouting for stray cattle. Cassidy's sunny disposition and savvy way with horses had impressed him, and he had invited George and his partner to join him and the rest of the boys in Hole-in-the-Wall. Much as he liked Cassidy, though, he couldn't warm up to Al Hainer with his sly looks and stand-offish ways. He didn't trust the man, and, for Nate, trust was paramount.

"What's with Hainer, anyway?" he asked casually.

"Al? He's OK. Just hard to get to know, is all."

"How well do you know him?"

"Well, we wintered together last year. Guess you get to know a man pretty good under those circumstances. You got a problem with him?" There was no edge to Cassidy's voice, but Champion got the clear impression the man would stick up for his partner.

"Reckon not. He just seems a mite too concerned about the legal niceties of things, if you know what I mean. He ain't going to rat on us, is he?"

George hesitated, framing his answer carefully. "I don't see nothing to rat about. You and the other boys got as much right to be here as anyone, and all those cattle down there," he waved toward the fields, "hell, the only brand I see on them is yours."

"I'm glad you see it that way. I just hope your partner does, too." Nate kept his voice non-threatening, but George knew he was being warned. Truth to tell, he occasionally had the same uneasy thoughts about Hainer. But a man didn't sell out his partner on the basis of vague suspicions.

"We're headed for some dicey times, Cassidy," Nate went on. "Coming off of last winter where everybody lost so many head, them big boys is going to come down hard on us. It's already happening. That damn' Stockman's Association tried to keep anybody who ain't a member from working the roundup this spring. And it ain't like the old days, when anybody could register his brand and stock his own herd. Hell, nowadays you do that, you get blacklisted . . . can't ever work for one of the big boys again. Or worse, and you know what I mean. Look what happened to Cattle Kate."

George was well aware of that lady's fate. The previous summer, two supporters of the small homesteader, Jim Averill, a journalist, and Ella Watson, known as Cattle Kate to the many young cowboys who partook of her favors, had run afoul of the Stockman's Association and ended up swinging from the end of a rope. The two had never stolen one cow themselves, but they had paid the ultimate price for their vocal opposition to the "big boys," as Nate called them. Their friends had been enraged, and many had vowed to seek revenge. George had had no idea that Nate was such a bitter enemy to the large landholders, but he could understand why he was—his own sympathies certainly lay with the underdog.

"I hear you, Nate," said George. "You can count on me, and I'll vouch for Hainer. He ain't got no reason to side with the big fellas. They never done him no favors."

The next day Nate showed them the property along Blue Creek, and both men were so taken with it, they decided to homestead it immediately. They set to work building a rough cabin in the shade of some tall cottonwoods, and, when that job was done, they joined Nate and the others in rustling forays over the Wall. After one or two such trips, however, Al refused to go along. His reasons were plausible enough—he had business in town, or some repairs to do around the ranch, or a sick cow to tend—but George knew they were mere excuses, and it puzzled him. He was certain Al's reticence wasn't due to any moral qualms—Al had never been above rustling a cow or two when the need arose—so he chalked it up to dislike of Nate Champion, who clearly had no use for the petulant Hainer.

It was no more than a niggling worry that George found easy to dismiss, for he was so content in this remote and beautiful valley that he began to think he could make it home. He had intended to stay only long enough to get a stake together to finance his return to Horse Creek, but now he wasn't so sure. As last winter proved, the Wind River region was harsh country where winter started early and spring thaws didn't come until June, whereas the Hole-in-the-Wall, protected by mountains on one side and the sandstone cliffs on the other, stayed relatively mild in the winter. He enjoyed the company here, too. Nate Champion and Tom O'Day were fast becoming close friends, and the rest of the gang—Walt Punteney, Flat-Note Currie, Sang Thompson, among others—were always good for a laugh. True, he had had nice neighbors in the Simpsons and Amorettis, but it was a lot more fun to be with a group of young men much like himself. Men who lived on the wild side, who thrived on taking risks. Men for whom "family" was something from their long ago past and not likely to be part of their future.

George had not forgotten Mary Boyd. Indeed, he thought of her quite often at first, conjuring up her face and voice at quiet moments or when he was drifting off to sleep. Her memory in the beginning caused his heart to ache, but, as the summer waned, heartache yielded to a bittersweet feeling. He knew he did not lead the kind of life that could be shared with a woman, and he regretted that in a way. But thinking of her now brought a smile to his lips and a warmth to his heart. Every now and then he toyed with the idea of asking her to join him, but then dismissed it as quickly as he had thought of it. Hole-in-the-Wall was no place for a woman, at least not a decent one like Mary.

Fall roundup was upon him before he knew it. The Hole-in-the-Wall cowboys drove their cattle to Casper for shipment. Given the bad blood that existed between them and the big ranchers, everyone agreed to keep their backs covered and the revelry to a minimum while in town. They knew two of the biggest ranchers, Carey and Nolan, would be looking for any excuse to take out one of the Hole-in-the-Wall gang. But, in spite of their caution, trouble managed to find them.

Cassidy and Walt Punteney, a big-boned, blond lad whom George had taken under his wing, had wandered in from their campsite on the outskirts of town, looking for a little entertainment. They ended up at the Lady Luck Saloon where they joined a couple of locals in a card game. George and Walt were cheerfully losing—neither had much of a knack for poker—when George became aware of two husky, mean-looking fellows hanging over Walt's shoulder.

"I ain't never seen two white men play a worse game of cards," said the first one, insolently propping a booted foot on the rung of Walt's chair.

"How you suppose they can be so bad at poker and so good at stealing cattle?" said the other, drawing his duster back to reveal two silver-plated six-shooters.

The two locals threw down their cards and scrambled away from the table. "Now look what you done," said George. "And I had a good hand for once. How about you, Walt? Do you have a good hand this time?"

"Best cards I've had all day, dang it!"

"Mmm-mm, what a shame." George shook his head. "What are we going to do about this situation, boys?"

"What are you going to do about all them stolen cattle, Cassidy?" said the first one, coming around the table to stand threateningly at George's side.

"Do I know you?" asked George evenly.

"Mister Carey sent me. Said I should be on the look-out for a couple of shit-eating cattle thieves"—Walt started out of his chair but sat back down at a stern look from Cassidy—"and, when I found them, to deliver a message. Well, it looks like I found them."

George thought quickly. There was no way he and Walt could survive a shoot-out. With one thug standing directly beside him and the other behind Walt, they would be dead before they got out of their chairs. He cursed himself for getting cornered and for not properly appreciating the danger they were walking into in Casper. On the other hand, he found it hard to believe that a prominent rancher like Carey would order his goons to gun people down in broad daylight in the presence of several witnesses. More likely they had been sent merely to intimidate. Well, that was a game two could play.

"I don't believe I know anybody named Carey," George feigned puzzlement. "Do you, Walt?" Walt shook his head. "We don't know a Mister Carey, boys, so go deliver your message somewhere else."

"Now listen to me, Cassidy. . . ."

Just then Al Hainer strode up, a frightened look on his face. "What's going on?" he asked nervously.

The thug next to George backed off a step, and the one behind Walt let his coat fall back over his firearms. They glanced at each other and at Al, their brows furrowed in confusion.

"Why, nothing," George said easily. "These boys was just paying us a friendly visit." He rose slowly and stared at the man next to him, a tight smile on his lips, his eyes flinty hard. "Too bad you got to be leaving now."

A long second ticked by. The man turned on his heel and, motioning to his partner, left the saloon, casting a backward glance at Hainer.

Walt let out a breath and grinned shakily. "You really called their bluff, George. I need a drink!" He signaled the bartender who sent three shots their way. George looked steadily at Al as they drained their drinks. His partner's face was blank.

"Did you know those guys, Al?" he asked.

" 'Course not. Why would I?" Al answered quickly, staring at his whiskey.

"Just seemed like you-all knew each other."

"Never seen them before in my life."

George raised his eyebrows. Something was wrong here, but he could not put his finger on it. He had no proof against Al, and, until he did, he would just have to take his partner at his word. He sighed. "OK. Looks like Nate was right. Carey and his kind mean business. I ain't one to run from a fight, but maybe it's time for a judicious retreat. Hope you boys have had enough of town to last you for a while."

George and Al prepared to winter on Blue Creek. They had made good money on the sale of their cattle, and that fact, plus the anticipation of a shorter and milder winter here in the valley, put George in a fine frame of mind. What's more, he finally felt that he could stop looking over his shoulder for the law on his tail. It had been a year and a half since the Telluride robbery, and, as far as he could tell, no one was pursuing him. While he was not yet ready to show his face in southern Colorado, he did feel as though he could relax his guard a bit. He had no idea if Matt Warner or Tom McCarty were still on the loose, but he, evidently, was going to stay a free man.

Then one evening, as he prepared to go to a barn dance over on Beaver Creek, Al Hainer galloped up and threw open the door to their cabin. Stumbling over the threshold, he leaned against the wall, breathing heavily.

"Whoa there, pardner. What's burning a hole in your britches?" George looked up from adjusting the spurs on his boots.

"I just heard something in town," Al gasped. "You . . . you got to leave, George. They're after you!"

George instantly moved to the door and looked out. He saw nothing. "Who's after me?"

"The law. I . . . . I heard one of Carey's men talking.

There's a warrant out for your arrest!"

Cassidy looked at him sharply. "What for?"

"Rustling. You got to hurry, George. They're coming for you tonight!"

"Hell, this is Hole-in-the-Wall. They ain't going to find me here."

Hainer hesitated, then took a deep breath. "They know how to get through the Wall. They just been waiting for the right time."

"What makes you so sure?" George stared at him intently.

Al looked at the floor. "Like I said, I heard some guys talking in a bar. You know, those two assholes who caused trouble before. They was whooping it up 'cause Carey finally got the Johnson County sheriff to go after the gang."

"So there's other warrants out, too?"

"No, just for you."

"Why only me?" Even as he questioned Al, he moved quickly about the room, gathering things he would need to take with him.

"I don't know. They must have an eyewitness seen you do it. Or thinks he seen you," Al's voice faltered.

George stopped in his tracks and fixed Al with his gaze. "Ain't nobody seen me rustle one fucking cow. Nobody outside the Wall, that is."

Al returned his look without flinching. "I know what you're thinking. It weren't me. I didn't rat on you. Why would I turn in my own partner, for God's sake? There's nothing in that for me."

"That's what I've been telling myself." George upended a large crock and shook out a pile of bills—his share of their earnings from the fall roundup. He stuffed the money in his belt, the same one he had used to carry his Telluride cash. This time the belt was not nearly so full. He found a piece of paper and a pencil and wrote as he gave Al instructions.

"I'm willing to give you the benefit of the doubt, Al. I'll know for sure you didn't sell me out, when you hunt me up and give me my share of this here claim. I'm writing out a paper . . . don't know if it's legal or not . . . deeding you my half of our property, including this land and the cattle. I expect you'll winter here, but come spring, cash out and come find me." He signed the document and handed it to Al.

"Sure, George. You got my word. Where will I find you?"

"I'm heading west," he replied vaguely. "Check with Tom Osborne or Emery Burnaugh." He buckled his saddle-bags and threw them over his shoulder. "So long, Al. See you when the snow melts." He held out his hand, and Al shook it firmly, but his eyes did not quite meet Cassidy's.

George secured his bags on Indigo and mounted up. He headed south and west, following the Middle Fork of the Powder River through steep cañons and densely forested draws. It was tough going, but it would be hard to track him through such wild country. He had no specific destination in mind, but, in a strange way, it felt good to be on the move again. He just wished that, for once, he was not running by necessity.

That night he camped in a cave carved into the cliffs that bordered the river. It was clear and quite cold, but he dared not start a fire, not even in the farthest recesses of the cave. The only food he had was some hard tack that he nibbled on sparingly. Finally, with the wind whistling past the entrance to the cave and snowflakes starting to fall, he rolled himself in his blankets and turned his thoughts to what he would do next. A vision of Mary flashed into his brain, the way she had looked on their ride by the creek when she had mounted Indigo Indian-style and tossed her long, dark hair away from her face. What spirit that girl had! But he was dreaming to think she could play any part in his future. For one thing, from what she had said about her father, the man would likely throw him out on his tail, if he showed up on her doorstep. No, he could not expect Mary's family to take him in, nor could he ask Mary to come away with him. It would be too much to ask her to share the hardships of a life lived on the run. For it appeared that was exactly what was in store for him. He had lulled himself into thinking he was safe, but events of the last few hours had given him a rude awakening. The rustling charge was unrelated to the Telluride job, he felt sure, but it would only take one smart lawman to put the two together and be hot on his tail for armed robbery.

For now, he would probably be safe once he got out of Johnson County. He would return to Horse Creek, although he did not have enough money to get through the winter without hiring out somewhere, maybe at the Amorettis or at Tom Osborne's *Quién Sabe* ranch.

He slept little that night, the cold and his need to stay on guard combining to keep him awake. When he rose just before dawn, the snow had stopped, but a film of ice had formed at the river's edge. He had kept Indigo saddled in case he had to get away quickly in the night, so now he needed only to tighten the cinch straps and tie on his bedroll. "Come on, boy," he said softly. "It's going to be a cold one today. We'll stay warmer, if we keep moving."

Indigo snorted white puffs of air and nudged him with his nose. George led the horse along the riverbanks, searching for a path out of the cañon. *Not another soul on earth knows where I am, or maybe cares,* he thought. *But I'm free. I'm free and aim to stay that way.* He saw a break in the rocks, and with a tap of his heels to Indigo's sides he disappeared into the forest.

Chapter Fourteen

The winter of 1890–91 was much kinder than its predecessor. Nevertheless, it seemed endless to George Cassidy who was beset with an uncharacteristic case of doldrums. He had frittered away his Telluride money, his Horse Creek venture had failed, and he was a wanted man. He felt like he was going nowhere fast. He got by doing odd jobs for Gene Amoretti, for which he was grateful, but he felt demeaned by the work; he was an experienced cowboy, yet chopping wood and mucking out barns was all Gene had to offer. He did the work and kept his mouth shut.

A couple of times, to relieve the monotony, he rode to Lander, and each time he passed the reservation he was sorely tempted to look up Mary. But he couldn't make himself stop. There was no future in it—why torture himself by seeing her again?

Things improved with the coming of spring. True to his word, and defying George's expectations, Al Hainer showed up with George's share of their money from the sale of the Hole-in-the-Wall property. He told Cassidy the Johnson County sheriff had shown up, indeed, with a warrant for Cassidy's arrest. Al said, truthfully, that he did not know where Cassidy had gone. The sheriff half-heartedly searched the area, then called it off after a day or two. Al surmised he had put on a show of looking for Cassidy to satisfy Carey, but that he really was not eager to get in the middle of a feud between the big ranchers and the Hole-in-the-Wall gang.

George accepted Al's explanation, and the two took up as partners once more. They still had the Horse Creek land and the few horses Gene had boarded. With any luck, they could spend the summer building up their herd and maybe make some money come fall.

The summer passed uneventfully, their days spent working on their own ranch or doing odd jobs for neighbors. In August, the two men stopped at the Mail Camp road ranch, halfway between Horse Creek and the *Quién Sabe* outfit, where they occasionally hired out to Tom Osborne. George's old friend, Emery Burnaugh, and his wife, Alice, were headquartered there, and it made a pleasant resting place, situated as it was at the base of the Owl Creek Mountains. Emery saw them coming and stepped out on the front porch of his cabin.

" 'Allo, boys!" came his familiar greeting. " 'Appy to see you! We 'ave a full camp tonight, but the more the merrier, eh? We 'ave a party tonight!"

"Hold on now, Emery," said George. "We don't want to cause no extra work for Alice." Alice Burnaugh was in the last months of pregnancy and tired easily, a fact George knew from previous visits.

"No, no, don't worry about Alice. She 'as a friend up from Lander 'elping out until the baby comes. Go on, stow your gear in the bunkhouse. I'll tell Alice we got two more for supper."

George and Al took the last two available bunks, the camp being full of fellow travelers. They knew most of their bunkmates, men like themselves who followed wherever the trail led and hired out wherever there was a job to be done. For most of them, the idea of marrying and settling down in one place, as Emery had done, was unthinkable.

When the supper bell rang, the men trouped to the

kitchen, already savoring the mouth-watering smells wafting out the door. A voice carried to them on the musky breeze—"Here, Alice, let me carry that. It's too heavy for you."

George stepped into the room, knowing what he would see, for there was no mistaking that distinctive voice. It resonated in him like the vibrating strings of a musical instrument. She had her back to him, preparing to relieve Alice of a large platter of meat. "Hello, Mary," he called softly. "Remember me?"

The platter slipped in Mary's hands, spilling food on the floor. "Oh my, look what you made me do, George! Shame on you for shocking me like that!" She smiled shakily and bent to pick up the mess.

"You two know each other?" asked Alice, eyeing them curiously.

"Yes. . . . Sure do!" They spoke simultaneously, then laughed nervously.

"George was an occasional customer at the store, and I helped him out once when he needed a horse." She smiled at him again, setting serving dishes on the table. George marveled at her intuition. She had known he would not want her to tell the whole story of his heroic ride to save Ella Simpson. It would only embarrass him in front of this unsentimental bunch.

"How long you been here, Mary?" George seated himself where he could get a good look at her. She was as lovely as he remembered, even more so now with her face flushed from working over the hot stove.

"About a month. Emery was at the fort on a mail run, and he told me Alice was having a hard time keeping up with the work here, so I asked if I could come help." She checked the table to see if she had forgotten anything, then sat down across from George. "I thought it would be a chance to get away, you know, from the store and everything." She finished lamely, wondering if he remembered or even cared about her unhappiness at home.

"I don't know how I would have managed without you, either. You're just an angel, Mary, to pitch in like you have." Alice turned to George. "And she won't let us pay her, if you can believe that. Does it all out of the goodness of her heart!"

Mary blushed. "Stop now, Alice. You're doing me a favor putting me up, and you know it." She gave her friend a pointed look, rising to refill the serving dishes.

Charley Willis, a lanky cowboy who would not have been bad-looking except for a mouth full of rotten teeth, glanced at Mary shyly as she set a bowl down in front of him. "Thank you, ma'am. This is sure fine fixin's." Mary gave him a warm smile, and Charley gazed back adoringly, clearly smitten. Alice started to giggle before Emery broke in to inquire after the news from all the travelers.

Later that night, after the men had tended to their horses and the women had cleaned up from supper, everybody gathered on the Burnaugh's front porch. It was still hot, even at this altitude, but a soft breeze made the evening bearable. George sat on the porch rail far back in the shadows, the lighted tip of his cigarette blinking like a beacon. He wanted to look at Mary without being observed. Since he had heard her voice this afternoon, he had been in a turmoil, alternately elated at seeing her again and despondent because he could not allow himself to get close to her. He intended to leave at the crack of dawn, whether Al wanted to or not, just to get away from the temptation she presented.

Mary sat on the top step of the porch, her back leaning

against a rough-hewn post. Her plaited hair fell over one shoulder in a thick river of darkness. As the talk flowed around her, she absent-mindedly stroked her arm, reacting to the conversation's currents without paying close attention. Her thoughts swirled around the dark figure, smoking in the shadows.

When he had shown up today so unexpectedly, all the feelings she thought she had finally vanquished came rushing back. How she had missed him! She had not even realized how much. After their ride together on Indigo, she had known she was in love with him, but, when so many months passed without his coming back for her, she had resolved to go on with her life, to find someone else and be content, if not happy. But this thing inside her, making her feel all warm and fluttery, was too strong to ignore. Now that he was back in her life, she was determined that he would not leave without knowing how she felt about him. Maybe he would run from her again, but, if he did, he would at least know for certain what he was running from.

Charley Willis ambled over and sat on the step just below Mary. He smiled at her crookedly, trying to hide his bad teeth. She gave him a friendly but not too encouraging look, scooting over an inch or two to put a little space between them.

There was a sudden lull in the conversation until Emery called out: "George, did you bring your mouth organ with you? Play us a tune!"

George started, wrenched away from his thoughts about Mary and that idiot Charley Willis. "Sorry, Emery. Don't have it with me." Truth to tell, he had not had his own harmonica since he left Circle Valley and doubted he could play much of anything any more.

"Here, use mine," offered Jeff Green, one of the cowpokes traveling with Willis. He drew the slim instrument from his back pocket and tossed it to Cassidy.

"Hell, I haven't played one of these in six, seven years. Don't know how to any more. You play, Jeff." He tossed it back to Green who shrugged and played a simple tune rather badly, although the group applauded his effort.

"George, you're lying," Emery said. "I 'eard you play not more than two years ago, at a Christmas party in Lander. Remember, you didn't want to, just like now, but Dora Lamorreaux wouldn't take no for an answer. You were damn' good, too."

George shook his head, ignoring the crowd's pleas, until Mary's throaty voice cut through the rest. "Surely, if you'd do it for Dora, you'll do it for us."

He looked at her from under his eyebrows. She gazed steadily back, her lips forming a half smile, daring him to rise to the bait. He leaped off the rail. "Give me that damn' thing, Jeff!"

He blew a few tentative notes to get the feel of it, then swung into a rousing version of "Clementine." Amazingly enough, he had not lost much of his technique, and, as the notes rolled out, he grew more confident, winding up with a fancy flourish. Everybody cheered and clapped and called for more. George turned to Mary, who was laughing and clapping along with the rest, and gave her a slight bow and a broad wink. At Alice's request, he played "Sweet Betsy from Pike," then performed several Stephen Foster tunes, ending with "I Dream of Jeannie with the Light Brown Hair." As the last plaintive notes died away in the soft summer night, Mary clasped her hands to her breast, transported by the music and the moment.

"Told you he was a liar," Emery said. "Don't ever believe it, if George Cassidy tells you he can't do something.

Give us another one, George!"

"Afraid I've exhausted my repertory, or whatever you call it. And I ain't lying this time." George wiped the harmonica on his sleeve and handed it back to Jeff Green.

" 'Ow about a game of cards, then?" Emery said.

A few of the men expressed their approval of that idea and headed inside, while others started ambling toward the bunkhouse. George glanced at Mary out of the corner of his eye. What he really wanted was some time alone with her, but, then again, he was afraid of what might happen. Things might be said and done that could not be taken back. He was about to follow Emery into the cabin, when Charley Willis held out a hand to help Mary up. Nervously crunching his hat, Willis said: "Miss, would you like to go walking with me a spell?"

Mary paused, searching for a tactful way to decline. "Well, Mister Willis, I, um, I. . . ." She threw a desperate glance toward George who hesitated in the cabin's doorway, clearly aware of her predicament but making no move to help her out. A hot flush rose in Mary's cheeks, and her eyes glittered. *All right then,* she thought. *If I have to do it all by myself, then so be it. God helps those who help themselves.* She took a deep breath and said aloud: "Thank you anyway, Mister Willis, but Mister Cassidy has already offered to take me to see his horse, isn't that right, George? You see, he bought Indigo from a friend of mine, and I've always had a special place in my heart for that silly thing." Flashing Charley a charming smile, she took a few steps toward George and waited expectantly.

George looked at her intently, his pale blue eyes strangely dark. "Miss Boyd's right. I almost forgot. Sorry about that, Charley."

Mortified, Willis clapped his hat on his head and

stomped off without a word.

George came down the porch steps and stood close to her. The air around them seemed alive, simultaneously pushing them together and pulling them apart. Then Mary's bravado deserted her, and she turned away, embarrassed. "I'm sorry about that," she managed to say. "I just didn't want to go walking with that Willis fellow. Please, go on to your card. . . ."

"Let's go see Indigo," he interrupted.

They walked down to the corral, the crunch of their boots on the gravelly rock the only sound in the still evening. When they reached the enclosure, George called out softly, and Indigo trotted over, pushing his nose through the rails.

"There he is. Hello, boy, how's my baby?" Mary cooed, rubbing Indigo's nose and ears. "I think he remembers me."

"Sure he does." George picked up a braided rope bridle draped over the rail and climbed into the corral. Fitting it over Indigo's head, he led the horse out the gate. "Come here," he said without looking at her.

She hesitated. "We're going to ride bareback?"

"Should be easy for an Injun gal like you." He bent over and cupped his hands for Mary to step into. She mounted up, and he handed her the reins, then swung up behind her. He took the reins back, his arms encircling her loosely. Mary clutched Indigo's mane, her heart pounding. Tapping the horse gently with his heels, they walked slowly down the road, away from the ranch. After a while, he turned Indigo onto a path that headed uphill and back in the direction from which they had come. They proceeded in silence, the only sound that of Indigo's hoofs scraping on the rocky path. Presently, George reined up and slid off the horse's rump, then helped Mary down. He led her to an outcropping of rock, and she realized they had doubled back above the ranch—she could look down and see the lights from the cabin and bunkhouse a few hundred feet below.

"I never knew about this place," Mary whispered.

"Good view of the whole valley in daylight." He took her hand and led her to the edge of the rocks. They sat with their legs dangling over the precipice. Mary felt the tension between them ease as they both tuned into the deep stillness of the night.

Finally Mary spoke, her voice hoarser than usual. "What did you do with yourself the last year and a half?"

He paused a beat, and, when he answered, there was a wistful note in his voice. "Found me a place east of here, in a beautiful valley full of tall grass. Built a cabin and had a few head of cattle. It was a nice place, Mary, you would have liked it."

"Why did you leave it?"

George shifted. "Had to," he said shortly.

Without thinking, she turned and put her hand on his arm. "George, whatever it is you've done that you won't talk about, whatever reason you had for leaving home, or for leaving this place you just were, it doesn't matter to me. I know the kind of person you are, and I know you wouldn't hurt anybody."

He stared straight ahead, his jaw muscles working. Just when she thought he was not going to respond, he said: "You don't know nothing about me. If you did, you wouldn't be sitting here."

"Well, you don't know me very well, either, do you? I've done a few things I'm not very proud of, but I don't dwell on them, for God's sake." She took her hand off his arm and leaned back on her palms, pursing her lips in irritation.

"I don't think we're talking about the same degree of

sin," George said, with a wry smile.

"Oh, George," Mary sighed in frustration, "you aren't making this easy for me. You say I don't know you, and it's true I know very little about the facts of your life. I mean, until tonight I didn't know you could play the harmonica, but I wasn't at all surprised that you could pick it up after several years and play so well. Somehow, I feel I know all about you, not the details, but . . . the essence of you. The goodness is there, I've seen it, and maybe there's a darkness, too, but it only makes me want to draw it out of you because I. . . ." She caught herself before she said something she would regret. "Well, I missed you and thought about you a lot this past year."

George ducked his head, embarrassed by her outburst, but also strangely thrilled. No woman had ever said things like that to him—not even Elizabeth Bassett had spoken with such passion—and it excited him beyond telling. His warning system had long been activated when it came to Mary Boyd, but the urge to override it came over him strongly. He stood and turned his back to her, squeezing his fist in an effort to control the struggle raging inside him.

"Mary . . . Mary, I thought a lot about you, too." It was all he could get out, and he hated himself for being so meek in the face of her boldness.

Her shoulders sagged, and she shut her eyes against sudden tears. She had not expected a declaration of love, but still she was disappointed. Foolishly she had created a romance where there was none, assumed things she should not have assumed. After all, he had never given her the slightest encouragement.

George spoke again, his voice strained. "Mary, I don't. . . ."

"Don't say anything, George." She stopped him before

he said something that would embarrass her even more. "It's getting late. You best take me back."

George helped her onto Indigo again, wondering how he could have made such a mess of things. He wanted to tell her how much she meant to him and that he dreamed of taking her away to wherever she wanted to go—even to California, if that was her heart's desire. But he simply could not get the words out, and now she was angry with him. Maybe it was for the best—he was getting dangerously close to becoming involved with this girl, and that was something he had vowed never to do.

He climbed up behind her and guided Indigo down the steep path. Mary had to lean back against him to keep her balance on the downhill slope. Her back felt tense and un-yielding next to his chest, but her hair was velvety and thick and loamy smelling against his cheek. When they reached the level road, he handed her the reins. Then, unable to resist, he untied the ribbon that kept her braid in place and slowly unraveled the three coiled strands until her hair fell loose down her back. He sunk his fingers into it, stroking it, gathering it in bunches to brush against his face. A tiny moan escaped Mary's lips, and her breathing became short and shallow. He pulled her long mane to one side and kissed the back of her neck, so softly she could barely feel his touch. She arched her back and drew in her breath sharply.

The sound of a rider overtaking them brought them to their senses. George slid to the ground, loosening his gun in its holster. The rider came into view. George relaxed. It was only Al Hainer, pulling up as he sighted them at the side of the road.

"What are you doing here?" Hainer said abruptly.

"I might ask you the same thing."

Hainer's horse breathed heavily. Wherever Al had gone, he had been in a hurry to get there and back. "Uh, I was out checking the horses, and I thought I heard a gunshot this direction. Decided I'd better look into it."

Not for a minute did George believe this explanation. If there had been any gunshots in the vicinity, he and Mary would certainly have heard them. But he was used to Al doing strange things, taking off at odd hours and returning late with little or no explanation, so he was not too concerned. Besides, he was occupied at the moment and did not want to prolong the conversation.

"You're crazy, Al." He waved a dismissive hand at his partner and took the reins from Mary. She sat tall and straight on Indigo's back, her eyes glowing warmly. George started to lead the horse back to camp. Al kept pace beside them.

"I see you got your squaw riding bareback," he muttered, half under his breath.

George stopped short. "Cut it, Al. Miss Boyd ain't nobody's squaw. Got that?"

Hainer kept walking. George reached for the reins to Al's horse and forced him to stop. "You got that straight?"

For a split second Hainer looked at Cassidy with raw hate and what might have been envy gleaming out of his eyes. His expression turned to mere sulkiness, and he nodded. George let go the reins. Wordlessly, Al spurred his mount past them. By the time they reached the ranch, Hainer had turned his horse loose in the corral and was nowhere to be seen. George did the same for Indigo and walked Mary up to the main house, holding her hand loosely.

"What was that all about?" Mary asked.

"Nothing. Al can be a mite peculiar is all."

"Well, he's certainly got lousy timing!"

George laughed out loud. He pulled her to him and wrapped his arm around her waist. With the other hand, he cupped her chin and smiled down at her. "That he does," he murmured. He kissed her, gently at first, then more urgently as the sweet taste of her went to his head. He held her tighter, entwining his hands once again in her long, luxurious hair. Mary's legs went weak. She felt as though all her strength came from him, that, if he stopped kissing her, she would collapse in a heap at his feet. He backed her against the rough wall of the cabin, his mouth almost bruising hers in his insistence. His hands slid under her arms, grazing the swell of her breasts, then down to her waist. He pulled her forward so their hips were touching. Bending his head, he nuzzled her neck. She threw her arms around him, pressing the whole length of her body against his.

"George," she breathed in his ear. "Do you know what I was trying to tell you back there?"

He grunted in response, so absorbed he barely heard her, much less understood what she said.

"George, George, listen." She put her hands on either side of his head and made him look at her. "I love you, George."

He stared at her with eyes that seemed clouded, heavy-lidded. Her words registered, and, for an instant, a panicky feeling swept over him, but then it was gone and all he cared about was holding her close. He took her hand from the side of his face and kissed her palm, then led her into the cabin and the small room off the kitchen where she slept. He closed the door behind them and not once that whole night did he get the urge to escape.

He slipped out of her room early the next morning, but

not early enough. When he opened the door to the bunk-house, most of the men were already awake, pulling on their boots and running fingers through snarled hair.

"Where were you?" asked Jeff Green, looking pointedly at Cassidy's undisturbed bedroll sitting at the foot of his bunk.

"Out," George said, pulling a bar of soap from his bags.

"Looks more like you've been in," Hainer sneered. "In real tight with that half-breed cook, that is."

George shot Hainer a withering look amid all the whistles and catcalls. "Drop it," he warned. "You don't know what you're talking about."

Hainer shrugged and said no more, but he looked around the room as if to say—"Ain't I right?" Charley Willis glared at Cassidy, and banged out the door.

Breakfast went smoothly to Mary's relief. Alice Burnaugh prattled on, oblivious to what had taken place under her roof last night. Mary had warned George to act as normal as possible, and he did an admirable job, catching her eye only once to offer a tiny wink. She, too, played her part, smiling and joking with the men, all except Charley Willis, who kept his sullen eyes glued to his plate. Once, as she leaned in to put a dish on the table, she braced her hand on the back of George's chair and allowed her fingers to softly caress his back. For some reason, this small proprietary gesture bothered him, but it was soon forgotten amid all the glorious memories from the previous night.

George had about decided it was worth it to get tied down, if it meant getting that kind of loving every night. Not, of course, that was all that attracted him to Mary. She was kind and generous, high-spirited and lively, a hard worker and a loyal friend. All in all, he counted himself a very lucky man this fine summer morning. If only she wouldn't already be acting like she owned him—fondling his back in public, for God's sake. But that was ridiculous. How different was that from the private little wink he had given her?

Later that morning George sat on his bunk, mending a tear in his shirt—a mundane task, but one a single cowboy was forced to do for himself. He and Al had planned to leave Mail Camp after dinner, but he was considering telling Al to go ahead while he stayed for another day or two. He wanted to be with Mary and put off making a decision about their future for as long as possible.

As he clumsily tied off the knot, the sound of several approaching horsemen reached his ears. Buttoning his shirt back on, he stepped outside to check on the commotion. Into the yard rode two men on horseback, one of whom looked vaguely familiar, trailing three horses behind them. George's expert eye roamed over the new horseflesh—a brown, a sorrel, and a gray. They were handsome animals.

Emery came down the porch steps, a wary look on his face. " 'Allo, Billy," he greeted the man whom George thought he recognized. "You staying long?"

"What kind of a welcome is that for a tired and hungry man?" Billy said in a thin, reedy sounding voice.

"Well, we got a full camp 'ere. Don't know as I can put you up, though you're welcome to stay to dinner."

"Cassidy and me is moving on," said Al, coming up behind George. "They can have our bunks."

Emery looked a bit put out, but he held his tongue.

"I ain't sure I'm leaving just yet," George said.

"Do I know you two from somewhere?" Billy pulled a dirty handkerchief from his pocket and wiped his sweaty face.

Al stepped forward, his thumbs hooked in the pockets of

his jeans. "Yeah, you came through the valley where we was last summer, east of here near Carey's C Y outfit. It's Nutcher, ain't it?"

George glanced at his partner. Something about Al's casual demeanor seemed forced. But Hainer was right about the newcomer. George now remembered. Billy Nutcher had stopped briefly in Hole-in-the-Wall the previous summer, but he and Nate had not liked his looks, and, after a few days, Nutcher had gotten the idea and moved on.

"Bingo," Nutcher said. "Cassidy and Hainer, if I remember right. This here's Frank Watts." He nodded toward his silent partner. Watts kept his face averted and made no move to acknowledge the men.

"I'll go tell Alice two more for dinner," Emery said reluctantly.

Nutcher turned to them with a sly grin. "Guess you boys got run out of Hole-in-the-Wall, too, eh? I never did like that asshole Champion. Acted like he owned the place."

"We didn't get run out, leastways not by Champion," said George. "What are you doing in this part of the country?"

"Riding through, mostly. Picking up a few horses here and there."

"This is a good-looking string right here." George patted the sorrel, admiring its sleek lines. "Where'd you get them?"

"Johnson County."

George shot him a questioning look. Nutcher shrugged, then climbed down from his horse. "I know what you're thinking, but I'm telling you, I traded for these beauties, fair and square."

"Ain't much goes on in Johnson County on the up and up," George said.

"Well, this deal was, or my name ain't Nutcher. You interested in buying any of them?"

George moved on to the gray, inspecting its teeth and running his hands along its withers. He did the same to the brown, then faced Nutcher. "I'd buy all three, if I thought they was yours to sell."

Just then the porch door banged open. Mary came out, shaking a rug. She paused when she saw the new arrivals.

Nutcher took no notice of the pretty girl. "I told you they're mine, and I meant it. I'll warrant the title, and I'll give you a good price, too."

He was too eager to make a deal. Given George's recent problems in Johnson County, the smart thing would be to walk away.

"I don't think so, Nutcher," Cassidy said. "If you ain't got any paper on these horses, I ain't interested."

"Wait a minute. I'm your partner. Don't I get a say?" Hainer broke in. George spread his hands, inviting him to speak. "I say we buy them. We could use a couple of good breeding mares, and the sorrel's a damn' fine horse, too. You ain't really worried about the title, either. You just don't want your girlfriend there to think you'd buy a stolen horse!"

"These horses ain't stolen, I'm telling you," Nutcher insisted.

"We heard you," Hainer said. "What do you want for them?"

"Like I said, I'm willing to make a deal. I got no use for them. Let's say fifty apiece."

"Hell, he's practically giving them away," Hainer said.

"Yeah, makes you wonder, don't it?" George tried to ignore Mary who still stood on the porch, pretending to be busy with her rug cleaning. "It smells, Al, and you know it."

"That ain't never stopped you before," Hainer muttered.

Mary suddenly went very still. She folded the rug and

held it tightly to her chest. George wished she would go back inside so he could conclude this business without feeling pressured by her disapproval. Hainer was wrong— his reluctance to buy Nutcher's horses stemmed from his caution about coming to the attention of the Johnson County authorities again. It had nothing to do with Mary's opinion of him. Yet, he knew if he held out, Hainer would accuse him of being a hen-pecked pantywaist. George pursed his lips and gave Mary an irritated look. What right did she have to stand there and listen in on his business? One night together and a few tender words exchanged, and, before you knew it, the woman was trying to run your life.

Scowling, George turned back to Nutcher. "Can you write me out something that says you traded for those horses fair and square?"

Billy squinted his eyes and twisted his mouth, considering. "That'll cost you more."

"I thought you said you'd warrant the title."

"My word is my warrant. You want something on paper, the price'll go up."

Hainer rolled his eyes impatiently. "Come on, George. You can't turn down fifty dollars apiece."

George willed himself not to look at Mary again, but, out of the corner of his eye, he could see her quietly step back into the cabin. He knew she had removed herself from the scene to let him save face, but he could not make himself feel grateful. Mostly he felt annoyed that she had intruded in the first place. It wasn't fair, he knew, but he couldn't help it. He turned to look at Hainer who stood waiting, hands on hips. *What the hell*, he thought. *I've done riskier deals than this.*

"OK, Nutcher, you got yourself a deal. I'll go get the money."

He turned to go back in the bunkhouse and saw Jeff Green and Charley Willis standing just outside the door. How long they had been there and how much they had heard he did not know, but, as he passed them, Willis gave him a sharp look.

Hainer followed him into the bunkhouse. "Think we just got ourselves a real bargain. Them is fine-looking horses. Glad you finally saw it my way."

George wheeled on him and shoved him hard. Al tripped over the corner of a bunk and sprawled on the floor. "What the hell was that all about, riding me about my girlfriend? I ain't got no girlfriend, and, even if I did, it wouldn't have nothing to do with dealing for horses. You know I ain't looking for no more trouble in Johnson County . . . that's the only reason I weren't too anxious to deal with that jack-off Nutcher. Christ, ain't you got any brains?"

"Jesus, George, I weren't thinking about that," Hainer said lamely. "Why didn't you just turn him down, then?"

" 'Cause you was all over my back for one thing. Oh, hell," George said in disgust, "it don't matter. How much money you got? I don't got enough for the whole thing."

Hainer dug in his saddlebags, and then handed George a wad of cash. "You told Emery you wasn't leaving today," he said.

"Well, I changed my mind."

Cassidy banged out the door. He found Nutcher and counted out the money to him. Within the hour, he and Al had packed their gear and were on their way, leading their three new horses. He had not seen Mary again, had made no effort to find her, and he felt like a coward and a heel. But what could he have said to her? *You mean more to me than any woman ever has before, but I can't take you with me, can't live the kind of life I want to live with someone depending on me, counting on me. I'd start to hate you, and even loneliness would be better than that.*

As they rode along side by side, Cassidy's black mood was not lost on his partner. Al frowned, not happy with the situation. Things had turned out the way he wanted, but it had not been as easy as he thought it would be. He had had to press too hard. And now Cassidy was angry at something or someone, most likely him. Time to back off, lay low, bide his time. Patience was the key now, and he was prepared to be very patient.

Chapter Fifteen

The late August sun beat down relentlessly on the town of Lander, baking its streets into a cracked jigsaw puzzle. The town seemed curiously empty for a week-day at noon. Most people had retreated indoors to escape the blazing sun. A lone horseman rode purposefully up the main street, kicking up clouds of dust. He was a compact man of about fifty, dressed in an expensive brown suit, a freshly minted Stetson hat, and Justin boots, the finest in the West. Halting in front of the sheriff's office, he pulled out a pocket watch, checked the time, and snapped it shut before climbing the sidewalk's wooden steps.

When the door banged open, the sheriff, in the middle of a post-dinner snooze at his desk, jerked awake, blinking rapidly. He took in the visitor's fancy clothes and new boots and quickly removed his own worn and dusty boots from the top of his desk. "What can I do for you, sir?" he asked, clearing his throat.

The man eyed him shrewdly, removing a pair of kid leather riding gloves before answering. "There's horse thieving going on in your county, Sheriff, and I want it stopped."

"We don't stand for that in Fremont County, sir," the sheriff said hastily. "Can you give me the details?"

"My name is Otto Franc," the man said, seating himself across from the sheriff and crossing his legs authoritatively. "You may have heard of me . . . I own the Pitchfork Ranch, one of the largest outfits in the Big Horn basin."

Sheriff Charlie Stough had not, in fact, heard of Otto Franc or the Pitchfork Ranch, although he didn't let on. He nodded noncommittally, and Franc continued.

"Earlier this month, three of my neighbor's finest saddle horses were stolen. I've done some investigating, and believe I know who has those horses now . . . two well-known scoundrels named Cassidy and Hainer."

The sheriff looked up in surprise. He knew both those men from their frequent forays into Lander and was not altogether pleased that they had run afoul of an influential man like Otto Franc.

"What makes you think they did it, and how come your neighbor ain't here himself, if they was his horses?"

"I didn't say they did it. I said they have the horses now. The evidence suggests they bought them from the original thief, knowing full well they were buying stolen property. As for my neighbor, he's not in the country at the moment. I frequently act for him in his absence, however, and I can assure you he would be quite eager to get his property back."

"What evidence is there, exactly?" Stough leaned back in his chair, a dubious look on his face.

Franc glared at him with growing annoyance. "Eyewitnesses to the felonious transfer, for one thing. Really, Sheriff, why the hesitation? I'm reporting a crime that occurred in your jurisdiction and offering to swear out a complaint against the criminals. May we procced?"

Sighing, the sheriff pulled out a piece of paper and started asking questions. "Name of the owner of the stolen property?"

"The Grey Bull Cattle Company."

The sheriff raised his eyebrows. "That's your neighbor?"

"In a manner of speaking. Mister Richard Ashworth is the proprietor of the company, but, as I said, he is in England most of the time." Franc pulled out a cigarette and impatiently tapped it against his gold cigarette case.

"Description of the stolen property?"

"One sorrel horse, a stallion, with one white foot and a white patch on its face, sporting the Grey Bull brand, of course."

The sheriff waited, his pen poised over the paper, but Franc was finished speaking. "Thought you said there was three horses."

"Yes, but naming one should be sufficient."

The sheriff shrugged. He wasn't sure what Franc's game was, but, if that's how the man wanted to play it, it was no skin off his nose. "Estimated value?"

"Around one hundred dollars, I should say."

The sheriff filled out a few more lines, then passed the paper over to Franc. "Sign here."

Franc signed, then folded the paper, and placed it in his coat pocket.

"Uh, Mister Franc, I'll need that complaint in order to execute a warrant for arrest."

Franc stood and headed for the door. "That won't be necessary, Sheriff. My man is on the thieves' trail, and I have reason to believe they are long gone from your jurisdiction. Thank you and good day." He exited into the undulating glare of the day, leaving the befuddled sheriff with a vaguely uneasy feeling.

"Alice, will you be OK for a little while? I think I'll go for a walk." Mary had looked in on Alice Burnaugh who sat nursing her newborn baby.

"Yes, of course, go on. Might as well enjoy this Indian summer while it lasts." Mary smiled and tucked a small pillow under Alice's elbow. "Oh, thank you, dear," crooned the beatific new mother, "you're so thoughtful, how would I get on without you?"

Mary smiled again and briefly stroked the baby's downy soft head. A sudden bubble of emotion welled up in her, and she turned away before Alice could see the tears in her eyes.

The day was bright and warm, although the air had the crispness of fall in it. She walked briskly, her hands in the pockets of her apron, taking deep breaths to calm herself. She reached the turn-off where the path jutted sharply up-hill and kept going at the same pace despite the steep slope. By the time she reached the rock outcropping she was quite winded and had to rest several minutes before her normal rate of breathing returned.

She had come to the place where George had taken her that night, high above the Mail Camp. It was not the first time she had returned to this spot—she came once or twice a week, whenever she could spare the time. With Alice busy with the baby, Mary had taken over most of the house and kitchen duties, but she came here every chance she got.

Mary gazed out over the valley below. It was a beautiful sight, as George had promised. The greens of summer were slowly but inexorably changing to browns and yellows, much like her own body was changing. Unconsciously, her hand went to her stomach, still flat as a washboard, but she knew even as she knew her own name that she was carrying a child, his child. There was the obvious sign, of course, but there were several subtler indications as well: her breasts felt fuller, her hair more lustrous, her complexion smoother. It was odd, she thought, that never in her life had she felt more beautiful, yet it was all a mistake, a huge mistake that she would undo, if she had the power to.

Somewhere behind her, a scurrying chipmunk scratched

over the ground and disappeared into a sliver between the rocks. She wished she could follow it into the deep recesses of the mountain and hide away from the world for a while. It was not that she was ashamed of her condition. Indeed, at times she felt thrilled to tears about the wonder of the miracle taking place inside her. But then she would remember the reality of her situation, and fear and anger and hopelessness would settle over her again.

Once her initial panic had passed and she had been able to think clearly, she realized she had two options. She could stay at Mail Camp, thus acknowledging her transgression to the Burnaughs and everybody else who stopped at the ranch, or she could go home and have the baby in relative obscurity. She knew, of course, which she would have to choose. She could not impose on the Burnaugh's hospitality. Her reason for being with them was to help Alice, yet, as time passed, she would become a burden herself. Nor was she anxious to advertise her predicament to every traveler who stopped by the camp. And who knows, one of those travelers might run into George Cassidy somewhere and casually pass on the gossip about the hired girl at Mail Camp road ranch. That was something she could not allow to happen, for, no matter how George reacted to the news of her pregnancy, Mary felt there could be no happy outcome. If he knew what had happened, yet chose to ignore her, it would hurt her beyond her ability to recover. If he acknowledged his responsibility and came back to her, any momentary happiness they enjoyed could not possibly last. He would feel trapped by her and the baby, and he would come to hate them both.

No, as distasteful as it was, she would have to go home, back to her family and her judgmental father who, no doubt, would take every opportunity to remind her that he had been right about the perfidy of men. Hot tears crowded her eyes, and she wiped at them viciously, struggling to climb out of the deep well of self-pity. But it was hard, for she did not really feel she had done anything wrong. She loved a man, and she had shared that love with him, body and soul. Now she was to be punished for this one act of love. She bowed her head and let the tears flow, giving in to the despair that weighed on her so heavily. *Oh, George,* she thought, *forgive me for needing you so much, but please come back, please come back.*

The butcher's clerk had just locked up the shop and flipped the sign to Closed, when a frantic tapping came at the door. Peering out the front window, the clerk smiled and admitted a portly little woman carrying several parcels.

"Five minutes later, Missus Morris, and I'd have been gone. But I was planning on delivering your order to you, if you hadn't come to pick it up."

"Oh, good heavens, how thoughtful of you! Well, I'm just glad I got here in time so you didn't have to go to all that trouble. I planned to be here a good hour ago, don't you know, but I got to talking to Betsy Phillips over at the dry goods store, and, well, you know how we jabber on!"

The young man crinkled his pale blue eyes at her, and she tittered self-consciously. One of her packages dropped to the floor, and he bent to retrieve it. "Have a seat, ma'am," he said, "I'll go get your order."

She sat in what she supposed to be a dainty pose and patted her hair. "Take your time, George, I don't mind waiting." Watching him retreat into the back room, she gave a small sigh. If only he knew that he had been the main topic of conversation between herself and Betsy Phillips this afternoon. They had agreed that he was the handsomest addition to Rock Springs since the new Methodist minister came three years ago, and so friendly, too. Why, he always had a smile and a good word to say, and he gave good measure on the meat to boot.

"Here we go. A side of bacon and a five-pound rib roast. I cut it kind of generous . . . hope you don't mind." He came out of the back room with her wrapped meat order.

"Mind? Of course not. Now you just add this to my bill, George." She rose and juggled her parcels. "Oh dear, I'm afraid I won't be able to carry all this myself. I wonder, would you . . . oh, but I'm sure you must be too busy."

"Not at all, ma'am. I was just heading out the door myself." He removed his blood-smeared apron and lifted the armload of packages effortlessly. She giggled again—wouldn't Betsy just die when she heard about this?

When they reached the Morris residence a few blocks away, she asked him to set the packages in the kitchen. He deposited them on the table and with a friendly nod, turned to go.

"George," she called after him, "the least I can do is offer you a drink. How about a lemonade?"

"Thank you, ma'am, but I best be going. I'll take a rain check."

"Well then, here. . . ." She opened her pocketbook and dug around for some coins. "I just can't let you leave without thanking you properly." She held the money out, her round little cheeks blushing a bright pink.

He stepped toward her and closed her hand around the coins, pressing it for just a second. "You don't need to thank me that way, Missus Morris," he said in a low, familiar voice. "Just keep coming back to the shop to see me every now and then . . . that's all the thanks I need." He gave her a quick wink and was out the door.

Mrs. Morris sank into the nearest chair, her mouth agape, clutching her hand, the very hand he had touched, to her breast. It was several minutes before her wits returned, and then all she could think about was what fun it was going to be to lord this over Betsy Phillips.

George strolled down the street, chuckling to himself over that fat old Morris dame. God, it was easy to bamboozle the ladies, especially the married ones whose husbands had long ago stopped paying any attention to them. He had practically every housewife in town eating out of his hand, and all it took was turning on the old charm. Business at the butcher shop had picked up considerably since he had been hired, and Mr. Gottsche, the owner, was even talking about giving him a cut of the profits. Not that chopping animal carcasses was what he wanted to do for the rest of his life, but, hell, it would get him through the winter in style.

He swung into his favorite saloon and was immediately greeted with calls of—"Howdy, Butch!" and "Well, if it ain't old Butch, the butcher boy!" Laughing and slapping backs, he made the rounds, accepting the good-natured teasing and giving as good as he got. Most of the men were in town for the winter to work in the nearby coal mines. George considered his present occupation to be a step up from that. In fact, he rather liked his new nickname and had taken to using it himself.

He drank a whiskey, then one more before settling at the faro table, where he stayed until he started to lose too much. Scanning the crowded, smoke-filled room, he spotted Patty sitting at the bar. Coming up behind her, he pinched the ample flesh of her bottom, then slid onto the stool next to her. "How's me fine Irish lass doing this bonny eve?" he asked in a poorly executed brogue.

SUZANNE LYON

Patty laughed broadly and leaned into his shoulder. "It's not an Irish lad you'll be making, Butch, me boy."

He shrugged and put an arm around her. "Lucky for me you ain't too particular!"

She laughed again and playfully poked him with her elbow. "That kind of talk'll cost you. Buy me a drink."

He ordered for both of them, and she downed hers with a practiced flip of the wrist. Butch regarded her fondly as she set her glass down, reached over for his drink, and downed it just as quickly.

"Help yourself," he said, after the fact.

"Don't mind if I do," she said with a wink. She was a large woman, not fat, but generously curved in all directions. Her curly blond hair was a bit too garish, and her voice, especially when she had been drinking, was on the brassy side, but she was funny and kind-hearted and always gave a fellow a good time.

"How'd you do at the faro table?" she said, wiping her mouth with the back of her hand.

"Got cleaned out. Spent the last of my money buying you a drink."

"Does that mean we ain't going to have any fun tonight?" She leered at him suggestively, rubbing his thigh with her dimpled hand.

"Not unless it's on the house," he grinned, knowing that Patty was a pushover when it came to sex.

"Christ, Butch, I'm going to go broke, if you don't stop gambling. I never seen a body lose as much money as you."

He flashed her a wicked smile. "Luck of the Irish, don't you know!"

She made as if to backhand him, then grabbed his wrist. "Come on, then, you lousy cheap-skate!" Pulling him along, she moved toward the saloon's staircase. Suddenly, one of

220

the men at the bar backed away, grappling with another, smaller man. They bumped Patty, knocking her hard into the stairs. Paying her no mind, the larger man proceeded to pummel the smaller man, although the latter offered little resistance.

Butch wheeled on the pair, his eyes blazing. He grabbed the attacker by the shoulder, whirled him around, and planted his fist squarely on the man's jaw. The man crumpled, knocked clean out. Butch turned to Patty who sat on the stairs, rubbing her leg.

"You OK, doll?" he asked.

"Sure. Just bruised my shin is all. Guess I'll go put a cold rag on it before it swells up too much." She headed upstairs, then turned back with a wry grin on her plump face. "Thanks for defending my honor, honey."

"We still got a date?" he said mischievously.

"Anything for my hero. Come up a little later."

Butch picked up his hat from where it had fallen on the floor and stepped over the unconscious man. Bar fights were common occurrences in Rock Springs, and nobody paid the stricken fellow any mind. The other party to the brawl stepped forward, his hand extended.

"Thank you, sir, for your assistance. I don't quite know how that got started, but I'm grateful that you put a speedy end to it. Allow me to buy you a drink." He spoke in cultured tones, his voice a deep baritone that belied his small stature.

They sat at a table, and the man wiped his face with a white silk handkerchief. He looked to be in his mid-thirties, although his hairline had receded far back on his forehead. He had a prominent nose and a square jaw, and his dark, intelligent eyes looked out from under bushy eyebrows. "In the future, I shall be more circumspect when defending my profession," he said, carefully folding the handkerchief and placing it back in his pocket.

Butch cocked his head at him. "Come again?"

The man laughed. "Evidently, I offended the poor man. He apparently has suffered at the hands of an inept lawyer, and, when I tried to explain that most attorneys, myself included, if I may be so bold, adhere to the highest standards, he became rather enraged. At any rate, thank you again for stepping in."

"You're a lawyer?" Butch asked, feeling somewhat dull next to this golden-throated orator.

"Indeed. Douglas Preston, at your service." The man held out his hand again. Butch was impressed with his firm grip.

"George Cassidy, but most people call me Butch. What kind of law do you do?"

"Criminal, primarily. Lots of opportunity in that field these days."

"Are you good?" Butch's only previous courtroom experience, his horse-thieving trial in Montrose, had not left him with a favorable view of lawyers, but this one seemed pretty damned smart.

"Yes. Yes, I am. Now you, Mister Cassidy, appear to be an upstanding citizen of this community, but, if you should ever need the assistance of counsel, please let me know. I owe you a debt of gratitude for what you did tonight." Preston passed him one of his cards which Butch perused carefully and pocketed. They shared another drink, and then Butch remembered his appointment with Patty.

Later that night, Butch moseyed down the plank sidewalk on his way to his room above the butcher shop. Patty had asked him to spend the night with her, as she always did, but as usual he had declined. Something didn't feel right about waking up in the morning with a woman who didn't mean anything more to you than a few laughs and a toss in the hay. He liked Patty well enough, and all the other whores he had been with in Rock Springs, too, for that matter, but only because they helped him forget for a while. Forget that there was a woman whom he had loved and left.

He hawked and spat into the dust. The rancid taste of whiskey flooded his mouth. He had been drinking far too much lately, much more than was his habit. *Booze and whores*, he thought. *What would Ma say about that?*

He reached the shop and climbed the outside stairs to his room. At the top, he turned on the landing and looked at the town spread out below. Nothing but cheap storefronts and shabby-looking shacks. And railroad cars, constantly moving in and out of the station, hauling their precious loads of coal. Rock Springs was a dirty, grimy little town, but it suited him fine for now.

Kicking open the door, he entered his tiny room. The slightly metallic odor of blood and raw meat wafted up from below, assaulting his nostrils. He fell asleep trying to remember the rich, earthy smell of Mary's hair.

It was Christmas night. Outside, the wind had picked up, blowing pellets of dry snow against the log walls, but, inside, the Boyd cabin was snug and warm. Although Bill Boyd had adopted many Shoshone customs, he was still a Christian and insisted on observing religious holidays. Earlier today the family had exchanged small gifts, and now Bill and his wife, Louisa, sat rocking comfortably in front of the fire.

Mary closed the bedroom door softly behind her. She had counted on this quiet moment at the end of a festive day, thinking there would never be a better time to tell them what she could no longer keep secret. She kissed her mother's cheek and squeezed her father's shoulder before settling in a chair beside them. For a moment, all three sat in silence, staring at the fire, lost in their thoughts. Mary knew what she had to do, but she hated to disrupt the spirit of calmness and contentment that enveloped the room.

Finally, Bill Boyd broke the spell. "I'm glad you were home with us for Christmas, Mary. After you went up to Mail Camp, I wasn't sure you'd come back. It's nice having the family together. Just wish Billy was here, too." Mary's younger brother, Bill, Jr., was spending the winter on a ranch in Sweetwater County.

Mary opened her mouth to speak, then closed it. She glanced at her mother, who she saw was watching her, a somber look on her dark, inscrutable face. Almost imperceptibly, her mother nodded at her, and Mary realized with a shock that she must already know. But how could she? She was only four months along and barely showing. True, she had had to let out her dresses a couple of stitches, but she had done that back at Mail Camp in the privacy of her own room. Nevertheless, her mother often seemed to know things that were not yet obvious to other people. Mary supposed it was some kind of Indian second sense—a way of looking closely and reading signs and allowing herself to be open to possibilities.

Taking courage from her mother's knowledge, Mary drew a deep breath. "Pa, I was planning on staying on at Mail Camp, but something happened to change my mind."

Boyd's face darkened, his brows drew down. "They weren't mistreating you, were they?"

"No, no, nothing like that. It's just, well . . . Pa, this isn't easy to tell you, but, well, I'm going to have a baby." She stared him straight in the eye, determined not to appear ashamed or apologetic. Her father stared back, a look of incomprehension, then disbelief, and finally anger crossing his face. He rose from his chair and grabbed Mary by the shoulders, pulling her to her feet. Louisa rose, too, but stood passively to the side, allowing her husband to have his say.

"You little tramp!" he roared, shaking her. "The minute you're out of my sight . . . I knew I shouldn't have let you go up there, but I thought . . . by God, I've done my best to raise her right, tried to warn her about. . . ." He pushed her away and wiped his hands on his shirt as though she were dirty. "Who did this to you? Or do you even know?"

Mary stared at him in shock, too numb to feel anything now but aware that she would hate him forever for saying that. "Of course, I know," she said, her voice low and husky, "but you never will, nor anyone else."

"Who do you think you're protecting, sister? Some no good son-of-a-bitch who thinks he can knock up a little half-breed girl and send her back home to the reservation? You're gonna tell me, all right, and I'm going to find the bastard. Nobody's going to make a whore out of Bill Boyd's daughter!" Turning his back on her, he stomped over to the fireplace and kicked at a log lying on the hearth.

"No, Pa. That's not how it's going to be." Mary stood, her hands trembling. "It wasn't like that. It was. . . ." She bowed her head and fought the tears. "I really think he loves me."

Boyd gave a short, mirthless laugh. "Sure. You bet. Loves you so much he deserted you."

"He doesn't even know, Pa," she pleaded.

Boyd changed tactics, a wheedling tone coming into his voice. "Now you tell me who it is, honey. Pa'll find him and bring him back to you. Now wouldn't you like that?"

She shook her head stubbornly, her lips pressed together, her eyes brimming. The thought of her father trying to coerce George into marrying her was horrifying. Boyd raised his hands in exasperation and made a strangled sound. Before he could do anything else, her mother stepped forward and put her arm around Mary's waist.

"When will the baby come?" she asked quietly.

"May, I guess," Mary said, pressing a handkerchief to her eyes and nose.

"Well, you ain't having no bastard baby in this house," Boyd said grimly.

"But Pa, that's why I came home!" Mary cried.

"You ain't having no bastard baby in this house," he repeated. "People ain't gonna talk about this family behind our backs!"

"But where will I go . . . what will I do?" Mary sobbed.

"Damned if I know. Your mother's got people she can send you to. Figure out what to do with the kid while you're at it."

"What do you mean?" Louisa said, a note of alarm in her voice.

"Just what I said, dammit! I ain't going to have no bastard baby living under this roof, so, if she expects to come back here, she better get rid of it to someone!" He glared at them both, then stomped into the bedroom, slamming the door.

Mary stared after him, the color drained from her face. "Get rid of it?" she whispered. "How can he say that? It's my baby, ours. . . ." She brought her hands over her stomach protectively. Her mother embraced her, stroking her hair gently.

"He's hurt, child, that's why he says those things. He'll

come around. But I do think it would be a good idea to go away until the baby is born. Your being here will just upset him, and there's no sense in that. Besides, I think you need time, too, to think about what to do. It's not easy to raise a child all alone. You must ask yourself if this is the wisest thing to do."

"I won't give up our baby," Mary said dully. "It's the only part of him I may ever have."

The next week, on New Year's Day, 1892, Mary went to stay with a friend of her mother's, an old Arapaho woman named Gray Hair who lived deep in the Wind River Mountains. As she climbed into the buggy to sit next to her stiff-backed father, she felt a rolling sensation deep within her— the first movement of new life. She clutched her stomach and felt another tiny twinge. Joyfully she turned to her father, but he stared straight ahead, sullen and angry. She closed her eyes and prayed with all her might that wherever George was and whatever he was doing, he had not forgotten her.

The sheriff of Uinta County prided himself on running a clean operation. Situated in the southwestern-most corner of Wyoming, just across the line from Brown's Hole, he saw more than his share of thieves, criminals, and general n'er-do-wells trying to escape the law by skipping across the border. They soon learned the folly of tarrying too long in Sheriff Ward's jurisdiction. Not content to wait for trouble to come to him, he and his deputies rode the county, seeking out undesirables and arresting them, if they had cause, or, if they did not, sending them on their way.

Mid-January was a slow time of year for criminal activity, however, and the sheriff was downright bored with the usual fare of barroom fights and domestic disturbances. So when his door opened one cold, blustery day and admitted a tough-looking *hombre* on the trail of a couple of serious rustlers, he perked up considerably.

"My name's John Chapman," the man introduced himself in a gravelly voice. He was tall and broad-shouldered with a grizzled, weather-beaten face. "I got a tip these two varmints was heading for Evanston. First one's tall, blond, blue-eyed, goes by the name of Cassidy. His partner's darker, wears a beard, named Hainer."

"Ain't come across either one," the sheriff said. "This time of year, though, everybody holes up. No telling where they might be. I'll put my best man on it, have him ask around. If they're in Uinta County, we'll find them. You got a complaint with you?"

Chapman pulled out a tattered piece of paper and pushed it across the desk. Sheriff Ward read it over and looked up. "You with the law in Fremont County?"

Chapman shook his head. "I was hired by the man that signed that complaint there. He's real interested in catching these fellas and thought I might have better luck at it than the sheriff. You might say I'm kind of a one man posse."

"Well, that's fine, Mister Chapman, but, if you find where these boys is hiding out before we do, I suggest you come get us to arrest them. From what you say, they ain't going to give up easy."

Chapman nodded and rose to leave. At the door, he turned back. "One more thing, Sheriff. Mister Franc, my boss, he wants them taken alive. Don't shoot unless you have to, and, if you have to, don't aim to kill."

"That ain't always easy," the sheriff said.

"You bring them in alive," Chapman said, "and Mister Franc will make it worth your while." With a sharp nod, he was out the door.

The sheriff pondered at his desk for a moment, then grabbed his gun belt and called for his deputy. "Calverly! We got us a couple of live ones!"

Butch came awake instantly, his ears attuned for danger, but all he heard was the steady *drip, drip, drip* of snow melting from the roof of the tiny shack. He lay back down on the cot, hands behind his head. He was not accustomed to sleeping during the day, but he had been out all the previous night, working the roundup, and was exhausted. It felt good, though, to be back doing what he liked best, riding and roping. His aching muscles told him he had gotten soft over the winter, and he was anxious to get back in shape.

It was cold inside the shack—the early April sun was not strong enough to penetrate its thin walls—and he had to relieve himself, but a lethargic mood had settled over him, and he continued to lie there and let his thoughts meander. He was glad Al had come to get him. Rock Springs was beginning to wear thin, and he had been looking for an excuse to leave. Not that he had relished hearing that the law was after them, but, at least, the news had got him out of the butcher shop and back out on the range where he belonged. Al had steered them to his friend's ranch on Ham's Fork in the far western part of the state, practically to Idaho. His friend had hired them to work the roundup, and they had holed up in this line shack on the edge of his property. Short of crossing the state line, there was no safer hide-out.

He reached over the side of the cot for his hat. A shout came from outside the cabin.

"George Cassidy! This is Bob Calverly, Uinta County deputy sheriff! I have a warrant for your arrest!"

Instinctively Butch rolled off the side of the cot and tipped it over so it was between him and the door. Fumbling for his gun belt, he cursed, then yelled out: "Well, get to shooting then!"

Silence. Then: "Come out with your hands up!"

Colt .45 in hand, he broke the cylinder and filled the chambers. He snapped it shut and steadied the gun on the edge of the overturned cot, aiming through the half-opened door. "Never to you sons-of-bitches!" he cried, and squeezed the trigger.

An answering shot *zinged* the wall above his head, showering him with splinters. "No!" a new voice cried, and he heard the sound of running feet. He scrambled from behind the cot and crouched beside the door. He had to figure a way to get outside this damned shack; inside it he was a sitting duck. Grasping his revolver in both hands, he lunged out the door, rolled to his right, and came up shooting. Shots came from his left—high and wide.

"God dammit! What the hell you doing?" Calverly's voice came from behind a boulder to his left.

"Don't shoot him!" growled the second voice.

Butch squeezed off more shots as he angled toward his tethered horse. Out of the corner of his eye he saw Hainer, his hands manacled, crouching next to the lawmen's horses. He motioned to him to run, but Hainer looked away nervously and stood his ground. *The hell with him,* Butch thought.

Shooting as he ran, he reached his horse, untied it, and swung up onto its bare back in one swift motion. Keeping low, he kicked the animal's flanks, when suddenly the air exploded around him, and his head jerked back painfully. Sparks colored his vision, and then everything was black and he was falling, and then there was nothing.

Mary sat outside the small cabin, her face turned to the

sun, soaking up its healing rays. She could almost feel the strength seeping into her bones and muscles, and, for the first time in two weeks, she felt her energy returning. The tiny bundle in her lap stirred. She moved aside the soft blanket to look at the baby's face with its delicate features and thatch of dark hair. Mary had labored mightily to bring this little thing into the world. The difficult delivery had so sapped her strength that she had been unable to lift her arms to hold the baby for a good three days after its birth. Old Gray Hair had had to hold the infant to Mary's breast and fit the nipple inside its mouth so it could suckle. But the baby was healthy, and Mary was on the mend and almost happy, as long as she could sit here, her mind blank, not remembering the past or worrying about the future.

She sensed movement and opened her eyes to see Gray Hair standing beside her, hands on hips. The old Indian woman could do that—move so silently you didn't hear her coming, but you'd turn around, and there she'd be, right where you needed her. Gray Hair had taken her in without question, had treated her kindly, and had never spoken of her leaving, but Mary knew she could not stay here indefinitely. But where could she go, a woman on her own with a baby, if she could not go back to her parents' home? And it seemed clear that she was not welcome there. The last message from her mother said that Bill Boyd refused to budge from his original, uncompromising position—Mary herself could come back, but not her bastard baby.

Gray Hair lifted her chin slightly and gazed into the distance. "Someone coming," she said, keeping still. Mary listened but could hear nothing. Nevertheless, she kept quiet, certain that the old Indian woman's instincts were reliable. Sure enough, before five minutes had passed, Mary could hear the soft *clop-clop* of an approaching rider. The two women turned to face the sound and saw Mary's brother emerge from the woods, leading a second horse behind him.

Mary stood to greet him. "Billy! Oh, it's good to see you! I was beginning to think everyone had forgotten about me!" He dismounted, and she threw one arm around him, the other still clutching her baby.

Awkwardly he backed off, and stared at the bundle she carried. His eyes, full of questions, met hers. Smiling, she drew back the blanket and angled the baby toward him. "Meet your new niece, Billy. She's two weeks old today."

The baby cooed and pawed the air with her tiny hands. She appeared to look directly at Bill, although she was still too young to focus on objects more than a foot or two away.

"She's got blue eyes," was all Bill said.

Mary pulled the cover back over the baby's head. "All babies do at this age. The color will probably change as she grows."

Bill nodded, but he looked sad, almost disappointed. "How are you doing, Sis?" he asked.

"I'm OK, now. Though I wouldn't mind sitting down again. I tire pretty easily."

He took her elbow and steered her back to the wooden stool. Gray Hair brought him a drink of water and then took the baby into the house. Bill seemed to relax some with the baby gone.

"I'm so glad you came to see me, Billy. But it's a long way from Sweetwater County. You still working on the ranch down there?" Mary said.

Bill nodded. "Gonna stay on through the summer, at least."

"This is a busy time of year on a ranch. I'm surprised they could spare you, just to go visiting your sister." Mary made her voice sound teasing.

Bill kicked at the dust, not meeting her eyes. "I didn't know I was going to come see you, but then, well . . . I was in Lander the other day on business, and I heard something I thought you might want to know. . . ." He paused and took a deep breath, exhaling slowly. Mary waited, her hands folded in her lap, struggling to keep her mind blank. "It's about George Cassidy. He's in the Fremont County jail, arrested on a charge of horse thieving." Bill cut his eyes to her, then looked away again. "Look, Mary, you don't have to say nothing. It ain't any of my business, except it is, I guess, seeing as you're my sister. I ran into Emery Burnaugh on my trip to Lander. He asked after you, said Alice misses you and couldn't figure out why you left so sudden. He'd heard about Cassidy, too, and he was telling me how George had just been to Mail Camp last August . . . that's where he picked up those stolen horses, they say. Anyway, he said you and Cassidy looked to be pretty good friends, and, hell, I guess that ain't no secret . . . I could tell you was sweet on him that day he came by the house. So, I'm just putting two and two together, and, well, you seen Cassidy in August, and here you are with a baby in May. . . ." His voice trailed off. Mary sat expressionless, her dry lips parted. "Oh hell," he slapped his thigh with his hat, "I just thought you might want to know where he is, even if it's in jail!"

"Thank you, Bill," Mary said, and then could not think of a single other thing to say.

Bill waited, shifting back and forth on his feet for a few minutes, then put a strong hand on Mary's shoulder. "Listen, Sis, for what it's worth, I like Cassidy. I mean, I don't know about this horse stealing business, but he don't seem like no hardcase to me. You just tell me what you want to do, once you figure it out."

Tears bit at her eyes as she patted his hand. He left her then, and her hand dropped lifelessly back in her lap. She sat for a long time before any particular thought came to her, and then, when one did, it was more of a feeling than a thought. A feeling that she should be somewhere else, that she was in the wrong place, almost as though the stars were out of alignment and would not be put right until she got herself to the place where she was supposed to be. But her rightful place was with her baby, wasn't it?—not chasing after a man who had abandoned her. Of course, it was, but none of that seemed to matter. George was in trouble and might need her. In fact, maybe she could be of some help; after all, she had been there when he bought the horses from that horrible Nutcher fellow, and she could testify that Nutcher had warranted the title. Yes, that was it! She had to get to Lander and tell them George was innocent, that he had been falsely accused! She rose quickly, full of plans, glad to have something productive to think about, although, even as she mentally made arrangements, she knew it was all a fraud, an excuse she had concocted to convince herself to return to him. But return she would, for better or worse.

She sought out her brother, who was brushing down his horse after his long ride. "Take me to Lander, Bill," she said.

He nodded once and went back to his work, his half-breed face dark and troubled.

Chapter Sixteen

Sweat dripped from his forehead, trickled down his back, dampened the front of his shirt. It had to be ninety degrees outside; inside this sun-baked, nearly windowless cell it was at least ten degrees hotter. Butch sat on the narrow cot, his back propped against the stone wall. Every few minutes he shifted one direction or the other, seeking a cooler spot not yet warmed by his body. He sighed and passed his hand over the ugly red scar that creased his forehead, courtesy of Deputy Calverly's bullet. Luckily that Chapman fellow had grabbed the deputy's hand just as he squeezed off his shot, or Butch would be pushing up roses right now. All in all, he preferred roasting in this hellhole to that alternative.

In the next cell over, he could hear Hainer pacing back and forth as he did a good part of the day, and the constant, repetitive noise—always four steps to the window, then four steps back to the bars of his cell—grated mightily on Butch's nerves. Why couldn't Al relax, for God's sake? It wasn't as if all that pacing was going to speed anything up. He was about to yell to Hainer to sit down, when the door to the cell block opened, and two dapper-looking men were admitted.

"Preston!" Butch leaped to his feet. "Where the hell you been? I ain't seen you in two weeks!"

Douglas Preston waited for the deputy to unlock the prisoners' cells. The lawman opened the barred doors and stood aside.

"We've raised your bail," said Preston. "You're free to go."

Butch let loose with a wild whoop, and even Hainer sported a rare smile. The lawyer held up a cautionary hand. "That's good news all right, boys, but we need to talk some things over before we spring you out of this oven they call a jail. I do not customarily remove my jacket in the presence of clients, but under the circumstances I'm sure you'll understand." He slipped out of his suit coat and sat on Butch's bunk. His associate, C. F. Rathbone, cast him a grateful look and did the same.

"Who posted the bond for us?" Butch asked, pulling his sweat-dampened shirt away from his chest.

Preston gestured to Rathbone who pulled some papers from a leather folder. "Fred Whitney and Leonard Short for you, Butch, and Bill and Ed Lannigan for Al."

"Ain't that a hoot! Couple of saloonkeepers holding your bond, Al, while I got me two of the finest citizens in town!" Butch laughed.

"The bondholders' occupations are irrelevant, obviously," said Preston. "The point is, they're guaranteeing your return to Lander for trial."

"When will that be?" asked Hainer.

"Well, that's up to you, to a certain extent," Preston said. "There's been a rather interesting occurrence . . . the prosecutor, Mister Vidal, has requested a continuance of your case until June of next year. Evidently they are having difficulty locating some of their witnesses and are not prepared to go to trial this term. Of course, you have the right to a speedy trial, so you could deny the prosecution's request and force them to try the case now."

"Hell, if they ain't got no witnesses, they ain't got no case! Let's go to trial and get this over with!" exclaimed Butch.

"It's not quite as simple as that," Preston said. "They do

have their main witness, Otto Franc, ready to appear. It could be they would win their case on the strength of his testimony alone. And we haven't been able to turn up our own witnesses yet . . . you know, the Green and Willis chaps you told us were there when you bought the horses. What's more, and I hate to bring this up, Rathbone and I have worked on your case so far without compensation. We've been happy to do so . . . after all, I do owe you a favor, Butch, from our Rock Springs days. But I'm afraid we simply could not go to trial on your behalf without some assurance of being paid. I'm sorry, but there it is. We all have a living to make. I'm sure you would have no difficulty raising our fee during the next year." Preston wiped his sweaty face with his clean silk handkerchief.

Stunned, Butch looked to Hainer who appeared equally flabbergasted. It had never occurred to them that their lawyers would quit on them unless they got paid. "Looks like you ain't leaving us much choice," said Butch. "See you back here next year."

"Now don't take offense, friend," said Preston. "I'm on your side, and that means you have a formidable advantage, if I do say so myself. We'll beat this charge, and it hardly matters whether we do it this year or next, now does it? On the subject of witnesses, incidentally, can you tell me who is Mary Boyd?"

Butch's head jerked up, his eyes narrowed. "What?"

"Mary Boyd. She came around to see me the other day. Tell me, what is your relationship to her?" Preston spoke matter-of-factly, his expression neutral.

Butch swallowed hard, raking his arm across his brow to wipe the dripping sweat. He was amazed at how rattled he had become at just the mention of her name. He lowered himself to the cot, elbows on his knees, and dropped his head in his hands. "I know her all right, but I don't got any relationship with her."

"She says she was at Mail Camp when the horse incident occurred, that she saw Nutcher and Watts there. Is that true?" Butch nodded without looking up. "Well, why don't you tell me about it? Did she actually see you close the deal?"

Butch rubbed his eyes, trying to remember the details of that morning. He couldn't think clearly; images of Mary filled his brain, confusing him. "She came out onto the porch kind of in the middle of the whole thing. She might have heard me ask Nutcher about the title to the horses . . . I just don't remember. I'm pretty sure she went back inside before we cut the deal."

"Is that how you remember it, Al?" asked Preston.

"Yeah. She definitely weren't there when we shook on it," Al said.

"Did she see you leave Mail Camp with the horses?"

Butch shook his head sadly. She had not seen them leave because he had sneaked away, too much of a coward to tell her he was going. He crossed to the tiny, barred window and stared out at the dusty alley, shimmering in the heat.

Preston rose and put on his jacket. "I think I see how it is, Butch, and it is as I feared. Wives and girlfriends make notoriously bad witnesses. They are far too eager to say whatever they must to help their men, and they wind up saying more than they actually know. Your Miss Boyd, for example, is absolutely convinced of your innocence, yet she is extremely hazy on the details of what happened that day. I would not dare to put her on the witness stand and subject her to Mister Vidal's cross-examination. You should consider yourself lucky, though, to have earned the loyalty of such a fine young woman. Now come along, you two will need to sign some papers for the sheriff."

When the paperwork was completed, the four men stood on the plank sidewalk outside the jail. Butch and Al looked up and down the busy main street, gathering their bearings after three months of incarceration. Preston told them to keep him apprised of their whereabouts during the coming year, and they shook hands and parted.

"By the way, boys"—Preston called them back—"did you hear the news about Nate Champion? You knew him, didn't you?" Both men nodded. "Well, I'm sorry to be the one to tell you this, but he's dead."

Butch and Al stared at each other in surprise. "What happened?" asked Butch, a sick feeling stirring in his gut.

"He was ambushed. Several of the local ranchers took it upon themselves to carry out the law. They hired some gunmen from Texas, fifty in all, so I'm told, to track him down. They had him surrounded for a full day before they burned him out of his hide-out, and then cut him down when he tried to run for it. Ghastly business, if you ask me. I don't sanction rustling, boys," he gave them a pointed look, "but there's a system for dealing with it, and those who act outside that system are as bad as the criminals themselves."

"Preston," said Butch fervently, "what they did to Nate, it's the same thing they're trying to do to me and Al, only not so obvious. This Otto Franc, whoever the hell he is, he's taking the law into his own hands. This whole deal was a set-up. It was fishy from the get go. They hired Nutcher to sell those horses to us. I know it! He was too damn' anxious to make a deal, and, when it looked like I wasn't going to bite, he named a price that was practically giving them away. I'm telling you, Preston, it's a war going on between the big boys and fellas like me that are just trying to get a few head together and live a peaceable life. We can't let them get away with it!"

Preston fixed Butch with his dark, intense eyes. "You find me evidence of a conspiracy, and I'll nail their hides to the wall. I'm no fan of bullies, as you well know, Butch . . . you rescued me from one." He grasped Butch's shoulder and gave it a quick squeeze. "Take care and keep in touch."

Butch watched his lawyer and Rathbone retreat down the sidewalk, and then turned to his partner who stood behind him with a sheepish expression on his face.

"We're free for a year, anyway," said Al. "What are you going to do?"

Butch removed his hat, wiped the sweat from his face with his sleeve, and clamped the hat back on his head. "Find me a woman," he said.

The dusty road unraveled before her, the buildings of Fort Washakie barely visible in the distance. It was already hot, despite the early hour, and Mary wished someone had thought to plant trees along the path for a little shade. On either side of her, rocks and low brush and an occasional cedar made up the landscape, but shade trees were a rare commodity on the reservation.

Her feet felt heavy this morning; little Mary had been up several times in the night, and, although Gray Hair had taken a turn calming the baby, the primary responsibility for the infant's care lay with her mother. Mary didn't really mind the night-time awakenings—now that she was back at Mr. Moore's store during the day, her only opportunity to be with the baby was at night. But spending all day on her feet and never getting an uninterrupted night's sleep had taken its toll—dark circles were visible under her eyes, and she felt perpetually tired.

It did seem as though Mary B' Hat, as Gray Hair called the child, had been particularly fussy lately, and Mary had a good idea why that was so. Since she had been leaving for work during the day, little Mary had been tended by a wet nurse, a young relative of Gray Hair's. Lack of use was causing Mary's own supply of milk to dry up, and poor Mary B' Hat was simply unable to draw enough from her mother's breast to nourish her through the night. Mary would have to talk to Gray Hair about finding a supplement for the baby, although she was still awfully young for anything but breast milk. Nevertheless, the baby had to be fed, and Mary was unable to do it on her own.

Thank God for Gray Hair. When Mary had decided to return to town, the old woman offered no protest and insisted on coming down from the mountains with them. She had found a place for them to stay with her relatives on the reservation and willingly agreed to look after the baby while Mary was at work. They shared a closeness now that, in some ways, Mary had never had with her own mother, whom Mary had not seen since her return. Old Bill Boyd still refused to see his daughter until she renounced her past, and his wife would not disrespect his wishes by meeting Mary on the sly.

She entered the gates of the fort, her dress already soaked under the armpits and her head pounding from the heat. Keeping her head down so the brim of her hat would block the sun's rays, she trudged along the fort's main thoroughfare which was quiet this early in the morning. She looked up at the sound of a horse blowing. A man stood before her, the sun at his back casting his features in shadow. But she had dreamt of that figure so often that there was no mistaking whose it was. A cry caught in her throat, and, before she knew what she was doing, she was flinging herself into the arms of George Cassidy, and he was lifting her off her feet and twirling her around and laughing and burying his face in her neck. She stood back and took him in. He was pale, and his hair was darker than she remembered it, and he had a fresh scar on his forehead, but there was the same broad-shouldered physique, the same square jaw, the same startling blue eyes that crinkled with pleasure. She hugged him again, and he spoke her name softly into her ear, and she knew that everything would be all right now, that her life could begin again.

She stood back, wiping the traces of tears from her eyes. "They let you out!" she cried, moving her hands up and down his arms as though to assure herself he was really there.

"For a year. My trial's been continued." He stared at her closely, and his brows drew together. "Are you OK? You don't look so good."

"That's a fine way to greet me after all this time." Mary laughed. "I'm fine . . . just tired is all. I haven't been sleeping very well. I've been . . . well, worried about you."

He started to reach for her again when suddenly he became aware of passersby in the street, casting curious looks their way. "Let's go inside," he said. "I've got a lot to tell you."

"Me, too," she said, although she wasn't sure she would tell him anything at all.

Mary ushered him into the store and locked the door behind them. She led him to the back room, stoked the stove, and set water on to boil for coffee. Now that they were alone together, away from prying eyes, an uneasiness settled over them, each remembering the last time they had been together. Butch was certain from the way she had greeted him that she still loved him, but how to pick up from here, after so much had happened?

"Remember the first time I saw you, out in the front room there, when you wandered in from the blizzard?" Mary broke the silence. "You practically scared me to death, with your clothes all snow-covered and eyes all bloodshot."

"Any other girl would have sent me packing." Butch smiled. "Mary"—he became serious—"how'd you know I was in jail?"

"My brother told me first, but I would have heard it as soon as I came back to town . . . everybody was talking about it. Most people are on your side, too, George. You're well liked around here, you know."

"You must have stayed at Mail Camp through the winter then."

Mary hesitated. "Alice asked me to stay on and help her after the baby came." That was true, as far as it went. My God, she had not seen him in a year—she couldn't just spring on him the fact that he was the father of her baby. He would haul out of here so fast he'd leave a breeze in his wake.

"My lawyer said you came to see him." Butch found a couple of tin cups and poured the coffee that Mary had forgotten about. "He said you wanted to testify for me."

"Yes. I tried to see you, too, but the sheriff said you weren't allowed any visitors except your lawyer. So I went to see Mister Preston and told him what I knew. He didn't seem too sure I could be of any help."

"He says wives and girlfriends don't make very good witnesses." Butch perched on the edge of the sawbuck table and stared at her over the top of his cup. She met his gaze.

"Is that what I am, George? Am I your girlfriend?"

"I want you to be, Mary."

A sudden chill came over her, despite the heat, and she hugged her arms. "What does that mean, exactly? I think we're past the point of making dates for the Saturday night barn dance and kissing on the front porch when you drop me off at home."

He smiled and set his cup down, pulling her to him until she stood between his legs. He drew the back of his hand down her cheek. "It means I want you to be with me. I got a year of freedom now. Don't know where I'll go . . . maybe back to Horse Creek . . . maybe up to the Owl Creeks . . . but I want you to go with me." He kissed her gently. "Maybe I'll take you to the land of milk and honey. How does California sound, darlin'?"

She searched his face, not sure this was really happening to her. It was what she had dreamed of for so long. "You've changed, George. You're not afraid of me any more."

"Afraid of you? I ain't never been afraid of you." He kissed her again, his hands moving on her body.

"I mean, afraid I might tie you down, be a burden to you."

He stopped caressing her and looked deeply into her eyes. "Preston told me I should feel honored to have the loyalty of a woman like you, and it dawned on me that may be the only thing I got in this whole world. I mean, I got my outfit and I got a little cash stowed away, but I'll be starting from scratch, just like I have a dozen times before, only this time, I want you by my side. Just you and me, honey, for as long as it lasts."

He kissed her forehead and her nose and her chin and finally her mouth, long and sweet. She closed her eyes and let the sensations ripple over her. Her breasts started to tingle, much as they did when she nursed little Mary, and she pulled away from his kiss. "Just the two of us?" she whispered, her brow furrowed.

"Just you and me." He pulled her closer, and she gave in to his embrace, forcing that other thing, that thing at the back of her mind, far, far away.

It was pitch black when she awoke, and she knew immediately, without moving or looking around the one-room cabin, that she was alone. He had not come back. He had left yesterday morning, his destination Mail Camp, no more than a half day's ride. He should have been able to get there, pick up his mail, visit with the Burnaughs and whoever else of his acquaintance might be there, and return to their cabin at the base of the Owl Creek Mountains by nightfall. But he had not returned at dark, and she had tired of waiting for him and gone to bed, thinking he would show up in the middle of the night and crawl under the warm buffalo robe with her. Yet, she had awakened alone, and a small wave of panic swept over her. *Don't be silly,* she thought, *he was delayed for some reason and decided to spend the night at Mail Camp, that's all.*

Mary stuck her cold nose back under the robe and tried to go back to sleep, but it was no good—too many unsettling thoughts swirled around in her head. Finally she decided to get up and stoke the fire. If he did come soon, the little cabin would be toasty warm for him. Shivering in the cold November air, she fetched more wood and got a good blaze going in the wood stove. Still wrapped in the buffalo robe, she sat staring at the dancing flames, mesmerized.

She should have gone with him to Mail Camp. He had asked if she wanted to go, but it had seemed a perfunctory request, so she had declined, thinking it would do him good to have some time by himself. After all, he was used to being on his own, and it must be trying at times constantly to have someone by your side, even someone as undemanding as Mary. And they had been together virtually twenty-four hours a day since he had taken her away from the reservation last summer. He had shown her the world, or so it seemed—at least, a large part of his world. They had visited Rock Springs, Green River, Boise, Billings, Miles City, even Denver on a whirlwind tour of his old haunts. She had loved every minute of it, loved the way people who knew him were always so delighted to see him again and then looked at her with admiration for being the woman who had finally snared Butch Cassidy. She had been somewhat disappointed when he had decided they needed to settle somewhere for the winter and then had chosen this isolated spot. She would have preferred spending the winter in a town where there would be other people and activity. Not that she wasn't happy just being with him—indeed, she loved having him all to herself—but she feared that, without the distraction of traveling and seeing new places, she would dwell on the past, on what she had left behind, and that might prove to be unbearable.

A pale, half-hearted light filtered through the window. Rousing herself for the morning chores, she filled the silence by humming tune after mindless tune. By midmorning, she had prepared, eaten, and cleaned up her breakfast, folded and put away the bedclothes and the straw ticking mattress they slept on, swept the hard-packed earthen floor, tended to her horse, and hung a set of curtains she had fashioned from a bit of muslin. Everything was clean and tidy, ready for his return, whenever that might be.

Now what to do? She stuck her head out the door, thinking she would gather some kindling, but the air was quite cold with a raw edge to it that suggested snow, so she

abandoned that idea. If he had left Mail Camp after breakfast, he would be back for dinner and would be chilled after
the long ride; perhaps a warm, freshly made pie would be a
nice thing to come home to! Checking her supplies, she
found she had one can of peaches left and set to work
mixing and stirring and rolling, once again humming indus-
triously. That finished, she sat down with her basket of
mending, enjoying the luscious pastry smell that filled the
room. Wasn't it lovely to fix and do for your man, to hang
curtains at the window and bake pies, all so that he would
feel warm and welcome and loved when he came back to
you? Only one thing could make this happy domestic scene
better, and there it was, that thing she had pushed away all
morning, tried to ignore for the past four months, but
couldn't avoid now as she sat in her warm, cozy cabin and
played housewife—*she had abandoned her child for this man!*

Her mending dropped into her lap, and she stared
sightlessly ahead, conjuring up little Mary B' Hat's image.
The child would be six months old now—Mary had been
away from her for half of her life. She was probably sitting
up on her own now, bouncing on Gray Hair's lap, looking at
Gray Hair's face, and in her little baby brain identifying that
face as her mother's, for she had spent many more hours of
her short life with the old Indian woman than she had with
her true mother. Or worse, what if something had happened
to her, some horrible infant illness, and Mary did not even
know about it? She shuddered and passed her hand over her
eyes. *You chose,* she thought. *You chose him over your baby,
even though she's his baby, too, and now you have to live with it.*

Maybe, when he came back, it would be a good time to
tell him. He would be so happy to see her after his absence,
and she would greet him with a fire lit and a meal made and
open arms—how could he help but be seduced by the

charms of domesticity? Surely he would come around to the idea of being a father. Oh, he would be shocked and confused, no doubt, but in time he would also be accepting—please, God.

She rose to take the pie out and then set it on top of the stove to stay warm. Poking her head outside, she looked up at the sky. On this gray day it was hard to tell the time, but it seemed to be well past noon. Well, he would be along shortly. She returned to her mending. Before long, the warm fire and rocking motion of the chair lulled her to sleep. When she woke, she could tell by the darkening sky it was late afternoon. Where was he, for God's sake? He should have been home this time yesterday.

Trying not to let her fears get the best of her, she reminded herself he was an experienced outdoorsman and was quite capable of handling any emergency that arose on the trail. But then she realized that it was not an emergency or accident of some kind that worried her; it was the possibility that he had left her, that he did not intend to return.

"Ridiculous!" she cried into the empty room, shaking her head in disgust. She was imagining things. He had not said or done anything before he left to indicate he would not come back as soon as he was able. He must have just decided to stay over an extra day at the Mail Camp, and what was wrong with that? Her stomach rumbled, and she realized she had not eaten since breakfast. She made herself a cold supper, covered the barely warm pie, and read by lantern light until it was time for bed.

The next morning, she busied herself as usual, confident he would show for dinner, but, when noon came and went with no sign of him, the fear returned, even stronger. She briefly considered saddling up and riding to Mail Camp to find out what had happened but then decided not to—what if he showed up hurt or sick, and she wasn't here to help him?

Darkness began to settle on the third day that he had been gone when her sharp ears caught the sound of a slowly approaching rider. She threw down the months-old magazine she had been worrying and raced outside, leaping on him almost before he had climbed down from his horse.

"Oh, George, George, you're back!" She covered his face with kisses, knocking his hat clean off his head.

"You miss me, honey?" he laughed, crinkling his eyes. He looked no worse for wear, outside of a day-old growth of beard that gave him a rakish appearance.

"Miss you! I was worried sick about you!" She knew it was the wrong thing to have said the minute it was out of her mouth.

His brows came down, and he looked at her skeptically. "What for?"

"Well . . . ," she tried to backtrack, "you were gone a little longer than I expected. But it doesn't matter, you're here now."

She leaned toward him again, but he turned his back to untie his saddlebags. "I don't recall saying how long I'd be gone," he said, his voice flat and hard.

"Maybe you didn't. I don't know. I guess I just thought you were going to Mail Camp and back all in the same day. Come on in . . . I've got a peach pie for you, only a day old."

He followed her into the cabin and sat at the sawbuck table. Mary set water on to boil for coffee and cut a generous slice of pie, then sat across from him and watched him eat. She couldn't take her eyes off him, she was so glad to have him back safe and sound. She asked him for the news, and he told her a few things—the Burnaughs' baby was toddling around now and getting into everything, which seemed to completely befuddle Emery and Alice. They laughed together, and it was on the tip of her tongue to broach the topic of babies and what he thought of them in general, when he cleared his throat and announced he had found a job.

"A job! What do you mean?" she asked, confused.

"You know, something you do for somebody else so they'll pay you." He was teasing, but she did not smile.

"I guess I thought we were set here for the winter."

"Well, we are. But we still need money. All that traveling around ate up my spare cash. So I moseyed on over to see Tom Osborne, and he hired me to work on the ranch some this winter."

"Tom Osborne? Isn't that the *Quién Sabe* Ranch?" she asked. Butch nodded. "But that's east of here quite a ways, isn't it?"

"Not so far. A day's ride in good weather."

Mary stood to fetch the coffee. "George"—she had never been able to get used to calling him Butch although he clearly preferred it—"do you mean to say you rode to Mail Camp, then turned right around and rode to *Quién Sabe*?"

"Sure." There was a note of challenge in his voice, and she knew she should let it go, but she couldn't. By God, she had worried herself sick for three days.

"But that means you rode right by here and didn't stop. Why not?"

He sighed and placed his hands flat on the table on either side of his plate. "That coffee ready yet?"

She poured him a cup and sat down opposite him again. "I just wonder why you didn't stop in for a while. I made a nice pie for you," she said in a small voice.

"Dammit woman, why would I give a good god-damn about your stinking pie?" he exploded. Her eyes got very wide, and she brought her hands to her mouth. "Jesus," he sighed in exasperation, "I'm sorry. I'm sorry, OK? I weren't by myself, that's why I didn't stop. I ran into a couple of fellas at Mail Camp, and we decided to go over to Tom's together. I just didn't want to . . . well, you know, surprise you with extra mouths to feed."

Wordlessly, she cleared his plate and started to prepare supper, her back stiff and straight.

"Christ," he groaned, "if there's one thing I can't stand, it's the cold shoulder." He slapped his hat on his head and started for the door.

"Wait," she called him back. "Don't go. I'm sorry. It was childish of me. Only, well, I always want to see you, no matter how many people you bring with you." She managed a feeble smile. Grudgingly, he sat back down. She came over to him and began to knead his shoulders. He pulled her onto his lap, and they nuzzled for a few minutes until she laughed and said in her husky voice: "Better turn me loose before the beans burn."

"Let 'em burn," he growled. Smiling, she pushed him away and put their supper on the table.

"Was there any mail for you?" she asked.

"Yeah, I almost forgot. A letter from Preston with some interesting news. You remember the Simpson family, used to be my neighbors up on Horse Creek?"

"Of course. It was Ella Simpson who was sick with the flu, when you rode all that way for the doctor." She cast him a loving look, convinced all over again of his nobility.

"Right. Well, listen to this. Will Simpson, Ella's father, went and became a lawyer, the son-of-a-gun. Not only that, he got himself elected prosecutor. He's prosecuting my case now!"

"Your old friend? That's good news, isn't it? Surely he

won't try too hard to convict you, not after what you did for Ella."

"Maybe. Or, like Preston said in his letter, he may try to bend over backwards to prove he's fair and . . . what was the word he used . . . impartial. He may try extra hard to get me. Hard to tell." Butch tried to shrug it off, but Mary could tell the possibility of being prosecuted by his good friend bothered him.

"No prosecutor on earth could convict you. You're an innocent man. The jury can tell that just by looking at you!"

Grinning, he reached across the table and lightly stroked the soft underside of her wrist. "I'm guilty of one thing for sure . . . being crazy for a certain beautiful, half-breed gal I know."

Later that night, as she lay wrapped in his arms underneath the heavy, buffalo robe, feeling the steady rise and fall of his chest, it occurred to her that she had not told him about Mary B' Hat, and that, most likely, she never would. For she knew perfectly well why he had bypassed their cabin on his way to the ranch, and it had nothing to do with wanting to spare her the trouble of feeding extra people. It was because he was embarrassed by her, or, more precisely, by their relationship. Oh, it had been fine when they were traveling and he could squire around a pretty woman on his arm, but now that they were settled somewhere, playing house, as it were, he could not bring himself to admit to his footloose and fancy-free cohorts that his life now had something of permanence in it. A stabbing realization came to her, and she literally stopped breathing as the stunning insight sunk in. She was the only one who thought there was any permanence to their relationship. He viewed this time as merely another episode in a life lived on the move. He had said he wanted her by his side "for as long as it lasts," but he had made no commitment to make it last.

Uttering a small, strangled sound, she started to pull away, but he stirred in his sleep and drew her close again, then, half awake now, began making love to her. She sighed and banished her disturbing thoughts to the part of her brain that shut out everything uncomfortable and unhappy. Only, there were too many such thoughts already there, and it was becoming harder and harder to keep the door closed on them.

Chapter Seventeen

Seven months later, on June 20, 1893, Butch Cassidy and his erstwhile partner Al Hainer rode into Lander to stand trial. They sat their mounts confidently, greeting friends and acquaintances they passed in the street, accepting handshakes and wishes of good luck. Preston had told them he thought they had an excellent chance of winning their case, although they still had not turned up any defense witnesses. Based on today's reception, it did appear that no jury made up of Fremont County citizens would convict the popular pair.

Butch's only regret was that Mary had not come to town with him. She had accompanied him as far as the reservation, and then had insisted on stopping, pleading some mysterious errand and maintaining she would be too nervous to attend the trial anyway. He tried to jolly her out of her trepidation, for he would have liked her to see how well received he was in Lander, but she remained adamant. They parted, he promising to return for her when the trial was over, she promising to come find him if, God forbid, something went wrong. Although she kissed him heartily and waved him off with a smile on her face, her dark eyes seemed pensive and somber, and he rode off, vowing to get to the bottom of her peculiar sadness as soon as all his legal troubles were behind him.

The two men hooked up with Preston and Rathbone and huddled outside the courtroom for last minute instructions. Preston informed his clients that he was going to move for a continuance on the basis that the two witnesses to the sale of the horse, Jeff Green and Charley Willis, could not be located.

"Why do that?" protested Butch. "If you think we got such a good chance of winning, let's go ahead and hold the trial. I don't want this hanging over my head for another year!"

"It's purely procedural," Preston replied. "There's virtually no chance the judge will grant another continuance, but, if things should not go well and you are convicted, I will have preserved my right to appeal on that issue. Do you understand?"

Both men nodded, although they still appeared a bit confused. "Say, Preston," Butch said, "you wrote me that Will Simpson got elected county prosecutor. Is he going to be trying my case today?"

"No, he recused himself. The judge appointed a special prosecutor, man by the name of M. C. Brown. I know him well . . . he's a former judge. I don't think we'll have any problems."

Smiling confidently, he escorted his clients into the courtroom. They sat at the defense table, only to rise again, when the clerk announced the arrival of District Court Judge Jesse Knight. A diminutive man with a shock of white hair entered the room and convened the court in the case of the State against George Cassidy and Albert Hainer. Butch felt a brief twinge, remembering the only other time he had been in court, on another charge of horse thievery, seven years ago in Montrose, Colorado. He was acquitted then, in spite of his greenhorn lawyer. Surely he would be here, too, with one of the best defense attorneys in the state by his side. He thought of Maxi, who had bailed him out at that first trial, and was suddenly very glad that his father was not here today to see his son brought to trial again, seven years older but arguably no wiser.

As predicted, Judge Knight denied the defense motion for a continuance, pointing out that they had had an entire year to find their witnesses, and that, if they had not been able to turn them up by now, it was doubtful they ever would. Preston sat without comment, and the judge proceeded with jury selection. It didn't take long to seat twelve "fair and impartial" jurors, some of whom Butch recognized, and almost all of whom cast sympathetic glances toward the defense table. Chortling inside, Butch played the part of the chastened defendant, maintaining a serious mien and making sober eye contact with each of the twelve men.

After the noon break, Prosecutor Brown gave his opening argument, an uninspired oration that left Douglas Preston desperately trying to repress an exultant grin. He leaned over and whispered into Butch's ear: "They've given up, my boy. They aren't even trying to win this case."

Then it was Preston's turn. He rose and surveyed the jury for a full minute before speaking. "Gentlemen of the jury," he began in his deep baritone, "there is no case here. None whatsoever. In his remarks to you a moment ago, my esteemed colleague, Mister Brown, offered no proof that a crime had been committed . . . not a shred of evidence! I ask you, where is the proof? My clients are accused of purchasing a stolen horse, but where is the proof that this horse was ever stolen? And even if it was stolen, where is the proof that my clients had any knowledge of that? Gentlemen, the law places the burden of proof on the state, in other words, the state *must prove* its case beyond a reasonable doubt, and I submit to you that it will not be able to do so in the case against George Cassidy and Al Hainer. Thank you."

Tempering his straightforward words with a folksy nod at the jurors, he strolled back to his seat. "That's it?" asked Butch.

"The first rule of a trial lawyer," Preston replied. "Be short, get to the point, and sit down."

The judge recessed for the day. That night Butch and Al hit the saloons, although on the advice of their attorney they kept to themselves. Sitting at a back corner table, they nursed their whiskeys, acknowledging friends who stopped by to talk, but carefully avoiding all discussion of their ongoing trial. During a quiet moment, Butch turned to his partner and asked: "I always meant to ask you, Al . . . when we was arrested at Ham's Fork, why didn't you try to run for it? You might have been able to make it even if they got me."

Hainer flushed and stared at his drink. "They had me cuffed. I wouldn't've got very far."

That wouldn't have stopped me from trying, Butch thought, but all he said was: "What are you going to do when all this is over?"

Shrugging, Al downed his whiskey. "Don't rightly know. Go back to Horse Creek, maybe."

"You want to stay partners?" Butch said, only half serious.

"I guess I figured our partnering days was over."

Butch was not sure if that was a reference to his new liaison with Mary or to the fact that their previous partnership had seemed to bring them nothing but trouble. "Tell you what," he said. "That Horse Creek land is damn' good property, but it don't look like I'm going to get back there. I'll sell you my share."

Al pursed his mouth and shrugged again. "Let's not go getting ahead of ourselves. Who knows what's going to happen."

"Hell, what are you so worried about? Preston says they ain't got nothing on us!" Butch exclaimed.

"Yeah, I know." Suddenly Al leaned in, a tense look on his face. "That's what worries me. Preston says they ain't even trying to convict us. Well, why not? Why go to all the trouble of having a trial? I keep thinking they're hiding aces up their sleeve."

Butch paused to consider. What Al said made a certain amount of sense, but, hell, he was just being a nervous Nellie. After all, their attorney, one of the top defense lawyers in the state, did not seem worried, so why should he be?

"The only thing M. C. Brown has up his sleeve is chilblains." Butch winked, and Al gave a half-hearted smile.

The next day, the prosecution presented its case, such as it was. The first witness was Otto Franc, who testified that the horse in question had been stolen from his neighbor, and that he, acting on his neighbor's behalf, had hired an investigator, one John Chapman, to track down the thief or thieves.

"Mister Franc," Preston rose to cross-examine, "who is this neighbor whom you have undertaken to protect so zealously?"

"Mister Richard Ashworth."

"So he is the owner of the horse in question?"

"Yes. Well, actually, the Grey Bull Cattle Company is the owner of record, but Mister Ashworth is the proprietor of that company."

"How do you know that?"

"How do I know that?" repeated Franc.

"Yes. How do you know that Mister Ashworth is the proprietor of the Grey Bull Cattle Company?"

"Well, he told me so." Franc appeared uncertain for the first time.

"I see. He told you so, and you believed him. Do you

have any proof that what he told you is correct?"

"Why, no, not really. But I have no reason to doubt him."

"So you know him quite well, then?"

"Well enough." Franc shifted in his seat.

"Where is the elusive Mister Ashworth, incidentally?" Preston threw the question out almost as an afterthought.

"In England, I believe. He is a native of that country, you know."

"Indeed. Does he spend much time in his native land?"

"A fair amount."

"How many times in the past two years, say, has Mister Ashworth visited his ranch next to yours?" Preston began to pace in front of the jury box, his hands clasped behind him.

"I couldn't say, exactly. Once or twice."

"Pardon me, Mister Franc, perhaps I've misunderstood you." Preston came to a stop directly in front of the witness. "We are talking about a man whom you say you know 'well enough,' whose affairs you handle in his absence, and who is your nearest neighbor, yet you aren't even sure when he is in residence at his ranch? Is that correct?"

"No, I misspoke. He has been at his ranch twice in the past two years, I believe." Franc looked at the prosecutor, hoping for a rescue, but Brown sat with his eyes averted.

"You believe or you know? Never mind, just answer this. Was Mister Ashworth at the ranch when the sorrel horse was stolen?"

"No, sir. His foreman came to see me about it."

"And how did the foreman know the horse had been stolen?"

"Well, the horse was gone, and it had not been sold, so it must have been stolen."

"So you went to the sheriff immediately to report the theft?"

Franc drummed his fingers nervously on his chair seat. "Not exactly."

"Oh? Why not?"

"Well, Steve, the foreman, thought he knew who did it . . . Billy Nutcher, a no-account drifter, who'd been hanging around. He didn't think Nutcher took the horse for his own use, but rather to sell for cash. Steve figured Nutcher would unload the animal as soon as he could, so there was no point in going after him. Better to go after whoever bought the horse from Nutcher."

"So you did not alert the sheriff to this crime, even though you knew who the criminal was, because the man you were really after was whoever bought the horse from the criminal? That seems to be rather odd reasoning. What if, as in the case of my clients, the purchasers were totally innocent as to the horse's status? Then not only would the true thief have gotten away, but you would have no redress against the purchaser. Didn't that occur to you?"

Franc gave the defense attorney an exasperated look. "It never occurred to me that anybody could think Billy Nutcher owned that horse fair and square."

"Why not?" Preston asked innocently.

"Because Billy Nutcher is a lying, cheating . . . ," Franc caught himself, and cleared his throat. "That is, Steve told me Nutcher was a well-known rustler, that he wouldn't fool anybody."

"Mister Franc, did you hire Billy Nutcher to steal that horse and sell it to my clients?" The suddenness of Preston's accusation drew gasps from the courtroom.

Franc cleared his throat and sat straighter in his chair. "No, I did not. That's ridiculous."

Smiling, Preston took his seat. "That's all for this witness, Your Honor."

A clearly shaken Prosecutor Brown moved for a recess which the judge denied. "Let's get this over with," he declared, glaring at the state's attorney.

Brown called John Chapman and asked him a few perfunctory questions about his pursuit and capture of Cassidy and Hainer, then fearfully turned him over to the defense. To everyone's surprise, Preston declined to cross-examine the witness, after which Brown rested his case.

"Is the defense prepared to offer evidence, Mister Preston?" inquired Judge Knight.

"Your Honor, the defense rests." Once again, gasps and murmurs rippled through the courtroom. Butch and Al exchanged nervous glances, not sure what their lawyer was up to. "The prosecution has not even begun to make a case. We have nothing to rebut."

"Very well. Let's proceed with closing arguments."

Recognizing defeat when he saw it, Prosecutor Brown kept his remarks mercifully short. Preston did likewise, merely pointing out that the state had failed to produce a witness either to the theft of the horse or its subsequent sale, and that even the original ownership of the animal seemed to be in question.

With that, the judge instructed the jury to return for deliberations first thing in the morning. Butch looked over and saw Otto Franc speaking intently to the prosecutor. Then he turned and stalked out, glaring at the defense table as he passed.

"Sore loser," grumbled Butch.

"I hope that's all it is," Al said, shaking his head sadly.

The little baby toddled forward on chubby legs, giggling happily at her newfound skill. Mary scooped her up and twirled her around, hugging her tightly.

"Look, sweetie, look at this shiny rock!" She picked a piece of quartz out of the dirt and showed it to the baby who immediately tried to put it in her mouth. "No, no, little one, not for eating. Are you hungry? Let's find you something you can eat." Holding the child on her hip, she entered Gray Hair's cabin and found a piece of bread for Mary B' Hat to nibble. She settled the baby on her lap and stroked her smooth skin, marveling at the changes that had taken place since she had seen her last, almost a year ago. She fought off sudden tears. How could she have let so much time pass without seeing her own child? What kind of a woman was she?

Gray Hair came up and put a hand on her shoulder. "She look like you."

"Do you think? Maybe a little, except for the eyes." Mary B' Hat did, indeed, have her mother's dark hair and high cheekbones, but her brilliant blue eyes bespoke an entirely different parentage. "Oh, I missed you so much!" Mary squeezed the baby to her, eliciting a high-pitched shriek of annoyance. Mary laughed. "I guess Mama's hugs are OK only so long as they don't get in the way of dinner!"

"That child do love to eat." Gray Hair shook her head dolefully.

Mary sat watching her daughter shred the piece of bread. "You think I'm awful, don't you? Leaving like I did."

Gray Hair looked at her with deep, clear eyes in which there was no hint of judgment. "You do what you have to then. And now."

Mary searched the old woman's face. "Yes. It's different now. I can't leave her again." Gray Hair smiled and left the tiny cabin. Mary B' Hat watched her go, but she seemed perfectly content to stay on her mother's lap. Mary's heart swelled, and she buried her face in the child's soft hair.

"It's time to meet Daddy, little one."

The jury filed back into the courtroom after only two hours of deliberation. Preston winked at his clients as Judge Knight instructed the jury foreman to rise. "How say you on the charge that George Cassidy and Albert Hainer did unlawfully, knowingly, and feloniously steal, take and carry away, lead away, drive away, and ride away one horse of the value of forty dollars of goods, chattels, and personal property of the Grey Bull Cattle Company, a corporation duly organized and existing under, and, by virtue of the laws of the State of New Jersey, and doing business with the County of Fremont, State of Wyoming?"

"Not guilty!"

The room erupted in whoops and hollers. Butch leaped to his feet, acknowledging the crowd with his fist raised in victory. Preston shook his hand and Hainer's, then crossed the aisle to commiserate with Mr. Brown. The prosecutor drew him in close, and they bent their heads for a private conversation that was lost amidst the bedlam in the courtroom.

Butch clapped Hainer on the back. "What'd I tell you, Al. Nothing to it! No aces in the hole!"

"I guess not." Al grinned sheepishly.

Butch enthusiastically pumped Rathbone's hand. "You guys are damn' expensive, but worth every penny!"

"Of course," said Rathbone, smiling. "That's the point."

Preston came back to the table, his mouth set in a hard line. "Looks like we better get while the gettin's good," said Butch. "What's the long face for?"

"I'm afraid you aren't going anywhere, at least not right away. You either, Al." Preston kicked the table leg in a rare display of anger. At this moment, Sheriff Stough walked up and planted himself behind the defendants, his arms folded in front of him.

"What's going on?" Butch looked around in confusion. Al closed his eyes and hung his head.

"You are being arrested again," Preston explained in a tight voice. "Apparently, it became quite clear that the state was going to lose its case against you, so our friend Otto Franc swore out a new complaint three days ago. The sheriff is here to take you back to jail."

"Wait a minute! I don't know much about the law, but I do know a man can't be charged with the same crime twice. Ain't that double jeopardy, or something?" Butch looked from Preston to Rathbone, a burning anger rising in him. His instinct was to flee, but he was sure this had to be a mistake that Preston could easily clear up.

"Quite right. But Mister Franc is smarter than we give him credit for. He named a different horse in this complaint and listed the owner as Richard Ashworth this time. Different horse, different crime . . . means you can be tried again. I'm afraid there's nothing I can do aside from raise your bail money." Preston nodded to the sheriff who stepped forward and grabbed Butch's elbow.

Butch jerked his arm away. "I don't believe this! This ain't right. You got to do something, Preston!"

Sheriff Stough drew his six-shooter and stuck it in the outlaw's ribs. "Don't give me trouble, Cassidy. I'm just doing my job."

"You're right, Butch, it isn't fair, and I intend to raise hell over it. But there is no legal reason why you cannot be arrested on this new charge, so you will have to go back to jail until we raise bail. I'm sorry." Preston slammed out of the courtroom, Rathbone trailing him.

With every fiber in his body, Butch wanted to shout and

fight and punch his way out of the courtroom, but the sheriff's gun nudging him along convinced him to go quietly. Back in the county jail where he had already spent three long months of his life, he sank down on the bunk and buried his head in his hands, wondering who he was up against and why they hated him so much.

Two days later, Al Hainer showed up outside the bars of Butch's cell, his bags thrown over his shoulder.

"We getting sprung?" Butch asked hopefully. "Gotta hand it to that Preston. Didn't take him no time to raise bail."

Al shifted on his feet, not meeting Butch's gaze. "Looks like they're letting me out but not you, Butch."

"What? What the hell's going on?"

"I don't rightly know. Sheriff Stough, he said I was free to go till this time next year but you was going to be sticking around for a while yet."

Furious, Butch grabbed the bars separating him from Al. "Who posted your bond?"

"Ain't sure. Sheriff wouldn't say." Al paused uncomfortably. "I feel bad about this, Butch, but you can't rightly expect me to stay locked up just 'cause you ain't free to go."

Butch gave the bars a frustrated shake and walked away. " 'Course not. So long, Al. See you next year," he said bitterly.

Al hesitated, torn between his desire to get out of there and his reluctance to abandon his friend. "Well, so long," he said. Then, more heatedly: "This whole deal's been crooked from the beginning, Butch. I feel damn' bad about that."

"Ain't your fault," Butch grudgingly admitted.

Al looked straight at him for once, and then dropped his eyes. "Reckon not."

"Listen, Al, do me a favor. Mary was expecting me a couple of days ago. She's probably wondering what happened. Look her up, would you, and tell her we got off but that something's come up, and I'll be there as soon as I can. Don't spill the beans about getting arrested again. You'll find her at Moore's General Store, or, if she ain't there, go to her folks' cabin on the reservation. They had some kind of falling out, and she likely won't be there, but they might know where she's staying."

Al nodded and started to leave, then came back and stuck his hand through the bars. "Good luck, Butch."

They shook, and Butch had the feeling that this was a final good bye, although he knew that wasn't so—at the very least, they would meet next summer for their second trial together.

Butch cooled his heels for two weeks in the Fremont County jail before the sheriff released him. Once again, two Lander businessmen had posted a surety bond on his behalf. Sheriff Stough continued to profess ignorance as to the identity of Hainer's bailors, saying the bond had arrived anonymously via messenger. Butch collected his gear and headed out of town, pondering the recent turn of events. Strange that Al should have gotten sprung by some mysterious benefactor who was only too happy to let Butch stay locked up. Now that he thought about it, Al's behavior in this deal had been peculiar all along. First, his insistence on buying the stolen horses, when Butch had held back, then his meek submission to being captured at Ham's Fork, and, finally, his reluctance to buy Butch's share of the Horse Creek property, as though he knew they weren't yet out of the woods. But it was hard to believe he was in cahoots with the law; after all, he was standing trial right alongside his partner.

Butch pushed these unsettling thoughts away. Loyalty to a friend, and especially to a partner, was so basic to him that he refused to lend credence to the possibility of Al's betrayal. Besides, he had the more pressing problem of how to break the news of his latest arrest to Mary. He knew she would be mightily disappointed; she had told him many times this past year that the only thing spoiling their happiness was the constant worry over his upcoming trial. Now they had to face another year in limbo.

He stopped at Moore's General Store and asked after her. Mr. Moore gave him a strange look but directed him to the cabin of some Indian woman named Gray Hair who lived about three miles away on the reservation. Wondering who this person was to Mary and why she had never mentioned her to him, he rode on and soon spotted the cabin, more of a shanty really, in the distance.

As he approached, the door opened, and Mary stepped outside, carrying a large egg basket. "George!" she cried in delight. Ducking her head back inside for a moment, she reëmerged and closed the door gently behind her. They embraced, and she buried her head in his shoulder so he would not see the tears of relief and happiness that filled her eyes.

He pulled her head back and kissed her tenderly, smiling at her joy in seeing him again. "Ain't you a sight for sore eyes. I didn't expect to be gone for so long, girl. It sure is good to see you again."

"Oh George, you're free! They didn't convict you . . . you're a free man now! Tell me all about it!" She fairly glowed with excitement, filled with the anticipation of finally being able to tell him about Mary B' Hat.

Butch raised one eyebrow in a quizzical expression. "Didn't Hainer come to see you?" he asked.

"Why, no," she replied.

"Bastard! He was supposed to tell you I got delayed." He shook his head in disgust. "I'm having serious second thoughts about that jackass."

"I never did like him much, although I didn't want to say anything. But forget about him, I have something important to tell you." Mary took his hand and led him to a small stream that ran by the cabin. Settling herself under a tall cottonwood, she picked up a leaf and started to shred it nervously. Although she had rehearsed her lines over and over again, now that the time had come, the words were jumbled in her brain, and she struggled to organize her thoughts. It was important that she say this right, for the manner in which it was presented to him might dictate his reaction. But whatever she said, she needed to say it quickly, because little Mary B' Hat, whom she had left sleeping inside, might wake at any moment and loudly announce her presence. The realization that her daughter and her daughter's father were so close to each other and would soon meet for the first time gave Mary chills.

Meanwhile, Butch knelt by the side of the stream and dipped his hands into the cold water, rinsing the dust and grime of the road from his face and neck. He, too, was nervous, hoping that Mary would understand about the new arrest and not blame him for anything. Running wet fingers through his hair, he sat down beside her, encircling his knees with his powerful arms.

"George, I've been meaning to tell you something for quite a while . . . ," Mary began.

"Wait!" he interrupted. She looked up sharply. "I know what you're going to say," he stumbled on. "You're going to say that now that I've been acquitted and am free for good, it's time you and I talked more seriously about, well, being together and everything. But the truth is, Mary, I ain't a free man, at least not yet. It's true I was acquitted, but it turns out this Franc fellow, the same bastard who swore out the first complaint against me, swore out a second complaint, accusing me and Al of stealing a different horse. It don't seem fair or even legal to me, but Preston says he's within his rights to do it. The long and short of it is, they arrested me, and now I got to stand trial again next summer. Same thing all over." He stole a glance at Mary. She stared at him, her eyes wide, her mouth slightly agape. "I'm awful sorry, honey, but there weren't nothing I could do about it. For some reason I can't figure, Otto Franc's got it in for me. He set me up, I swear it, from planting Nutcher at Mail Camp to bribing Hainer somehow." He paused to let himself calm down, then went on. "It ain't fair of me to ask you to stick with me through all this. I know it's been hard on you, not being able to count on me. If you wanted to go your own way, I'd understand."

He dropped his chin to his chest, feeling completely sorry for himself, and waited for Mary to offer words of encouragement. When none came, he looked up, and what he saw made his stomach roll over. Her face had gone ashen gray, and her eyes stared ahead blindly. True, he had worried she would be upset, but he had expected tears and recriminations, not this silent emptiness.

Suddenly she gathered her skirts around her and stood, wavering slightly. He put out a hand to steady her, but she hurried away. Halfway to the cabin, she stopped and hugged herself tightly. Butch came up behind her and touched her shoulder. He could feel her trembling.

"I'm sorry, honey," he repeated. "I didn't think you'd take it so hard."

She turned to face him. Her eyes were not vacant now but were filled with a hurt the likes of which he had never seen. Not even his mother's face, when he had left Circle Valley, had appeared so grief-stricken.

"Please leave now," she whispered.

"Listen, honey, it ain't that bad. Hell, I'd give anything to be shut of all this for good, but it's only one more year. Like as not, they won't be able to convict me next time, either." He spoke earnestly, but something in the back of his mind resented the pleading tone in his voice. A small knot of anger started to form.

"What if you do get off next year? How do you know you won't get arrested a third time, or a fourth time?" she said harshly.

"Well, hell, there was only three horses. Sooner or later they're going to run out of things to charge me with." His attempt at humor fell flat. With a look of contempt, she turned to run, but he caught her arm.

"I'm sorry, Mary. I didn't mean to make light of the situation. But I think you're making too much of this. And I'm getting damn' tired of hearing myself apologize."

She pulled her arm away and rubbed the place where he had held it. "Then don't. I don't want to hear your apologies, anyway." Suddenly her husky voice lost its angry edge. "There's so much you don't know. And now you never will. Good bye, George." She opened the cabin door and disappeared inside, closing it softly behind her.

"God dammit!" Butch kicked the dust violently. What the hell was she talking about . . . so much he didn't know? Well, he knew one thing, all right—he wasn't going to waste any more time pining after Mary Boyd. He had gotten sucked in to the point where he was practically on his knees begging the bitch to stay with him. Well, good riddance! He was back where he started—free as a bird, able to go anywhere, and do anything he damned well pleased, as long as he showed up in Fremont County court next June.

He dug his spurs violently into his horse's sides, and it bolted into a breakneck gallop. Gritting his teeth into the wind, he gave the horse its head, not caring what direction it chose. North, south, east, or west, it was all the same to him, just as long as it took him far away from Mary Boyd.

Chapter Eighteen

"All rise."

Chairs scraped, and the din in the courtroom subsided as Judge Knight mounted the bench and solemnly surveyed the scene. It looked much the same as it had one year ago with one exception—representing the state this morning of June 30, 1894, was Will Simpson, the duly elected prosecutor of Fremont County. Douglas Preston had forewarned his clients of this circumstance and, to Butch's pained inquiry as to why his former neighbor had decided to try the case himself this time around, replied that Simpson undoubtedly felt he needed to prove his impartiality and commitment to the rule of law. How better to do that than to be willing personally to convict an old friend? Despite having taken this strong moral stand, however, Simpson refused to look Butch Cassidy or Al Hainer in the eye.

Butch slumped in his seat, seeming to take little interest in the proceedings. He assumed this trial would follow a similar course as the previous one, although his lawyer had warned him that things were a little trickier this time around. For one thing, the original ownership of the horse in question had finally been pleaded correctly. Preston's focus, therefore, would be on his clients' states of mind when they purchased the horse—did they know it was stolen property or not?

As the judge and lawyers droned on through various preliminary matters, Butch's mind wandered. The past twelve months had been the most miserable of his life, filled with tragedy and disappointment. He had rambled throughout the Rocky Mountains, unconsciously trying to recapture the fun and excitement he had shared with Mary on their Western tour, but it had been hopeless. Oh, for a while he had relished the freedom and independence of solitary travel, but soon enough he found himself missing the beautiful girl's companionship. Perhaps seeking to replace her, he had traveled to Rock Springs to look up his old friend, Patty. But that poor, doomed soul had succumbed to pneumonia the previous year. Then he had ventured over into Utah, only to run into some acquaintances who informed him that his brother, Dan, was serving time in the Wyoming penitentiary for robbing a mail carrier. His spirits had plummeted at that news—no doubt his parents were devastated to have a convict for a son. Dan had not even had the good sense to change his name in order to spare his family's pride. He had spent the rest of the year roving from one haunt to the next, picking up odd jobs here and there, putting away cash to pay his lawyer's bill. It had been a nomadic existence that even he, a confirmed wanderer, found unsatisfying. In his more rational moments, he could not blame Mary for refusing to live that kind of life, but he rarely thought rationally about that woman. Although he had tried to put her out of his mind, she was constantly there, and her memory made him alternately depressed or angry or wistful or a combination of all three.

He struggled back to attention, aware that a lackadaisical attitude on his part might alienate the jury. He did care what happened—he had no desire to be the second Parker sent to prison—but it all seemed a bit unreal to him, as though it were not his life that hung in the balance.

Butch glanced over at Al, who sat at the other end of the table staring morosely at the proceedings. They had not seen each other since Al had walked out on him in his jail cell one year ago. Still not certain what rôle, if any, Al had played in setting him up, Butch vowed one thing for sure—if they got out of this mess free and clear, he would have no more to do with the silent, mysterious Al Hainer.

The next day, July 1, the prosecution presented its case. Will Simpson competently led his witnesses through their testimony, displaying none of the temerity or indecisiveness of his predecessor, Mr. Brown. Otto Franc had obviously learned a lesson from the first trial—he testified only as to what he actually knew and refused to let Preston rattle him on cross-examination.

On July 2, Douglas Preston took the floor for the defense. Rising slowly, he picked up a piece of paper and turned to face the audience. Rathbone stood at the back of the courtroom; he moved to a spot behind a man sitting in the back row and nodded imperceptibly. Sighing, Preston dropped the paper to the table. "The defense rests, Your Honor."

"Are you sure, Mister Preston?" Judge Knight had great faith in the defense attorney's abilities, but resting his case without presenting any evidence seemed bizarre in the face of the strong effort put forth by the prosecution this time around.

"Quite sure. Once again, the state has utterly failed to prove its case."

"Very well. Mister Simpson, are you prepared to begin closing argument?"

"I am, sir." Simpson presented a workman-like argument, not flashy or filled with oratorical excesses, but thorough in its summation of the evidence and convincing in its entreaty that the jury show no mercy to men who committed the crime of horse thievery, a crime on the par with murder in this part of the country. Preston did his usual splendid job; nevertheless, Butch left the courthouse that day feeling a little less confident than he would have liked.

"Preston, why didn't you use that bill of sale?" he asked as they walked together down the plank sidewalk. The piece of paper discarded by Preston just prior to resting his case was, on its face, a bill of sale showing the purchase of a group of horses, the stolen horse among them, by Billy Nutcher from a Nebraska horse dealer. Preston had been prepared to argue that the bill of sale convinced Butch and Al that Nutcher held legal title to the horse.

"Did you see Rathbone identify that man in the courtroom?" Preston said.

"Yeah, who was he?"

"The horse dealer. We got word late yesterday that Simpson had located him and would have him in court today. I instructed Rathbone to be on the look-out and give me a signal if he was there. When I saw him point out the man, I didn't dare introduce the bill of sale into evidence for fear the prosecution would re-open its case, call the dealer to the stand, and elicit damaging testimony from him."

"What kind of damaging testimony?" asked Al.

"To the effect that he knew nothing about any such transaction and that the bill of sale was a fraud," said Preston acidly. "Come now, boys, you didn't really expect me to believe that paper was genuine." Butch and Al looked at the ground and did not reply. "Buck up, fellas. We're facing stiffer odds this time around, but the jury's with us, I think." He smiled gamely, but his dark eyes remained troubled.

The jury deliberated for one full day. On July 4, it announced it had reached a verdict. "Independence Day," joked Butch, as they sat at the defense table for the last time. "That's got to be a good sign."

Judge Knight read the jury's verdict silently, then handed it to the clerk who rose and intoned the following: "We the jury find the above named defendant George Cassidy guilty of horse stealing, as charged in the information, and we find the value of the property to be five dollars. And we find the above named defendant Albert Hainer not guilty. And the jury recommend the said Cassidy to the mercy of the court."

Pandemonium broke out. A reporter rushed out to file his story; a woman who had sat through the entire trial burst into tears; several people came forward to congratulate Will Simpson. Judge Knight rapped his gavel over and over in a futile effort to restore order. Finally he gave up and dismissed the jury. Butch sat motionless through it all, trying to comprehend what had happened. *George Cassidy, guilty of horse stealing . . . Albert Hainer, not guilty.* How could that be? How could he be found guilty and not his partner, the very man who had urged the shady deal on him in the first place. Butch gripped the arms of his chair tightly. A white hot rage started to build as he realized all his suspicions about Al were justified—the man had betrayed him. It had taken a long time to play out, but how else to explain this outcome? Otto Franc had used Al to frame Butch, with the promise that Al would never do time. Just exactly how that was accomplished Butch did not know, but he had no doubt that a man like Franc would stoop to anything, including jury tampering, to pull it off.

He leaped to his feet and grabbed Hainer's shirt. "You bastard! You sold me out, you fucking stool pigeon!" He drew his arm back to land a punch, but, by this time, the sheriff's deputies were all over him, wrestling his arms behind him. "Rot in hell, Judas!" Butch spat in Hainer's face. The last thing he saw as he was forcibly removed from the courtroom was Will Simpson watching him with a look of utter dismay.

Later that afternoon, Douglas Preston visited Butch in his cell. Because of his outburst in the courtroom, the prisoner had been handcuffed. Preston asked the deputy to remove his shackles.

Butch rubbed his wrists and glared at his attorney. "What happened in there?"

"I don't know. One never knows what a jury will do, of course, but it appears that on this particular day, Mister Simpson simply got the better of us." Preston made no excuses, a fact that Butch grudgingly appreciated.

"You don't think Franc bought off that jury?"

Preston regarded him closely. "I think Otto Franc conspired with Nutcher and Hainer to set you up. I think he instructed Chapman to take you alive so you could be put to trial as an example to other rustlers. Whether he engineered Hainer's acquittal or not, I don't know. I do know jury tampering is a very serious charge. One must have overwhelming evidence of it to overturn a verdict."

"It's pretty damn' clear to me the jury was fixed. It don't make no sense to convict me and acquit Hainer, not unless that's the verdict they was paid to deliver."

Shaking his head, Preston drew some papers from his litigator's bag. "If you want to fight your conviction, Butch, there are a number of avenues to pursue, but alleging jury tampering is not one of them. I've already filed a motion for a new trial, raising several technical points, but, frankly, I doubt the court will give any of them the time of day. Our other option is to appeal on the basis that Judge Knight failed to instruct the jury that you could be found guilty of a lesser offense than grand larceny."

Butch leaned forward and put his head in his hands. God, how he hated all this legal mumbo jumbo. "What happens if we do that . . . appeal, like you said?"

"You'll be retried, probably next year. Of course, this time you would have to stay in jail until your trial."

"Another year? I've already wasted two years of my life waiting to get this thing over with." Butch slapped his thighs impatiently.

"Butch," Preston said slowly, "there is another way, but you might not like it."

"It couldn't be any worse than what I've already heard today."

"I could talk to the prosecutor, try to cut you a deal. Despite his vigorous effort to get a conviction, I get the feeling Mister Simpson rather likes you. It's entirely possible he would be willing to recommend a light sentence, say only two years, instead of the maximum five, in return for our promise not to appeal."

Butch laughed mirthlessly. "So that's what it's come down to. Bargaining for years of my life with a man whose daughter I saved."

"What?" Preston asked, confused.

"Never mind." Butch pondered a moment, then looked his lawyer in the eye. "I want this to be over, Preston. I don't want to go through a third trial just to get convicted again. Anyway, I can't afford to pay you no more. I'm plumb broke. Go ahead and talk to Simpson. Two years in the pen ain't all that bad. I can stand that."

Preston stuffed the papers back in his bag and stood. For once in his life, he had nothing to say. He had represented this man to the best of his abilities, and it had not been enough. He was frustrated that, in spite of his suspicions

about Otto Franc, he could prove nothing, and was, therefore, obligated to remain silent. And, now, a man whom he
considered his friend, who once helped him out of a tough
situation, and whom he sincerely believed was striving to
lead an honest life, was forced to pay the price for one
stupid, if not totally innocent, mistake.

"I'll come to see you after we've talked." Preston called
for the deputy to let him out. "I'm sorry, Butch, I'm truly
sorry," he said as the bars clanged shut behind him. But he
got no response from the tall, square-jawed cowboy who
looked so out of place in the confines of the tiny cell.

Will Simpson bought the deal. On July 10, he recom-
mended to Judge Knight that, in view of the prisoner's lack
of prior convictions, he be sentenced to two years out of the
possible five. Judge Knight agreed and ordered Sheriff
Stough to transfer the prisoner to the Wyoming State Penitentiary in Laramie forthwith.

Back in his cell, Butch sprawled on his wooden bunk,
listlessly dealing a game of solitaire onto the dingy, gray
blanket. The cell-block door banged open, and Deputy
Harry Logue shuffled down the aisle to stand in front of
Butch's cell. "You got a visitor," he announced.

"So?" Butch did not look up from his card game. "Bring
him in."

"It ain't a him," the deputy leered.

Butch's heart skipped a beat. Very deliberately, he
stacked the cards, rose, and hooked his thumbs in his
pockets. "Bring her in then."

Logue snickered as he retreated to the sheriff's office. A
moment later he returned, leading Mary Boyd. Catcalls and
whistles followed her as she walked down the row of cells—
the jail was full of prisoners being transferred to the state

lock-up. She ignored them, looking straight at Butch, her hands at her side.

"We had to frisk her, you know. Couldn't let some half-breed slip you a weapon or nothing like that," Logue chuckled. "Fifteen minutes, that's all." He turned to go.

"Logue!" Butch called after him. "Couldn't you let her in the cell? Kind of hard to talk with all these jailbirds looking on."

"Can't do it, pal. Hell, I ain't supposed to let anybody in to see you at all, except your lawyer, only she sweet-talked me into it." He gave her a lascivious wink and strolled out.

Mary took no notice of the deputy or the other inmates. Her eyes, large and limpid, were all on Butch, drinking in the sight of her lover whom she had not seen in a year. Slowly she stepped forward and put her hands through the bars. Butch met her there, and they intertwined fingers, holding on to each other in the only way they could. They stayed that way for several minutes, not speaking, until the other inmates grew tired of heckling and left them alone.

Finally Butch disengaged his hands, reminding himself that this woman had hurt him like no other ever had. He must be careful not to set himself up for further rejection.

"Why did you come?" he whispered.

Mary ducked her head, then looked at him with full, dark eyes. "I couldn't let you go off without telling you . . . telling you that. . . ." Her head dropped, and her shoulders shook with silent sobs.

"Mary, look at me." Wiping her eyes, she met his gaze. His pale eyes were curiously shrouded. "You told me once that there was so much I didn't know. What did you mean by that?"

She had not intended to tell him about Mary B' Hat, but

now she hesitated. Maybe the knowledge that he had a daughter would help him get through the next two years, would give him something to live for. Or, maybe, it would fill him with loathing, for her for keeping such a secret, and for himself for not being the type of man who could be entrusted with the rôle of father. She thought of her little girl, now a happy, carefree toddler. She would be four years old by the time George got out of prison, too old to accept some stranger as her father. And that was assuming George would return to them when he got out, something Mary knew better than to count on. Mary Boyd knew for a fact that George Cassidy loved her, but there were limits and conditions to that love that made theirs an impossible romance to sustain. Nevertheless, when she had heard of his fate, she knew she had to see him once more before he disappeared from her life forever.

Touching his raspy cheek, she whispered: "I just meant that you don't know how much I love you."

His eyes lit up with a soft smile. "It's only two years. That ain't so long. When I get out, I'll . . . I'll come find you."

She smiled back, but in her heart of hearts she did not believe him. There were things in life that George Cassidy loved better than her, and she doubted even a lifetime in prison would change that. For their remaining time together, they spoke quietly of this and that. Mary promised to write to him, and he promised to take her to California when he got out. Then the deputy came to get her, and they said a restrained good bye, clasping hands again briefly. Mary walked out the door with her back straight and her head held high, but, when she reached the street, she collapsed against the side of the jail. She was sure she would never see George Cassidy again.

★ ★ ★ ★ ★

On July 15, 1894, Prisoner Number 187 was booked into the Wyoming State Penitentiary: *Name, George "Butch" Cassidy; Age, 28; Nativity, New York City; Occupation, cowboy; Height, 5'9"; Complexion, light; Hair, dark flaxen; Eyes, blue; Wife, no; Parents, not known; Children, no; Religion, none; Habits of life, intemperate; Education, common school; Relations address, not known; Weight, 165 pounds; Marks scars: features, regular, small deep set eyes, 2 cut scars on back of head, small red scar under left eye, red mark on left side of back, small brown mole on calf of left leg, good build.*

The prison mug shot revealed a grim, haunted young man with disheveled hair, a three-day growth of beard and a shiner under his left eye. Prisoner No. 187 was stripped, given prison garb, and taken to his cell, a room about eight feet square with one tiny window so high up he had to stand on the bunk to see out. The cell door clanged shut, and he was alone. Slowly he stretched his arms straight out. He could almost touch the walls on either side of him, the room was so small. He closed his eyes and tried to imagine being on a wind-swept plain with the buffalo grass whipping at his legs and hawks soaring overhead, but it was no good—all that came to him was a dank, moldy smell and the sound of a rat skittering in the walls. Panic started to overtake him. He fought it down by conjuring up a vision of a beautiful, dark girl who whispered to him in a deep, husky voice: "Two years, only two years." Prisoner No. 187 drew a deep breath of stale prison air and sat down on his bunk to wait.

Chapter Nineteen

1896–1897

A raw, biting winter wind whipped into him as he stepped off the train platform. Dust and coal smoke blew into his eyes, tearing them up as they fought to flush out the grit. He turned his back to the wind and glanced up at the station sign swinging from its hinges: **Rock Springs**, it announced. *Still as grimy as ever,* he thought, clutching his light coat around him, the same coat he had worn when he entered prison eighteen months ago. They had given him his old clothes and enough money to buy a train ticket that would take him out of the state of Wyoming, but Butch Cassidy had no intention of leaving Wyoming. Not yet, anyway. Not until he had taken care of unfinished business.

He walked through the station house, pausing only to wipe his eyes with his large kerchief and then knot the cloth around his neck. Heading down the town's main street, he marveled at how much it had grown and changed since he was last here. Rock Springs, untamed and ugly although it might be, was on the way up, no doubt about it. He turned the corner at a familiar side street and was happy to see Gottsche's butcher shop anchoring the same spot as before. He pushed open the door and entered the warm space gratefully, rubbing his frozen hands together.

"Mister Gottsche in?" he inquired of the young man behind the counter.

"Yes, sir, he's in back," came the reply, accompanied by a

disdainful look at the tall, pale man, wearing clothes that looked too big for him. Butch stared back, and something in his face caused the boy to go pale himself and scurry into the back room. Passing his hand over his eyes, Butch sighed. *My face never used to scare kids,* he thought. *I must look like the ex-con I am.*

"Butch! God Almighty, man!" Bill Gottsche bounded into the room, holding out a welcoming hand. "Hell, I thought . . . well, never mind that. Come on back here where we can talk."

Gottsche led him past the curious eyes of the clerk into his office and offered Butch a chair. "I didn't want to say anything in front of the boy out there, but I heard you got sent away for a long spell, son. Was damn' sorry to hear it, too."

Butch nodded, warming to the first friendly contact he had had with anyone in so long. "You heard right, Bill. Got sentenced to two years, but somebody finally wised up to the fact I got framed, and the governor pardoned me, so I'm out six months early." He saw no reason to tell his former employer that the true reason for his pardon was his promise to leave the state and never come back.

"Ain't surprised at all!" the butcher exclaimed, slapping his knee. "I figgered there had to be something slippery about that deal. Why, I ain't never met a man more honest than you, Butch. Yes, sir, the minute I heard you was in trouble with the law, I said no, uh-uh, not the Butch Cassidy I know, not the man who worked for me and never took a penny out of the till!"

"Thanks, Bill. I appreciate it. I ain't gotten a hell of a lot of praise lately, and it does a man good." Butch smiled and scratched at his prickly chin.

"You look in need of a place to clean up and rest for a

while," said Gottsche, taking in his friend's worn, dirty clothes and wan complexion.

"You read my mind," said Butch. "If it ain't too much trouble, I could use a place to stay for a few days, just until I get an outfit of sorts together. And maybe the loan of some cash . . . I'd pay it right back, soon as I'm able."

" 'Course, you would. Run on upstairs. My new clerk lives there now, but he won't mind sharing. Stay as long as you like, and, listen, me and the missus will be mighty put out if you don't take your meals with us. Looks like you need to put some meat back on those bones!"

"You're too good to me, Bill," said Butch with a tired smile.

"Naw, I ain't," the butcher said, suddenly serious. "I know a good man when I see one, just like some men can judge prime horseflesh. When you walked in my shop and asked for a job, I said to myself this fella's first rate, and I ain't had no cause to change my mind about that. Now, go along, get out of those filthy duds, and I'll send them home for Frieda to launder."

Staked by the loan from Bill Gottsche, Butch bought winter clothes, a horse and tack, a Winchester and supplies to last until he got to Lander where he could pick up his meager belongings from Douglas Preston. Two weeks after arriving in Rock Springs, he rode out, looking considerably healthier after having dined on Mrs. Gottsche's generous portions of sauerbraten and potatoes. In fact, he appeared much the same as he had before entering prison, with the exception of a few scars—legacies from the prison guards— and a distant, wary look that was a new constant in his icy blue eyes.

On his way north he stopped by several outfits where he had friends or where he had hired out during his previous wanderings. All of his old acquaintances greeted him warmly and were happy to feed and house him overnight, but none offered him a job. Although it was the middle of winter and not a prime time for hiring a cowpuncher, Butch thought it strange that none of these Wyoming ranchers wanted him on their payroll. Used to be they'd be tickled pink to have such a crack hand working for them.

Finally he reached the banks of the Popo Agie. Lander lay just ahead. He reined up and swung one leg over the saddle horn, resting it sideways on the cheap saddle he had purchased in Rock Springs. Staring straight ahead, toward the little town that lay just over the next rise, he realized the time had come to decide what to do about Mary Boyd. He had avoided thinking of her, to the extent he was able, but he could no longer put it off. He pulled tobacco and paper from his pocket and rolled a cigarette, more because he thought better when his hands were busy than because he needed a smoke.

She had not written to him in prison as she had promised. At first, when he did not hear from her, he worried that something might have happened to her—that she had fallen ill or met with some accident. But he knew that was unlikely, and anyway, if either of those things had occurred, surely Douglas Preston would have mentioned it in one of his occasional letters to Butch. No, odds were she had not written him because she wanted him out of her life, and who could blame her?

He tossed the half smoked cigarette into the swirling river waters and hunched his shoulders against the cold February wind. *Ride on, cowboy,* he counseled himself. *There ain't nothing for you here. How many times does the woman have to tell you to leave before you get the point?* But still, she had come to him that day in jail, just before he was shipped off to Laramie. She came and cried and held his hands through the bars of his cell. Would a woman with no love in her heart do those things?

Uttering a soft curse, he urged his horse into the frigid water and up the bank on the other side. He would find her, would give them one last chance to be together, but he would not go to her as he was now—broke, without a job, with no prospects. Somehow, he would get back on his feet, and then he would see what Mary Boyd had to say about things. Precisely what *things* he wanted to say to her he deliberately skirted in his mind. An offer of marriage was out of the question—he was not the marrying kind. But would she be willing to live like they had before—on the move and with him gone a large part of the time? A cold finger of doubt shuddered down his spine.

He stopped in Lander only long enough to retrieve his gear. From there he continued north and east, asking at all the larger operations if they needed an experienced ranch hand. The answer was always no.

For the hell of it, he headed up the Powder River to Hole-in-the-Wall, that hidden paradise he had enjoyed so long ago. Of course, his old friend, Nate Champion, was no longer riding the valley, stirring up trouble for the big outfits, but some of the other boys were still hanging around and a new man, named Harvey Logan, had drifted in and become part of the gang. Logan was a true hardcase, on the run for having murdered a man in Montana two years before. His brusque manner and quick temper hid a soul crying out for kindness and acceptance, and he quickly fell under the charms of the jovial, good-natured Cassidy.

One evening, Butch and Logan, Flat-Nose George Currie, and Ben Kilpatrick sat around a table, playing a relaxed hand of gin rummy. Flat-Nose took a swig of whiskey and wiped his mouth with the back of his hand. "Too bad old Nate ain't here to jaw at us . . . he always said how gin rummy was a game for Nellies."

"Hell, what did Nate know about it?" said Kilpatrick with a crooked smile. "He was too damn' serious to ever play cards."

The men, all except Logan, laughed softly, remembering their friend and former leader. Butch gathered up the cards and shuffled. "I heard some of the story," he said, "about how the ranchers around here hired gunslingers to ambush him and then burned him out. I'd bet you a twenty-dollar gold piece he died brave."

Flat-Nose nodded solemnly. "He weren't alone, you know. There was four of them all together. The first two got captured right away, but Nate and Nick Ray . . . you remember him, he homesteaded up near Pine Ridge . . . stayed holed up for a day. Then when Nick thought the coast was clear, he snuck out and got shot. Well, Nate, he dragged Nick back in the cabin and tried to doctor him, but it weren't no good . . . Nick died. Then they burned Nate out and killed him. But the funny thing was, all that time he was holed up he wrote a kind of diary of what was happening. Last thing he wrote was . . . 'The house is all fired. Good bye boys, if I never see you again.' "

The men fell silent, contemplating the last few hours of their brave friend's life. They were the boys he had thought of in his final moments on earth.

"It ain't right," said Butch. "Not just what happened to Nate, but everything that's going on around here. The little guy ain't got a chance against the big outfits. Hell, even a small-time cowpuncher like me can't get a job no more . . . the fucking Stockman's Association done blacklisted me. Even my friends are too scared to hire me!"

288

"It ain't getting any better, either," Kilpatrick chimed in. "Just last August, Jim Baldwin from Fremont County led a raid up here. We fought them off good . . . they went scrambling with their tails between their legs . . . but they'll be back soon as the weather turns warmer."

"So what are you yellow bastards going to do about it?" They all turned to stare at Harvey Logan who had issued the challenge. He stared back, his black eyes cold and dangerous-looking.

"Not much to do, but fight back whenever they come a-callin'," said Flat-Nose.

"You sure about that? I don't wait to get snakebit before I go hunting rattlers." Logan laid his cards on the table. "Gin," he announced in a lethal-sounding voice.

With narrowed eyes, Butch studied the darkly fierce man beside him. "I think you got something there, Harvey." Smiling, he gathered the other men in with his gaze and then dealt a new hand.

Butch lingered at Hole-in-the-Wall for a month or so, but as the snow melted and the creeks and rivers filled with spring run-off, he realized he had accomplished nothing since his release from prison. He was living in limbo, unable to find work in the State of Wyoming, yet unable to leave until he settled things with a certain husky-voiced beauty who invaded his dreams all too often. On a fine, warm day when the breeze was touched by the first ripe smell of summer, he left the valley, nervous and apprehensive, but also full of hope. The sky was clear; the trees were budding; he was a free man; and he was riding to his love. True, he was coming to her as a pauper, as a man with a checkered past, to say the least, but if she truly loved him, what difference did that make?

He supposed he should start looking for her at the cabin

where he had last seen her, the one belonging to the old Indian woman called Gray Hair. But, first, he decided to stop in town to fortify himself with a quick drink and to get the lay of the land. He had a lot of friends in Lander still, and they would be eager to fill him in on the latest news around the region.

Lannigan's Saloon was just as he remembered it—dark and smoky, a few beat-up tables here and there, a long pock-marked bar with a painting of a voluptuous, naked woman hanging behind it. It was packed with its usual clientele: soldiers, townspeople, cowboys, and the occasional Indian, although the bartender refused to sell the last any alcohol. Butch stood at the bar and greeted one friend after the other, most of whom bought him a round to celebrate his release from prison. He was thoroughly enjoying himself, basking in the confraternity of the gin palace, when a tall man with thick features elbowed his way to the bar and exhaled drunkenly in his face. "Welcome back from the jug, Cassidy. Here's hoping you don't stay long."

Butch recognized Deputy Harry Logue, obviously well in his cups. "Thanks for the sentiment, Harry, but, in case you hadn't heard, I'm a free man now. Pardoned by Governor Richards himself. That being the case, reckon I'll stay where I want as long as I want." He spoke with a smile but fixed Logue with a steely blue stare.

"I heard all right. They're letting all kinds of riffraff out these days." Logue signaled the bartender and downed a shot followed by a beer chaser. " 'Course, it's a matter of opinion how long you'll stay a free man," he sneered.

"Meaning . . . ?"

Logue glanced around, then leaned in closer. "I shouldn't be telling you this, but there's a warrant out for your arrest."

Butch's stomach flipped and his throat tightened so he thought he would not be able to breathe. But his face revealed nothing as he calmly ordered Logue another drink and muttered: "You don't say."

Logue downed the drink, then hawked and spat on the sawdust-covered floor. "It's a fact. The same bastard who swore out all those other warrants on you. This time he says you rustled fifty of his own horses."

"Fifty!" It was so preposterous Butch had to laugh. "You're out of your mind, Logue. I ain't been near the Pitchfork, and, even if I had, I wouldn't be stupid enough to rustle one of Franc's horses, much less fifty!"

The deputy shrugged and said nothing. His eyes started to glaze over, and Butch wondered if this whole thing was a story concocted out of a drunken stupor. But he could not afford to assume that. He grabbed Logue by the arm and propelled him to a table in the corner. "Listen, Harry," he said casually, "if there's a warrant out on me, why ain't you locking me up?"

Logue stifled a belch and looked at Butch with woozy eyes. "I ain't actually seen no warrant. I heard Sheriff Stough talking about it, but he ain't told nobody to do nothing yet. My guess is he don't trust Franc no more'n you do . . . that he wants to check out his story 'fore he goes bustin' his ass arresting people. But I'd be careful, I was you. Franc's got a way of gettin' his way, if you know what I mean."

Butch tugged his hat brim low over his eyes and rose to go. "Thanks, Harry. I'll be on the look-out."

He was halfway to the door when Logue called him back, a maudlin look on his fat face. "Say, Butch, I ain't never forgot that pretty little half-breed what came to see you in jail. I figgered at first she was, well, you know, but then I could tell by the way she carried herself she weren't no chippy." He paused and sighed dramatically. Every muscle in Butch's body tensed as he waited for Logue to go on. "Well, anyway, I thought somebody ought to tell you not to go looking for her, if you had a mind to."

A roaring sensation filled Butch's ears. He could barely hear himself ask: "Why not?"

" 'Cause she went and got herself married about a year ago. Hitched up with Ole Rhodes, 'member him? Naw, you probably wouldn't. He's a two-bit cowboy what's drifted around some, but he ain't the type people take much notice of, you know what I mean? Well, anyway, I thought you ought to know . . . you and her seemed pretty sweet on each other . . . ," Logue trailed off.

Everything disappeared, the noise, the smoke, the drunken fool before him, and the next thing he knew he was out on the street, unhitching his horse. He acted automatically, his movements jerky and sudden, so that the animal sensed something awry and shied away. Grabbing the horn, he swung into the saddle and loped out of town, suppressing his urge to race away for fear of calling attention to himself. Even in his misery, his survival skills served him well, telling him how to look and act when all he wanted to do was ride out flat and hard until his mount frothed at the mouth and dropped in its tracks.

He found himself on the banks of Squaw Creek, where he and Dora Lamorreaux had ridden together years ago. He could picture everything about that scene—Dora's pert little face and high-pitched giggle, the white-socked bay she rode, even his own gloved hands lightly holding the reins as they rested on the saddle horn. His gaze dropped to his uncovered hands, scarred and callused from the hard work of cowpunching. Suddenly he could see those hands as they looked touching Mary, brushing her cheek, playing with her hair, caressing her soft skin. He pitched forward over his horse's neck, a soundless cry twisting his mouth, and fell to the ground, panting shallowly. What had she done? My God, what had she done?

Butch laid there for a long time until the sky deepened and the warmth of the day began to seep away. He got to his knees and sat with his hands braced on his thighs, drawing in deep breaths of air. Slowly his head cleared, and he became aware of a new feeling that, if he could have named it, would have been called despair. Even in all of his dark and lonely prison days, he had never felt so completely bereft of hope. Mary had given up on him. She did not love him, maybe never had. Not only had he lost Mary, but his name had become synonymous with outlaw and rustler in this state. No one believed in him any more. With Mary at his side, he would have been willing to try the straight life again, but no more. They wanted an outlaw; they'd get one. And, by God, they'd get a hell of a lot more than they bargained for.

His face set, his eyes hooded, he mounted up and rode south and east. Behind him the sun slowly sank below the purple line of mountains, casting his lengthening shadow before him.

Chapter Twenty

"Elzy! Ho, there, Elzy Lay!"

Grinning ear to ear in anticipation of seeing his friend after seven long years, Butch leaped off his horse and pounded on the door of the small cabin. He heard rustling noises inside, and the door opened, revealing a short, dark-haired woman with wide-set, green eyes and luscious, full lips. She leveled a Colt revolver directly at his heart. Butch backed away, his hands held out from his sides. "Beg pardon, ma'am. I didn't mean to startle you. I was looking for Elzy."

"Who are you?" the woman asked, the gun steady in her hand.

"An old friend of Elzy's . . . name's Butch Cassidy." He gave her a tentative smile. She lowered her weapon, although she did not return his smile or invite him in.

"I've heard of you," she conceded. "Elzy talks about you all the time." Her gaze was diverted over his shoulder, and Butch turned to see Elzy Lay, approaching on a tall chestnut mare.

"Elzy!" he called. "You mind telling your woman I'm a friendly native? She's making me a little nervous, swinging that there Peacemaker."

"George?" Elzy climbed down and started toward Butch, disbelief written all over his handsome face. "I'll be damned! Maude, honey, this is George Cassidy. You remember me telling you about him." Elzy grabbed Butch's hand and shook it heartily.

"He didn't call himself George just now," Maude said, eyeing the newcomer skeptically.

"Well, that's right. I plumb forgot you're going by a new moniker. It's Butch Cassidy now, ain't it?"

"Yup. Reckon I'll stick with this name for a while. I'll allow as how I'm partial to it." Butch crinkled his eyes at Maude, trying to win her over.

"I see you've met my wife. Ain't she a beauty?" Elzy wrapped one long arm around the pretty girl and hugged her to him.

"Your wife! Holy sh . . . , I mean, I didn't know you was married." Butch pushed his hat back on his head and stared at the couple in amazement. Elzy had gone and done the one thing Butch was convinced he himself could never do.

"Damn' right! Couldn't take a chance on this one getting away." The tall cowboy leaned down and planted a kiss on his bride's voluptuous mouth.

"Elzy, for heaven's sake," she protested, but the look she gave him was long and low and full of promise. Butch found himself thinking of Mary, remembering what it felt like to have sweet young lips brushing his own. Now those lips belonged to someone else. He looked at his friend and forced himself to smile.

"Congratulations are in order, I reckon."

Elzy laughed and clapped him on the back. "Maude, honey, whip up something special for supper. We got reason to celebrate tonight! Come on, bud, let's go put up these horses, and you can tell me what brings you back to Brown's Hole."

In the barn, the two men busied themselves unsaddling and combing down their mounts. They talked easily, the years since they last saw each other melting away. "The old place looks good, Elz," said Butch. "You've really fixed her up." Elzy had brought his wife to an abandoned ranch on Diamond Mountain and had set about restoring the place.

"Something about having a woman around makes you want to fix things, I reckon. It ain't like the old days when any old shack would do," Elzy said almost wistfully. "What about you? I thought for sure some gal would've hooked you by now . . . they always was crazy for you."

Butch was silent for a moment, then murmured: "I got sidetracked."

Now it was Elzy's turn to pause. Brushing his chestnut in long, smooth strokes, he thought for a moment, then said quietly: "Me, too. I got in some trouble up near Lander a couple of years ago but managed to stay out of the hoosegow. I hear you wasn't so lucky."

Then Butch told him the whole story—how he had tried to go legitimate with his partner, Al Hainer, but was double-crossed and set up to take the fall. How the big ranchers, and one in particular, Otto Franc, had it in for him so that he was blacklisted in Wyoming. How he had endured prison and had even gotten out with the notion of abandoning the outlaw life, but that his subsequent treatment had convinced him the only path open to him was exacting revenge against the greedy cattle barons. He told his friend everything, save for any mention of Mary Boyd.

"That's why I'm back in Brown's Hole," he finished. "I'm hunting up some of the boys to see if they want to come with me. It's time somebody did something to get back at the god-damned ranchers and the god-damned bankers and railroad owners they're in cahoots with. You're the first one I've asked, Elz. Ain't nobody I'd rather have riding with me. 'Course, things have changed for you now, I guess, being married and all."

Elzy shot him a sharp glance. "I ain't carrying around no

ball and chain. Reckon I'll do what I have to no matter what."

Butch nodded, secretly pleased that Elzy's loyalty to him seemed to outweigh any responsibility he felt toward his new bride. It was troublesome, coming between a man and his wife, but, hell, Elzy had brought it on himself by getting hitched in the first place. And married or not, a man had to attend to business.

That night after supper, Maude left the two men alone with their cigars and whiskey. They sat outside, leaning against the hitching rail, gazing up at a sky full of stars. They shared a companionable silence, and Butch found himself wondering how things might have been different, if the man next to him had agreed to partner with him when they left Brown's Hole seven years ago. If Elzy had gone in with him on his horse ranch, he would never have hooked up with Al Hainer, would never have wound up on Horse Creek, would never have gone to prison, maybe. *Well, hell,* he thought, *better late than never.* Although the partnership he had in mind now was of a different nature entirely.

"You never told me why you left here so sudden before," said Elzy, also in a reflective mood. "It ain't my habit to ask a man his reason for moving on, but I always wondered."

"You probably got a pretty good notion why," smiled Butch.

Elzy smiled back. "Reckon so. That Elizabeth Bassett was one wild and beautiful woman."

"Was? You mean she's lost her looks already? Hell, she can't be that old. Matter of fact, I was thinking of riding over there one of these nights . . . see if I couldn't rekindle the old flame," joked Butch.

Elzy looked down at his boots and sighed deeply. "She's dead, Butch."

The words hit him hard. He drew in a sharp breath of air that seemed full of her rich, earthy aroma. She had been his first real love, and the knowledge that she was gone left a void in his heart. No matter that he had not seen her in seven years or that he might never have seen her again. She was still a part of him, as was his one true love, and their absence from his life hurt more than he cared to admit. "What happened?" he asked, taking a slug of whiskey.

"The family says it was appendicitis, but rumor has it she had a bad miscarriage."

"How long ago?"

"Four years now. I guess things ain't going too good at the Bassett place these days. She kind of ran the show, you know."

"Josie's got a lot of spunk. Maybe she'll take up the slack." Butch removed his hat and creased its edge, remembering how the petite, red-headed girl had blushed so prettily when he asked her to dance.

"Well, Josie's another story," Elzy went on. "She married Jim McKnight just a few months after Elizabeth died."

"Go on," Butch scoffed. "How did McKnight manage that?"

"The oldest trick in the book, if you get my meaning. I hear tell the bride looked a little thick around the middle on her wedding day." Elzy gave him a wink, and suddenly Butch had to laugh.

"Those Bassett women are sure as hell hot-blooded little fillies, ain't they?"

"Poor old Herb. How he ever married one and sired another is a puzzle sure enough." Elzy and Butch shared a good chuckle, and then Butch headed to the barn to bed down. As he tucked the saddle blanket under his head and tried to find a comfortable position on the scratchy, straw-covered floor, he thought of Elzy, lying in a soft bed in the arms of his sweetheart. Envy momentarily overtook him. Maybe Elzy had it right—find a pretty young girl and settle down and stay out of trouble. But he had ruined his one chance at that kind of happiness, or, rather, Otto Franc and his cohorts had ruined it for him. For after much soul-searching, he had concluded he could not blame Mary for abandoning him—no woman in her right mind would wait around for an ex-convict destined to live life on the run. But he could blame Franc and all the rest of the ranchers, bankers, lawmen, and tycoons who had conspired against him, and, by God, he would make them pay.

Once again, Butch's thoughts turned to Elzy. Perhaps it was not fair to ask his friend, newly married and with no significant criminal record of his own, to join him in his escapades. But Elzy seemed game, and Butch got downright excited thinking about the great team they would make. Together, they would lead the toughest, smartest, most feared gang in the West, and the best part was that it would be so much damn' fun!

He rolled over and closed his eyes, but sleep eluded him as his mind raced, posing questions and considering options. Who besides Elzy would he recruit?—where would they strike first?—how would he train his gang?—where would they hide out after the job was done? Success, he knew, lay in attention to details. As dawn broke, he rose refreshed and energized even after his sleepless night. Eager to share his plans with Elzy, he strolled toward the cabin for breakfast, thinking that maybe, just maybe, there was no one better suited to the risky profession of outlaw than Robert Leroy Parker, alias Butch Cassidy.

Two days later, Butch was out in the yard, cleaning his gear in preparation for a trip to Hole-in-the-Wall. He and

Elzy had discussed who they wanted to join their gang and had agreed on Butch's old buddies Flat-Nose George Currie, Harvey Logan, and Ben Kilpatrick. Butch planned to head north in the next day or so to recruit them. At the sound of trotting hoofs, he looked up and saw a lone horseman slowly approaching. The man's face was mostly hidden by a black hat pulled low over his eyes, but Butch could make out a thick, brown mustache, neatly trimmed. The rest of the stranger's appearance matched his tonsorial elegance. Although his clothes were covered with road dust, they were obviously new and of the highest quality. Butch noted the ivory-handled Smith and Wesson stuck in the waistband of the man's striped trousers and quickly took stock of the location of his own weapon—it lay holstered in the gun belt at his feet.

"Howdy," said Butch, squinting into the sun.

The man regarded him silently, his eyes still hidden. He did not have a particularly imposing physique, but something about the cool way he sat his horse convinced Butch he would be quite capable in the event of trouble. Finally the man spoke. "Looking for Elzy Lay."

"You a friend of his?" asked Butch casually.

"Maybe. Depends on if you is." The stranger leaned over and spat in the dust.

Butch wiped the sweat from his face with his sleeve and chuckled. "Appears you and me is circling each other for no good reason. I'm Butch Cassidy and, yeah, Elzy's a friend. Believe he's down to the barn, if you want to see him."

The stranger tipped his hat up, and Butch got his first look at the man's eyes. They were small and a bit narrow-set and right now were gazing at him with great interest. "You're Cassidy, eh? You and me know some people in common."

"Yeah? Who?"

"Bill Madden and Bert Charter, for starters." For the first time, the man smiled, a small turning up of the mouth that was barely visible beneath the heavy mustache.

"You don't say! Good men, those two." Charter and Madden, of course, had held the relay horses for the Telluride robbery. "Introduce yourself, friend."

"Harry Longabaugh's the name. Don't imagine you've heard of me."

"Longabaugh," Butch mused. "Sounds familiar."

Just then Elzy strode up from the barn. "Sundance!" he shouted. "Good to see you, man!"

It all fell into place for Butch now. The newcomer was none other than the Sundance Kid, so named because he had once been jailed in Sundance, Wyoming. As Butch recalled, the charge had been horse theft, although the Kid was rumored to have committed many more serious crimes, train robbery among them.

"Say, Harry," Elzy went on enthusiastically. "Lucky thing your riding in today. Butch and me got big plans, and you're just the man to join us. If I know you, you'd be more than happy to screw the big boys to the wall."

Sundance alighted from his horse in one fluid, graceful motion. "How you going to do that?" he asked, his tone indicating he could care less.

"Well, we're going to pick a few banks, maybe a train carrying a payroll or two, and we're going to redistribute the wealth a mite. Butch here, he's got it all figgered. What do you say?" Elzy smiled broadly, and Butch, although he would have liked to have time to consider the offer, seconded the invitation. After all, he trusted Elzy's judgment, and the Kid was reputed to be a cool-headed customer.

Sundance looked from one to the other with calculating eyes. "I'm in," he said.

Butch laughed and held out his hand. "Welcome to the Wild Bunch."

"The Wild Bunch?"

"We was going to call it the Train Robbers Syndicate, but we didn't want to limit ourselves to just robbing trains." Butch winked conspiratorially, and Sundance actually laughed, an unusual phenomenon for him.

"It ain't got the same ring to it as the Wild Bunch, that's for damn' sure," he said.

As the three men headed to the barn, Sundance filled them in on news from outside the Hole. "Did you hear what happened to Matt Warner?" he inquired.

Butch's eyes narrowed. Was he about to find out another old friend had passed away or was in trouble?

"We ain't heard nothing. We've kind of been sticking to ourselves out here," Elzy said.

"Well, Matt's got himself in a real jam. He's in jail over in Vernal accused of killing two men and crippling a third. Unfortunately for him, they wasn't just a bunch of no-good drifters but fine, upstanding citizens, or so the story goes, and now the whole town's in an uproar. I hear tell the sheriff's had to post armed guards to keep the lynch mob away." The outlaw shook his head, more in bewilderment at Matt's stupidity in getting into such a fix than in sympathy.

"Christ, Matt always did shoot first and ask questions later," Butch said in disgust. Thinking back to the story Matt had told him about shooting the federal officers, he had no doubt Matt was guilty of this latest crime. Nevertheless, he owed the man a debt and maybe the time had come to repay it. "Do you know if he's got a lawyer?" he asked.

"Nope." Evidently Sundance had exhausted his ability to make conversation.

"Well, shit, this throws a kink in the works." Butch grimaced and looked off to the west at the Uinta Mountains, glimmering in the distance. Vernal was an easy ride from here—less than a day, if he pushed it. He hated to disrupt his well-considered plans, but he was nothing if not loyal to old friends. If there was anything he could do to help his former partner, he needed to find that out. "I'm going to go see him," he announced.

"You sure it's safe, Butch?" Elzy said.

"Hell, yes. I ain't wanted for anything in Utah." He paused and then smiled mischievously. "Yet."

Butch Cassidy loped into Vernal, Utah late afternoon the following day. Located in the lush Green River Valley, the town was a bustling, prosperous community, nothing like the sorry little Mormon villages of his youth. Why, there was even a saloon here which Butch was sorely tempted to visit after his long, dusty ride. But it was getting on in the day, and he was eager to see Matt.

The jail was easy to find; as Sundance had warned, an armed deputy was posted at the door. The guard pulled back on the hammer of his Winchester and blocked Butch's path. "What's your business?" he demanded.

"Here to see Sheriff Pope," replied Butch, unbuckling his gun belt and hanging it over his saddle. The deputy relaxed and stepped aside to let him enter. The jail was like every other jail Butch had ever been in—small, dark, and full of the smell of unwashed bodies and moldy food. He automatically cased the joint, noting the location of doors and windows and the sheriff's gun rack, although he was not really considering staging a breakout.

" 'Afternoon, Sheriff," he greeted the only occupant of the room. "My name's Butch Cassidy. I'm here to see your prisoner."

The sheriff's expression did not change; apparently the name Butch Cassidy meant nothing to him. *That's about to change,* thought the incipient outlaw wryly. *One day this old coot will be telling his grandchildren how he had Butch Cassidy, the leader of the Wild Bunch, in his jail and didn't even know it.*

"Which one?" the sheriff asked in a bored tone.

"Warner."

At that, the sheriff perked up. Matt Warner was his star inmate at the moment and any of his visitors warranted a closer look.

"I'll have to frisk you," he said, coming around his desk. Butch complied, spreading his arms and legs. "Why do you want to see him?" the lawman asked when he was done patting him down.

"We was friends from 'way back . . . grew up together in Levan. I told his family I'd check up on him," Butch lied cheerfully.

The sheriff rubbed his chin, considering this co-operative, open-faced stranger. He seemed harmless enough. "OK, but only for a few minutes and not alone. I'll be listening to every word you say."

Butch shrugged as if to say: "Fine with me." The sheriff fished keys out of his desk drawer, unlocked the door to the cell block, and led the visitor to the last cubicle in the row. Matt sat slumped on his bunk, idly picking at the frayed cuff of his shirt. At the sound of activity, he looked up. A wide smile broke over his round face. "Cassidy! You wily bastard, I should've known you'd show up!"

Butch was surprised to hear Matt call him by his adopted name, but he supposed the outlaw network had kept Matt informed of his old partner's twists and turns in the last few years.

"Howdy, Matt. It's been a while. I'd ask how you're

doing, but from the looks of it things could be better." Butch was saddened by Matt's appearance. Although the man was only thirty-two years old, his belly looked soft and ample, and the whites of his eyes were closer to the color of parchment, the result of too many years of hard drinking.

"I'm in a hell of a fix, pardner, I can't deny it. Funny thing is, this time I don't even deserve to be."

"Maybe you ought to tell me about it some other time," Butch said, nodding his head in the direction of the listening sheriff.

"It don't matter. I've already told him and everyone else my side of the story. But ain't no one buying it. They done charged me with murder!" Matt sounded so shocked Butch was almost tempted to believe his claim of innocence until he remembered what a ruthless killer Matt could be. "There I was," Matt went on, "just sitting at the bar, when this fella I'd never seen before, Coleman was his name, comes up and says he's got a proposition for me. Tells me he's found this copper deposit worth a lot of money, but he's being shadowed by three guys trying to horn in on his claim. He swears he can't shake these guys, so he offers me five hundred dollars to ride back up to Dry Fork with him and scare them off. Well, hell, sounded like an easy piece of work for that kind of money, so I go with him. We get to their camp right around dawn, and before I can say horseshit, my horse gets shot out from under me. Well, naturally I grab my rifle and give them everything I got. Meanwhile, Coleman's high-tailed it, the lily-livered coward. Anyway, when the shooting stops, turns out the men following Coleman was Dick and Ike Staunton and David Milton. Jesus Christ, if I'd've known that's who they was, I never woulda gone up there. But it's too late now. I sent for a wagon and got all three of them into town to see a doctor, but Dick and

Milton died, and I hear Ike ain't never going to walk again."
Matt dropped his head to his chest.

Good show, thought Butch, certain that Matt's real regret
was his own precarious situation, not the death of two men
and the crippling of another, although it was to his credit
that he had not left them to die in the wilderness. Aloud, he
said: "Have you got a lawyer?"

"Shit, no. Can't afford one."

"You're going to need a good one. I'll see what I can do."

With that, Butch headed back to Brown's Hole. Drawing
Elzy and Sundance away from Maude's curious and increasingly hostile stare, he described his visit with Warner. "He's
in a bad way, boys. Charged with murder in a town that'd
just as soon hang him as try him and too broke to hire a
lawyer. We got to do something."

"Let's bust him out of there," Sundance suggested
coolly.

"Don't think it's possible," said Butch. "The sheriff's got
him too closely guarded, and that jail looked pretty damn'
tight. Not that I wouldn't fancy giving it a try, but we'd be
writing our death sentences. I think our best bet's getting
him a lawyer, the best damn' one money can buy."

"Only problem with that is we ain't got no money," Elzy
said. "Reckon we're going to have to hurry up our plans a
mite."

"You're reading my mind, pardner. Here's what I'm
thinking. We got to have at least three men to pull a job . . .
two inside the bank and one to hold the horses. Thing is, I
don't think the three of us ought to work together, at least
not this first time. Right now, we're all there is to this gang,
and, if something goes wrong, there ought to be one of us
free to round up the rest of the fellas to help out." Elzy and
Sundance seemed to agree with this reasoning. "Sundance,

you know all the boys up in Hole-in-the-Wall. Why don't you go on up there, get them on board, and stand by in case Elzy and I get in trouble. Meantime, the two of us," he nodded to Elzy, "will scout out banks and look for a third man. I got a notion there's some boys out there who might be looking for some excitement."

The plan met with approval, and the next day they rode out, Sundance heading northeast to Hole-in-the-Wall, Elzy and Butch heading northwest to Idaho. For on the ride back from Vernal, Butch had decided through a process of elimination that his gang's first strike should be in that rugged state. He intended, for now, to keep his promise not to cause more mischief in Wyoming, and, besides, his name and face were well-known to every lawman west of Cheyenne. Using the same reasoning, he thought it wise to steer clear of Colorado where some enterprising sleuth might still connect him to the Telluride robbery. Utah was crossed off the list because it was his native state and people there might recognize him. Montana was wide open territory but too far away—this job had to be done quickly. That left Idaho, and it did not take long for the two bandits to identify their target—the bank in Montpelier, a small town in the far southeastern corner of the state just over the border from Wyoming.

For cover, they hired on at a ranch near Cokeville, Wyoming, also just over the state line. This turned out to be the perfect place to hone their plan, for it was run by an unsuspecting woman whose curiosity was never aroused by the mysterious activities of her newest gun-toting employees.

Furthermore, it was in Cokeville one day that they ran into Bub Meeks, Butch's old neighbor on Horse Creek, who had since fallen on hard times. He enthusiastically signed on to be their third man. Their team complete, they spent considerable time in preparation—casing the bank, scouting their getaway trail, choosing relay points.

Finally, they were ready. On August 13, 1896, only eight months after Butch Cassidy had walked out of prison, he stepped into the Montpelier bank and back into the outlaw life. It went down just as planned, smoother than the Telluride job, for Elzy Lay, who held the bank employees at bay, was not about to lose his temper and beat some poor teller senseless. Butch grabbed as much money as he could carry, and, within ten minutes, they were out of the bank and racing down the street on the horses Bub held for them. They rode east and were soon across the state line and mounted on fresh relay horses. No one followed them that they could tell, but they knew that sooner or later a posse would be on their trail.

Traveling only at night, hiding out and sleeping during the day, they soon made it to the Wind River Mountains, a part of the country Butch knew like the back of his hand. There, they split up, agreeing to meet back at Brown's Hole when it was safe. Before leaving, they counted their loot and discovered they had $6,165.00 in greenbacks and $1,000.00 in gold and silver. No one wanted to take the bag of coins—it was too heavy to carry and too difficult to conceal on one's person—so Butch decided to bury it. Someone could always come back for it.

"Are you nuts, Cassidy?" protested Meeks, pointing at the tall mountains and rugged landscape. "There's a million places in these mountains that look just like this spot. Nobody will ever find that loot again."

"I will," Butch said. He drew his revolver and with the butt started digging a hole at the base of a lightning-scarred stump. Meeks grew tight-lipped but said no more.

They decided that $3,000.00 ought to be enough to hire Douglas Preston for Matt Warner's defense, and Elzy agreed to approach the lawyer in Lander. Butch was too well-known in that town to risk showing his face. That left precious little to split between the three of them, but the job had not been undertaken with the idea that anyone would personally profit, at least not by much. Butch figured he had just enough to live on until the next heist, but for now he needed to disappear.

Continuing east, he hid out on ranches belonging to old friends, all of whom welcomed him and gave him news about the various posses that were looking for him. And looking they were, in all directions. Apparently, it was no secret who had pulled the Montpelier robbery. Wyoming had become too dangerous, that was clear, but where to go? They would expect him to flee to Brown's Hole, or even that desolate part of Utah, known as Robbers' Roost, that Butch had crossed so many years before when he had been on the lam the very first time. With that in mind, he hatched what he was sure would be a foolproof escape plan.

From his friend Frank Burns, he borrowed a fancy suit of clothes, a bowler hat, and dress boots. All done up, he was a dead ringer for one of the bankers or businessmen he so despised. In the town of Hanna, on the Union Pacific line, he boarded a train and bought a ticket all the way to Chicago. As he headed east, over rolling prairies and verdant farmland, his blood surged in rhythm with the pulsing wheels of the train. He had always wanted to travel, to see more of the country and the world, for that matter. Now it seemed that instead of fleeing his past, he was seeking his future, pacing some marvelous adventure that was sure to be waiting for him at the end of the line. He pressed his face to the window and watched the world rush by, every turn of the wheel taking him farther away from what was familiar, yet dangerous, and closer to the safety of the unknown.

Chapter Twenty-One

The first thing he noticed when he stepped out onto the street from Chicago's cavernous Union Dépôt was the smell. From the nearby river came an incredible stench of human waste and garbage. A quick look confirmed that this unfortunate tributary was more dumping ground than river. Eclipsing even this odor, however, was a smell he recognized right away—the stockyards. Although used to the odor on a working ranch, he had never encountered anything like this. Manure, blood, and decaying flesh all mixed together in an indescribable stew that took his breath away.

The second thing he noticed was the dense fog of coal smoke that hung over the city, filling his lungs with its noxious fumes. Finally, wrinkling his nose and half tempted to pull out his bandanna to shield his face from the smoke, he noticed the people, hundreds of them on this one street alone, some rushing away purposefully, some malingering, some plying a trade of one sort or another, but all apparently oblivious to the stench and heat and noise of their surroundings.

He picked a direction and started walking, trying not to look like a rube fresh off the farm. He had, after all, seen pictures of big cities in magazines and knew that such things as ten-story buildings existed. But up until now, the largest city he had ever been in was Denver, a veritable cowtown compared to the Windy City. Yes, Denver had paved streets and its share of wealthy magnates, but one was just as likely to see a cowboy in chaps and six-shooter sauntering down the street as a banker or shop owner. Here, a cowboy would most likely attract stares from pasty-faced men wearing side-whiskers and tight pants.

In what he thought was a neat trick, if a bit foolhardy, he asked a ruddy-faced policeman for the name of a clean, inexpensive hotel, and he was directed to Clark Street. To get there, he rode a strange, elevated trolley car pulled by a little steam locomotive that gave him a birds-eye view of the city's teeming streets but left him sweat-soaked and even a bit nauseous from the constant starts and stops.

After he found a room and cleaned up from his long trip, he was back on the streets, eager to discover the pleasures that this big, dirty, noisy metropolis must certainly offer. The hotel clerk told him many of the saloons offered free lunch counters and suggested he would find quite a selection from which to choose on State Street. Indeed, that venerable avenue sported more beer gardens, gambling joints, flop houses, wine rooms, and theaters than it was humanly possible to sample in one month, let alone one afternoon. Nevertheless, he made a valiant effort, consuming more of the food than the booze so as to keep his wits sharp and his wallet full.

He struck up several conversations with the local patrons, although he had some difficulty understanding people at first. Many of the men were immigrants, and what little English they spoke was delivered with a heavy accent that suggested German or Slavic heritage. Even the home-grown Midwesterners required his close attention for they talked too quickly, dropping the ends of their phrases and pronouncing their vowels in a strange, flat tone. He tried to disguise his own lilting Western twang but knew that it was impossible to do so completely.

It was getting late in the evening and Butch was on his

fourth or fifth saloon when two dandies, Irv and Joe as they called themselves, became quite friendly with him, asking him his business here—visiting relatives, he told them—and enthusiastically describing the many and varied charms their city had to offer a man looking for entertainment. Butch laughed and joked with them, but he had seen his share of grifters and confidence men, and he could tell they were trying to work some kind of scam on him. When they invited him to accompany them to a different bar, he decided to act dumb and play along—it might be fun to see how they planned to roll him.

Sure enough, the route to the second bar took them into a dark alley. Butch walked between the pair, affecting a shuffling gait and a bleary look although his senses were perfectly clear. Halfway through the alley, at its darkest point, Irv stopped and put his hands on his hips in disgust.

"Wait a minute," he barked. "This ain't the way to the Continental. You turned down the wrong alley."

"No I didn't," said Joe. "This is a short cut, you idiot. We've taken it a dozen times. You're just too pie-eyed to remember."

"Who are you calling an idiot?" Irv poked his partner in the chest.

"You, you bohunk piece of shit. Now keep your stinking hands off me." Joe turned his back and started walking. Irv grabbed his arm and swung him around.

"Why don't you make me, asshole?"

Joe, the bigger of the two, uttered a low growl and pushed Irv up against the soot-covered wall. Butch stood aside, a half smile on his face, watching the drama unfold. Glancing over at their intended mark, Joe picked up his partner by the lapels and threw him to the ground. Butch propped one foot against the wall, hands in his pockets, the picture of relaxation and repose.

"Help me, man!" cried Irv, prone on the filthy bricks of the alley. "He's going to wallop me for sure!"

Butch shrugged and grinned. "This quarrel looks to be between the two of you. Reckon I'll sit it out." By now, he knew their game. They had hoped he would step in to break up their fight, leaving himself open to attack. While he was busy rescuing Irv, Joe would mug him from behind. But they had misread their man.

Irv raised himself on his elbow, and for a moment both of the would-be thugs appeared completely perplexed. Then anger settled over Joe's face, and he charged like a bull, his large, flat head lowered. In a split second Butch had his revolver out from where it had been hidden in his waistband. He brought the barrel down hard against Joe's temple, sending him sprawling senseless to thc ground. Irv stared at him, open-mouthed. Smiling, Butch pointed the muzzle of the gun. "So long, Irv," he said. The unfortunate man yelped and scrambled to his feet, then took off running down the alley. Laughing, Butch returned the gun to its hiding place. These greenhorn shysters had not seemed to know one end of a gun from the other. Why, he could have rolled them if he'd had a mind to.

With the toe of his boot, he nudged at the prostrate Joe, then bent over and felt for a pulse. Satisfied that there was nothing seriously wrong with his foiled attacker, he strolled away, back to the bright lights of State Street.

A sign advertising **Free Show—Dancing Girls** caught his eye. He started to pass it by but paused. The idea of returning to his stifling room with its one tiny window stained black from soot and trying to sleep on hot, sweaty sheets was unappealing, to say the least. For one second, a feeling of total displacement gripped him. What was he doing here in the midst of a steaming, noisy mass of humanity, when he should be sleeping under the stars on a cool, crisp, silent Wyoming mountainside? Someone jostled his arm, breaking his reverie.

He stepped through the theater's swinging doors and immediately realized there was plenty more entertainment here than just dancing girls. The first floor was given over to slot machines, roulette wheels, and craps tables. Fingering the rapidly diminishing wad of money in his pocket, he bypassed these, climbing the wide, red-carpeted stairs to the second floor where the stage show was just getting started. Leaning against a column, he watched for a while, enjoying the lively show and the pretty girls with their brightly colored petticoats, fishnet stockings, and high-button boots. Little did he know that several of the dancers noticed him as well—a well-dressed man with crinkling blue eyes and sandy blond hair that fell in a cowlick over his forehead. When the show was over, the girls circulated through the audience, collecting tips and taking drink orders. More than one was disappointed to find that the handsome gentleman with the fetching smile was no longer there.

Butch had already ascended to the third floor where he found a long, mahogany bar and more gambling tables, these seating games of poker and faro. He watched the faro table for a while but declined to join it when a seat opened up. One more beer and call it a night, he decided. The bartender had just set the bottle in front of him when a young girl, not more than seventeen he guessed from the fresh, unused looks of her, planted herself beside him and smiled nervously.

"Hey, mister, looking for some fun?" she asked, vainly trying to make her little girl voice sound bold and alluring.

Restraining a laugh, he gave her a once-over. She was a

pretty little thing, with big round green eyes and an up-turned nose that sported a smattering of freckles that peeked out from under layers of powder. Her light brown hair fell in ringlets over creamy white shoulders, so thin the bones stuck out. The low-cut dress she wore revealed a figure still maturing, and Butch imagined she had a hard time attracting men who preferred the buxom type.

His silent perusal made her uncomfortable. She shifted on her feet, dropping her eyes and blushing. Butch suddenly felt very protective of this veritable child who looked as if she should be reciting her lessons in grammar school, instead of hustling grown men in a bar.

"Just what do you think you're doing here, sweetheart?" he asked gently, propping one elbow on the bar.

She gave him a frightened look. "I . . . what do you mean?"

"I mean you don't look like you belong here." His smile was kind and reached all the way to his eyes.

Her blush deepening, she tossed her head in attempted bravado. "If you aren't interested, just say so."

"Oh, I'm interested all right. I ain't sure in what, though." He continued to look at her, and this time she stared back in puzzlement. Finally he asked if she wanted something to drink. She gave a slight nod, and he ordered her a sarsaparilla. She took it, wondering if she should feel insulted.

"What's your name, sweetheart?" he asked.

"Candy," she replied, a bit defensively. "What's yours?"

"George." Upon arrival in Chicago, he had reverted to his previous alias.

More comfortable now that the conversation was back in familiar territory, Candy sidled closer and made big eyes at him. "Why, George is one of my very favorite names. I bet you and me could have a good time together, George."

"We might at that. What do you like to do for a good time?" There was no suggestiveness in his voice, and he continued to look at her with clear, kind eyes. She hesitated, not certain how to answer his question. Was it meant innocently, or was he speaking as a potential customer, as a john would to a whore? She almost shuddered as those words passed through her mind; six months ago she would barely have known their meaning and would have died rather than speak them out loud.

Butch saw the pain and uncertainty flash over her face and took pity on her. "Listen, sweetheart, it appears to me this ain't the right line of work for you. If you don't mind my asking, how did you come to be here?"

Candy stared at him for a long second. Lily Ann, the woman in charge of the girls here at the Ontario, had warned her about men who wanted to know her life story. Don't talk about yourself, Lily Ann said. Keep the conversation light and to a bare minimum. Talk ain't cheap. But this man was different. There seemed to be no artifice to him. Lord knows she was not the best judge of men, but something about this one rang true.

"Mister, I don't know who you are, but you seem to be a real straight-shooter, so, if you really want to know about me, I'll tell you."

Without a word, he took her arm and smoothly steered her to a corner table. "Go ahead, Candy," he urged when they were seated.

"First of all, it isn't Candy. It's Candace. Nobody ever called me Candy until . . . well, until lately. And I'm not from Chicago. I'm from Quincy, a little town downstate," she explained when he did not register recognition of the name. "My father owns a shop there. We never had much money, but it wasn't so bad, except my pa, he's kind of strict and he never, well, you know, let me go out with boys or anything. Anyway, one night I met a man at a dance, a fine-looking man like you, George." She blushed again, and Butch smiled back. "He was older than me by quite a bit, but I didn't care. He was just so handsome and jolly and carefree and he treated me like a queen, like no one ever had before. He wasn't from Quincy . . . he said he was a salesman just in town for the season. I know it was wrong to keep seeing him since he wasn't going to be sticking around, but I couldn't help myself. I fell in love with him, or thought I did."

Butch knew where this story was going. It was the classic case of the traveling salesman and the wronged woman. But now that she had started telling it, he would let her finish. To her, the tale was unique.

" 'Course, I couldn't tell my family, and we had to sneak around to be together, but finally we decided to get married, and I told my father everything." Her face became grim, remembering the ugly scene. "He wouldn't hear of it, he said, wouldn't have his daughter running off with some no-good drummer twice her age. He hit me, even. Lord, he'd never done that before. So I ran away and married the man, and he brought me here." She looked up in embarrassment, wanting now just to get through the next part. "You can probably figure out the rest. He couldn't get any work, so I started working in a shop, but then he told me I could make better money working here. I thought he meant as a maid or something, but he didn't mean that. He wanted me to be one of the girls who work on a percentage. Well, I wouldn't do it at first, told him I'd leave him before I'd do that, but he made me," her voice faltered. "He beat me pretty bad and told me if I tried to run, he'd find me and do it again." She took a deep breath before going on. "So I did it. I started . . . well, you know. And then one morning I came home, and he was gone. Cleared out without leaving me a dime. But he did leave a note that said we weren't ever legally married, so I had no claim on him and shouldn't bother looking for him. As though I'd ever want to see him again, the lying. . . ." Candace was still too much of a lady to say what she was thinking. Her story finished, she looked across the table timidly. Was Lily Ann right about not sharing her personal life with strangers in a bar? Would this strong yet seemingly gentle man laugh at her, or scorn her, or try to take advantage of her as others had?

Butch leaned back in his chair and crossed his long, elegantly attired legs. He didn't know how much of Candace's story to believe. It had the ring of truth, and the girl seemed to have a good heart, but, if she really hated working on a percentage, as she put it, why didn't she quit and find other work or go back home? Butch firmly believed in taking responsibility for one's own life, or so he thought.

"That's a hell of a story, sweetheart," he said sympathetically. "But tell me, now that you're here, it ain't so bad, is it? The money's good, you get three squares a day, the work ain't all that hard. You really want to give it up?"

Candace's eyes flashed, and she pushed back from the table. "I knew I shouldn't have confided in you. You're just like all the rest, rotten and selfish and . . . oh!" Flushed with anger, she rushed by him. He grabbed her hand and pulled her back.

"Hold on now! Calm down, sweetheart. That was just a little test to see if you was sincere about things. I admit it was a mite cold. I apologize. Forgive me?" He looked up at her with those pale blue eyes that seemed warm despite their icy color and she couldn't stay mad.

"I forgive you," she said. "But you shouldn't doubt I mean what I say. I'm trying as hard as I can to get out of here. I've moved in with my cousin so I can save more money, and as soon as I can, I'm leaving, heading West."

"Now you're talking!" he grinned. "I like your gumption, sweetheart!" Suddenly, Butch wanted out of there. He was tired of boozy crowds and smoke-filled rooms. All he wanted to do was escape with this pretty, brave young girl.

"Come with me," he urged. "Let's go find a park bench somewhere and talk."

Her eyes lit up at the idea, but then her face fell. "I can't. I don't get off here until morning."

Butch knit his brows for a moment, hatching a plan. "I got it! I'll leave and then send a message that your cousin has gotten very sick, and you have to go to her right away. They'll let you leave for that, won't they?"

"Maybe. Yes, I guess so." Candace started to get excited. "But you must make the note look real . . . Lily Ann will be sure to read it carefully."

"Trust me, sweetheart. I'm good at this sort of thing." Butch winked, and she laughed gaily.

Half an hour later, she met him at a street corner two blocks away. At the last minute, he almost backed out, afraid once again of getting too close to someone. But then he decided that was silly, he only meant to have a little fun. So he was there, waiting for her underneath a street lamp as she ran up, giggling and a little breathless. They walked and walked, Candace doing most of the talking, although when she discovered he was a Westerner, she pressed him to answer her questions about that part of the country. Finally they wandered into Grant Park and rested against the stone wall that fronted Lake Michigan.

"There ain't no lakes big as this out West," Butch said in

awe. "I used to think Salt Lake was big, but it's nothing but a puddle compared to this."

"The lake is the one thing I like about Chicago," Candace said, resting her palms on the seawall and leaning out over the dark water. "I love looking out into nothingness, into total blackness, except for a ship's flashing lights every now and then. Makes me feel . . . I don't know . . . limitless."

Butch gazed at her thoughtfully. Suddenly it came to him that this girl was a lot like Mary—strong-willed, proud, willing to take life by the hands and live it her way no matter what others said. The unbidden reminder of his lost love pained him. He turned his back to the water and propped himself against the wall, hands thrust deep in his pockets. "Everybody's got limits," he said quietly. "Sometimes you don't find out about them till it's too late."

Candace smiled and placed her delicate hands on his broad shoulders. "I know you're right, George, but for tonight, anyway, I feel as though I could do anything! Come on, let's run!" And, picking up her skirts, she dashed away, laughing as the brisk wind tossed her long hair into tangles. Butch jogged behind her, knowing that in a tight corset and long skirts she could not go far. When she came to a halt, still laughing between pants for air, he lifted her high and swung her in a circle. As he lowered her to the ground, her laughter died down, and they looked straight into each other's eyes, feeling the joy of being young and alive, but feeling something else, too, something that gave Butch a jolt and made him drop his hands and step back.

Still breathing heavily, Candace brushed the hair back from her face and gave him a tentative smile. "Only a few hours till dawn," she said.

"I'll take you to your cousin's," Butch murmured, still

unnerved by what had just passed between them.

"No, I don't want to go there," she said firmly.

"Where then?"

She took his hand and started walking. After a few minutes she said, so softly he could barely hear her: "Take me to your room, George."

He took a deep breath and let it out slowly. "No, sweetheart. That wouldn't be right."

"It isn't what you think," she said. "It's not that I want to be with you . . . that way. It's just that right now I feel like you're my best friend in the whole world, but I know that, after tonight, I'll never see you again. So I just don't want tonight to end yet."

She was so young, so sweet, so full of hope in spite of all she had been through. He knew it was a mistake, knew that the current that had arced between them was a dangerous thing, knew that he would regret ignoring the warning signal that was blaring in his brain. Even so, he heard himself assenting, saw himself wrapping his arm around her waist to pull her thin, boyish body close to his as they walked on.

But, when they reached his cheap hotel and were inside his tiny room, his uneasiness disappeared. They were comfortable with each other, unembarrassed to be alone together. Candace sat on the edge of the single bed while Butch picked up the sole chair in the room, turned it around, and straddled it, resting his arms on its straight back. They talked for another hour or two until the girl's eyes drooped with fatigue.

"I don't want to go to sleep, but I can't seem to help it," she said. "Maybe I'll lie down for just a minute, but promise to get me up soon. I mustn't sleep the rest of our time away."

He promised, but when she dropped off almost immediately into what appeared to be a deep sleep, he spread a blanket on the hard floor, rolled up his jacket for a pillow, and fell asleep himself. The next thing he knew, she was beside him on the blanket, naked, stroking the hair on his chest which she must have laid bare while he slept. He started, but she pressed him back down, shushing him as she covered his face with kisses.

"This ain't right," he protested feebly between kisses, not knowing what he would do if she agreed with him and stopped her lovely ministrations.

"It is right," she whispered. "For the first time in my life, it feels right."

Then he gave himself up to her, and it was as if he were the child and she the wise, all-knowing teacher. He lost track of time; it could have been minutes or it could have been hours before the sun filtered weakly through the blackened window. Butch looked down at the tousled, heavy-lidded, freckled girl/woman in his arms and said the words he had never been able to say to anyone before: "I love you." Pushing up on one elbow, he brushed a strand of hair from her cheek and said: "And I'm going to send you far away from here."

Chapter Twenty-Two

The train whistle's long, shrill cry announced the departure of the westbound express from Union Dépôt. To many of the passengers, the sound was exciting—a call to the beginning of a new life in that mythical place of hope and opportunity known as the Wild West. For others, both on the train and on the platform seeing off friends and relatives, the whistle seemed the loneliest, most mournful sound they had ever heard—a final good bye to loved ones who might never be seen again.

Butch Cassidy stood beside Track Number Nine, watching with a mixture of sadness and satisfaction as a small, freckled face disappeared into the unknown. He knew he had done the right thing putting Candace on the train, but he could not deny the emptiness he felt at once again losing someone he loved.

Had it really been love? Maybe a little bit of the real thing, he decided, combined with an overwhelming feeling of protectiveness. He had simply wanted to rescue the girl from the harsh life she had fallen into, so he did the only he could think to do—bought her a ticket to Seattle where she had relatives to take care of her, gave her $500 to make sure she got there safely, and kissed her lightly on lips that tasted salty from her tears as he handed her up the steps of the train. She had wanted him to come with her, but he had said no, not bothering to explain that the company of a noted outlaw still being hotly pursued by the law would place her in a dangerous situation. *I'm better off on my own anyway,* he thought, cramming his hat on his head and walking briskly back along the platform. *Who needs the burden of a woman to take care of, especially one barely out of short skirts?*

Intent on what his next move should be now that his nest egg had been cut in half, he did not hear his name being called from the other end of the platform. Suddenly a hand reached out and grabbed his shoulder. "Butch! Holy shit, man, so this is where you're hiding out!"

Butch's hand automatically went for his gun. Luckily, it was stuck in his waistband beneath his buttoned coat; if it had been any more accessible, the man standing before him would be dead. "Buck!" he expelled the name on a breath of air. "You ought to be careful coming up behind a fella like that."

"Sorry, Butch. Guess I was so surprised to see you, I plumb forgot myself. Hell, the entire population of two states is looking for you, and, by God, if I ain't the one to find you!" Buck Williams laughed and gave Butch a friendly punch in the arm. An old acquaintance from his cowboy days, Buck posed no immediate threat. Nevertheless, Butch cautiously pulled him behind a gurney piled high with luggage where they could talk without being seen.

"What are you doing in Chicago?" Butch asked casually.

"Came in with a shipment of cattle from the E Y outfit. Jesus Christ, I still can't believe it's you! How'd you slip through anyway? They got the law watching every train leaving Wyoming." Buck, so called because of the unfortunate appearance of his teeth, was caught between excitement, fear, and awe at encountering his famous friend.

"Never mind that," Butch said. "Tell me what's going on back there."

"You ain't going to believe it, Butch, but for a while

there everyone thought you was dead."

"What?"

"That's right. There was a report you got killed down near Elk Basin. Your old lawyer, Preston, went down to claim your body, and damned if it weren't some cowpuncher named Johnny Herring, instead of you. Reckon that Preston fella must think a lot of you, 'cause word has it he was so happy he stayed drunk for a week!"

An ironic smile creased Butch's face. "Would've been better if Preston let them think it was me. Then nobody'd be looking for me no more."

"That's a fact." Buck nodded his head thoughtfully. "But I'll tell you this, Butch. The law may be looking for you, but not all of them want to find you. Hell, old Charlie Stough practically had tears in his eyes, leading the posse out of Lander."

"Yeah? Well, I aim to keep Charlie happy, then. Thanks for the news, Buck. I gotta be going."

"Hold on! Don't you want to see the other boys? They'll be hopping mad, if they find out they missed seeing Butch Cassidy!"

"What other boys?" Butch asked warily.

"Well, there's Jimmy Morgan and Toot Herford . . . and, let's see, Harry Long." Buck ticked them off on his fingers. Butch recognized the names and was none too sure that one of them might not turn him in for the reward money.

"Tell you what, Buck. You'd be doing me a big favor, if you keep it to yourself that you saw me here. I wouldn't forget it. You can count on that." Butch turned his most winning smile on the buck-toothed cowboy.

"Well, OK. Reckon I could keep it quiet," Buck said reluctantly. "But if you is worried about being recognized, you better skedaddle from Chicago. We's only the first of the fall shipments, and there's likely to be plenty of boys you know coming to town."

"Yeah, I kind of figured that out," Butch said with a wry smile. Peering from behind the baggage cart, he made sure the coast was clear before scooting down the platform and out of the station.

Once on the street, he proceeded with caution, walking at an unhurried pace but keeping his eyes peeled for anyone who might be following him. For he now knew, if Buck Williams was to be believed, that the pursuit of him had not died down in the least. Although he had managed to slip out of Wyoming, he had to assume that lawmen were questioning every ticket clerk in every train station in the state, and that they might soon trail him to Chicago.

A boy on the corner was selling newspapers. Butch tossed him a nickel and then boarded a crowded trolley car. Hanging on to the strap with one hand, he managed to unfold the paper. Scanning the front page, he came to a screeching halt at an item halfway down the left-hand column: **Butch Cassidy, Notorious Bandit, Seen in Chicago, Rewards of $15,000**—read the headline. The car lurched, and the paper slipped out of his hand. A woman seated on the bench next to him bent to retrieve it and handed it to him with a smile. Nodding his thanks, he hoped against hope his face did not betray the shock he felt.

He read the rest of the short article. It did not say where or by whom he had been sighted which probably meant the authorities were going on an anonymous tip. He racked his brain, trying to remember if, among all the people he had encountered in this city, any of them had flashed recognition upon seeing him. Nothing came to mind, but he knew one thing—he dared not return to any of the places he had been, not even his hotel. In fact, the sooner he got out of Chicago, the better.

Glancing out the windows of the trolley car, he tried to get his bearings. The car was heading east, along what street he wasn't sure, but eventually it would stop at Lake Michigan. A plan started to form. With the train stations under surveillance, his chances of getting out that way were extremely poor. But what about a boat? It was possible the piers were being watched, too, but maybe he would get lucky.

At the end of the line, which fortuitously turned out to be at one of the city's largest piers, he hopped off and strolled along the lake shore, eating a hot dog purchased from a sidewalk vendor while trying to determine if he was being followed. Satisfied that he was not, he inquired at the ticket office and decided to board a boat bound for Frankfort, Michigan, across the lake and some two hundred miles to the north. The *City of Petoskey* was a steamer with several decks. Butch found a secluded corner, and, when night fell, slept in a deck chair with his hat pulled low over his face.

The next day, still anxious to put miles between himself and Chicago, he boarded a train heading inland. He got off at a small junction called Mancelona, for no reason other than it appeared to be in the middle of nowhere. Remote as it was, however, it attracted its share of visitors, for Butch was given the last available room in the only hotel in town. The hotel clerk warned him that there were two beds in his room, and, if another traveler checked in, he would have to share the room. Not wanting to make a scene, he agreed to the conditions.

That night, before he went to bed, he moved a chair in front of the door so, if someone tried to open it, the chair would tip over and wake him. He laid down fully clothed, removing only his hat, coat, and boots. It seemed impossible that anyone had been able to track him to this remote town in the middle of the Michigan woods, but until he was absolutely certain of that, he intended to be ready for anything.

The night was hot and still; no breeze stirred the shabby curtains. Unfamiliar night sounds came through the open window—tree frogs and cicadas made such a racket he wondered how anyone around here ever got any sleep. His mind wandered, and after a few moments it came to rest on Mary, as it always did whenever he allowed himself the luxury of reflection. What was she doing right now? Was she lying contentedly in the arms of her husband or was she, like himself, tossing and turning with unfulfilled desires and unrealized dreams? Deep in his soul, he knew Mary had loved him with a passion that comes along only once in a lifetime. Why had he squandered their chance to be together? Why had he been unable to say to Mary the words he had spoken so easily to a virtual stranger?

Sighing heavily, he turned on his side and stared out the window. The stars did not shine as brightly here as they did out West. The air seemed heavy and sapped the energy right out of a body. With an empty feeling in the pit of his stomach, he realized he did not belong here where people might know his name but knew nothing about the real man. Why, he would probably be safer back in Wyoming where, at least, he had plenty of friends willing to help him. The more he thought about it, the more it made sense. Where better to hide than where you were least expected? Now that the law knew he had made it out of Wyoming, that would be the last place they'd go looking. As sleep finally settled over him, he determined to make his way back home, home being just about anywhere west of the hundredth meridian.

He did not know how long he had slept, when a soft tapping woke him. He lay still, hoping whoever was at the door would go away, but the knock came again.

"Who's there?" he called, affecting a voice thick with sleep.

"It's the landlord, sir," replied the hotel proprietor. "Another guest needs to share your room."

Butch cursed silently but, nonetheless, got up to remove the chair from in front of the door. Getting back in bed he called: "All right. Come on in."

The door opened, and he could hear two people enter, stumbling around in the dark. "I'm afraid I'll have to light the lamp, sir," the clerk said, "just long enough for this gentleman to get his bearings."

"Go on then," Butch said, throwing his arm over his face to shade his eyes. From this position, he could observe his new roommate without being seen himself.

The lamp flared up, revealing the broad back of a tall, muscular-looking man. Closing the door after the clerk, the man turned around and removed his coat—a shiny star sparkled on the front of his vest. Butch inhaled sharply, then coughed to hide his surprise.

"Sorry to disturb you," the sheriff said. "I'll douse this light right quick."

Grunting his response, Butch turned on his side, his back to the unwelcome newcomer. A few minutes later, the light went out, and he heard the springs squeak on the bed not three feet away from him. The sheriff sighed deeply and no more than thirty seconds later was loudly snoring.

Butch lay awake the rest of the night, mostly from his need to stay on guard, although the sheriff's clamor would have been difficult to sleep through under any circumstances. At the first hint of light, Butch rose, quietly pulled on his boots, and stole out of the room.

Stopping at the office, he addressed the sleepy-eyed clerk. "Say, I'm curious who that was shared my room last night."

"My apologies, sir, for having interrupted you at such a late hour. You see, that was the sheriff of Manistee, and he arrived so late because he had been tracking a dangerous criminal all day and into the night. Said the man had been seen getting on a train at Frankfort, so they're checking all the station stops. Terrible, isn't it, what goes on these days?" He shook his head sadly.

"What sort of criminal?" asked Butch, feigning alarm.

"Bank robber from way out West somewhere. Named Butch Cassidy, if I remember right."

"I see. Well, thank you, sir. I'll be on my guard today." Butch tipped his hat and left. The hotel clerk had given him some useful information. Manistee was a little town on the shores of Lake Michigan, just south of Frankfort. The *City of Petoskey* had docked there briefly. That meant someone had seen him get on the boat in Chicago and had alerted the law at each of its stops. Damn! Whoever was trailing him was doing a hell of a job—Butch thought for sure he had gotten away clean from Chicago. No matter. The trick now was to get out of Mancelona before his erstwhile roommate awoke and discovered he had bunked with his outlaw prey the previous night.

He hopped a southbound train and by the end of the day found himself in Bay City on the shores of Lake Huron. The hobo who shared his freight car had been only too happy to trade clothes with him; thus, the notorious bandit now appeared to be nothing but a down-on-his-luck drifter.

Butch wandered down to the docks, not certain what his next move would be but keeping his eyes and ears open for possible opportunities. Playing the part of a bum, he stationed himself outside one of the many bars that crawled with crews from the numerous boats that plied the waters of Lake Huron. Along about midnight, a jaunty little man, wearing a sailor's cap, strode by and paused before Butch's tattered, slouching figure. "Looking for a hand-out, feller?" he said brusquely.

"No, sir," replied Butch, straightening up. "Looking for a job, if you know where I might get one."

The sailor looked him up and down with an appraising eye. "You seem hearty enough. Ever done any sailing?"

"Yes, sir," Butch lied.

"Well, we'll see about that. Show up at the *Eagle* at dawn. The captain might hire you, if he likes your looks." With that, the man sauntered off with the peculiar rolling gait common to men who lived on the sea.

Butch did as he was told. The *Eagle*'s skipper, a Frenchman by the name of La Croix, gave him one quick glance and offered him a job. He was in dire need of additional crewmen so was willing to hire virtually any able-bodied man.

The *Eagle* was a double-rigged schooner, a small boat but well cared for. It was bound for one of the small beach towns on Michigan's eastern shore. Butch was told to help with the raising and lowering of the mainsail. Using careful observation and general good sense, he managed to acquit himself of his duties despite his total lack of sailing experience. During the twelve-hour voyage, he tried to remain inconspicuous, following orders without comment and keeping to himself the rest of the time. He would have liked to engage the crew in conversation for they seemed a jolly, tight-knit bunch, but he did not dare make an impression.

As they neared their destination, a sharp gale blew up,

and the captain began barking out orders that the crew rushed to carry out, their faces full of concentration. Butch gathered the wind was complicating their efforts to enter the narrow harbor. At one hundred yards out, the captain gave the order to lower the mainsail. As Butch tugged at the heavy ropes, he felt the boat veering to starboard, then, just as they cleared the breakwater, the vessel righted itself and slipped into the harbor easy as a breeze. Novice that he was, he recognized an impressive feat of piloting, and he joined the rest of the crew in cheering the smiling Captain La Croix.

Safely moored, the skipper invited all the crew to go into town for a meal, his treat. Reluctantly Butch declined, accepting his pay and then departing. He wished he did not have to, for he had enjoyed the trip and these men, and he was hungry for laughter and camaraderie. But it seemed to be his fate to keep moving through life. He bade them good bye and turned his attention to his next mode of flight.

It did not take long for him to discover what form it would take. The circus was in town, and, when the manager learned Butch was adept at handling a six-horse team, he put him to work driving one of the wagons that hauled their gear from one town to the next. They spent two days in the town of Bad Axe, then moved on to Cass City. Butch figured he had lucked into the perfect hide-out. Who would think to look for him in a traveling circus making the rounds of tiny, backwoods towns?

On their second day in Cass City, Butch left the big tent in the middle of the show to check on the horses. Rounding the corner of one of the wagons, he pulled up sharply—he was face to face with a man he knew well, Deputy Sheriff Jess Walker from Evanston, Wyoming! Startled, Walker fumbled for his gun, but Butch had him beat. He rammed his six-shooter into the lawman's belly.

"You here to see the show, Walker?" he said, grinning in spite of his shock and dismay at being discovered.

"I'm here to take you in," the deputy said through clenched teeth. "Drop your piece and give up quietly."

"I'll give you points for having nerve, that's for damn' sure. Come on, move!" Butch jabbed him with the gun and started walking him toward the woods, looking right and left to see if they were being watched. Luckily, they were alone.

"Don't look and don't talk, just keep walking or you'll be coyote bait," warned Butch. He walked him two hundred yards into the woods, then told him to stop.

"You the one been following me all this time?" he asked.

"Me and about half a dozen others. You're the man of the hour, Cassidy." Walker grinned sardonically, and Butch remembered that he had always liked this man. He had moxie and a sense of humor to go with it.

"Ain't it nice to be so popular. Sorry to do this to you, bud, but I'm going to have to tie you up."

"Out here? Nobody'll ever find me. You want to add murder to your rap?" Walker's eyes narrowed, and his hand strayed close to his gun belt.

"Throw it down, Walker. I've got you covered. You ain't got a chance." The deputy hesitated but then threw down his weapon. "That's better. Now listen," Butch went on as he switched his gun to his left hand and unbuckled his belt with his right. "You ain't going to die. I'll make sure of that. Better get yourself a drink of water before I tie you up." He gestured toward a nearby creek. Walker glared at him but knelt and drank. Then Butch tied him to a tree with his belt making sure the cinch was not so tight that it cut off the man's circulation.

"You ain't going to get away, Cassidy. If it ain't me that

gets you, it'll be somebody else. Your days are numbered." Walker spoke almost sadly, feeling something akin to respect for his captor.

Butch sat back on his heels and regarded the lawman with amusement. "All our days are numbered, friend. But at least I'm still counting mine." With that, he removed Walker's handkerchief and gagged him with it. Promising to send help, he bounded away, his mind already assessing the best means of escape.

Deciding he would have to risk the trains, he gathered what few things he owned from the circus wagon and walked to the dépôt. The next train was not scheduled to leave for two hours. Not knowing when he might eat again, he bought a meal, then returned to the dépôt and penned a short note describing where to find Deputy Walker. Addressing it to the Postmaster, he dropped it in the box just before boarding.

The train was heading south for Detroit. On the outskirts of Pontiac, he jumped off and started walking down a dirt road. As soon as he had put enough distance between himself and the train tracks, he laid down in a cornfield and went to sleep, exhausted from his efforts.

When he awoke, the sun was high, although the tall corn shielded him from its rays. He sat up slowly, muscle-sore and foul-mouthed. He spat several times and rolled his shoulders, trying to work out the kinks. This constant running was getting old. He needed to get back home, wherever that was. *Somewhere I can lay my head for longer than two hours at a stretch and not be worried about waking up with a gun pointed at it,* he thought.

Creakily, he got to his feet and made his way out of the field. It was September, and the corn was taller than he was, about ready to harvest, he judged. That gave him an idea.

He started walking along the road, looking for the farm-house that belonged with these fields.

No more than five minutes later, a white frame house and several outbuildings came into view. There was nothing pretentious about any of it, although everything appeared to be in good repair. Approaching cautiously, having learned to expect the unexpected, he knocked on the door. A kindly-looking woman answered.

" 'Morning, ma'am." He tipped his hat. "I was wondering if you might have need of an extra hand."

The woman regarded him closely, a Mona Lisa smile on her face. She appeared to be about fifty, although a farm wife's age was difficult to estimate. Maybe the years had been hard and she was closer to forty.

"You'll have to speak to my husband when he comes in," she said. Butch nodded and turned to sit on the porch steps to wait. "Come on in the kitchen," she urged. "You look like you could use a cool drink."

"Yes, ma'am. Thank you, ma'am." He followed her into the house and her kitchen, neat as a pin.

"I'm Marie Goodloe," she said, setting a glass of water in front of him.

"George Maxwell," he said, throwing out the first name that came to him. He drained the glass, and she took it to refill.

"What brings you to this area, Mister Maxwell?"

Butch opened his mouth to answer, not knowing, even as he started to speak, what lie he would utter this time. Their eyes met, her's large and brown and trusting, and, suddenly, he was tired of lying, tired of pretending. Not that he intended to tell her the truth, but maybe he could just say nothing. He smiled and shrugged, and she dropped her eyes.

"I didn't mean to pry. Of course, it's none of my business," she said softly.

"I guess, if I'm asking you to give me a job, it is your business. So if you really want to know why I'm in these parts, I'll be on my way." He set the glass down on the table and turned to go.

"Wait!" she said. He turned around, and once again their eyes met. "It's all right, Mister Maxwell. My husband has the final word, but I'd like you to stay."

Marie Goodloe's husband and teen-aged son returned to the house for the noon meal. Ordinarily Everett Goodloe was wary of hiring strangers, but this one seemed to have gained Marie's approval and he did need help with the harvesting, so he told George Maxwell to stow his gear in the barn. It turned out to one of the best decisions he had ever made for the new hired man worked tirelessly, laboring in the hot, scratchy fields with nary a complaint. In fact, he had little of anything to say, although he seemed pleasant enough. Occasionally he would straighten up from his back-breaking work and catch the boy's eye, and he never failed to offer a friendly wink or grin.

The boy, Jack by name, was at that age where manhood was tantalizingly close yet frustratingly out of reach, and thus everything that had to do with home and family and responsibility and routine seemed an unbearable burden. Butch looked at him and remembered what it felt like to want more than anything to bust loose and yet still be scared of what lay ahead in that big, wide world. Jack watched Butch closely, too, fascinated by this hard-working, confident man who kept to himself yet seemed to look at the world through eyes touched with intelligence and humor. He lay in his bed at night conjuring up all manner of possible backgrounds for George Maxwell, sometimes coming closer to the truth than he ever imagined.

One evening after supper, Jack wandered down to the barn where Butch was busy currying the horses. The Goodloes had all noticed how expertly and lovingly their hired man handled the stock. Jack stood unobserved in the door, listening to Butch murmur soft words to Jack's own sorrel pony.

"You aiming to steal my horse's affections?" the boy said with a smile.

Sheepishly, Butch looked at him over the pony's back. "I didn't hear you come in. Guess you caught me, so I might as well admit it . . . I'd just as soon palaver with these old plugs than most people I know."

"Can't blame you." Jack left his post by the door and came forward to stroke his horse's neck. "You seem to know a thing or two about animals. You grow up on a farm?"

Butch snorted derisively. "I reckon you could call it that."

Cursing himself for bringing up a sore subject, Jack cast about for a new topic. "I ain't going to stay on the farm much longer. Ma and Pa want me to go off to the university, but I ain't decided yet. Maybe I'll do that or maybe I'll just roam around, see what happens. Either way, I ain't coming back here."

Butch grabbed two pitchforks and tossed one to the boy. "Help me with this hay," he said. Cutting open a bale, he began spearing it into the stalls. "I ain't one for offering advice, kid, especially if it ain't wanted. But I think I been where you are, and I'll tell you one thing. Don't go thinking that what your folks want you to do is necessarily the wrong thing. I know you got your wild oats to sow but don't get it in your head that's all there is to life."

"Are you saying I ought to do like Ma and Pa want and go off to school?"

"I'm the last one to tell you how to live your life, kid. Hell, when I was your age, I was champing at the bit. Still am, I reckon. I ain't got no regrets, leastways not many, but I wouldn't recommend a life on the road for everybody." He caught himself before saying "a life on the run."

Jack leaned on his pitchfork. "Why don't you settle down, if you're tired of being on the move?"

"It ain't that easy. Reckon I got roaming in my blood, whether I like it or not." Butch smiled, but, for once, it stopped short of his eyes.

Later that night Butch walked up to the house to tell Everett Goodloe he would be leaving in the morning. He had no way of knowing if the pursuit had died down, but it was time to move on, time to head west to his familiar and much missed stomping grounds. Marie Goodloe sat alone on the porch swing, idly pushing herself back and forth with one foot.

" 'Evening, ma'am," Butch removed his hat. "Mister Goodloe around?"

"He's retired for the night. Anything I can help with?"

He told her of his plans. She stopped swinging and sat silently for a moment. "I'm sorry you have to go, George, but I know better than to ask you to stay. Nevertheless, please remember that you have a place here with us if you ever need it."

He swallowed, touched by her kindness. "Thank you, ma'am, that's right nice of you."

"I should be thanking you, George. I don't know what you said to Jack, but he came up from the barn this evening and told us he'd decided to go to the university, after all. Why, Everett and I had talked ourselves blue in the face, trying to convince him of that, to no avail. Yet it seems a few well chosen words from you did the trick. What did you say to him?" She rose and leaned against the porch rail. The moonlight caressed her face, erasing the lines and making her look younger and quite pretty.

"Nothing much. He's a good boy. He would've done the right thing no matter what I said." Butch gazed out over the newly harvested fields, suddenly seeing himself at Jack's age—brash and impressionable and altogether full of himself. He, too, had taken the advice of an older man whom he had admired, for better or worse. He took a deep breath and leaned his head back to look up at the sky, homesick for . . . what? Brown's Hole, Hole-in-the-Wall, Horse Creek? No, it wasn't a place he yearned for, it was a person, a person forever lost to him. Or was she? An odd feeling came over him, a chill that made the hair on his arms and the back of his neck stand up.

Marie was saying something about how they appreciated his hard work. He wrenched his gaze away from the star-filled heavens, and, when she saw his face, she stopped in mid-sentence. "Oh, George. I know there are things about yourself you don't want to tell and it isn't my place to ask, but I see such sadness in your eyes. A sadness that seems out of place for a man like you. I've only known you a short time, but I can tell you're not normally a sullen or unhappy person. You've got a zest for life that . . . well, that anyone can see." She paused, out of breath, amazed that she could talk like this to a man she barely knew. He said nothing, but he held her gaze, unembarrassed by her outburst.

"Whatever it is that's making you so unhappy, you must confront it. You're a strong person, George. You can shape your own fate, with God's help."

He stayed silent for a long while. Finally he sighed and put his hat back on, tugging the brim low. "I don't reckon God's on my side, ma'am, but there's some truth in what you said. I'll remember it." He started down the porch steps, then turned back to her. "I'll remember you." With a quick nod of his head, he was gone.

Marie Goodloe put her hand to her tired, worn face and sat back down on the porch swing. A minute later she put her foot out and slowly pushed off, swinging in the moonlight.

Over the next few days Butch slowly made his way to St. Louis, sometimes walking, sometimes hopping trains, sometimes hitching rides in the backs of wagons. He never got the feeling of being followed, but he took precautions nonetheless, staying away from major thoroughfares and changing clothes as often as possible. Once, he even took the tattered coveralls off a scarecrow in the fields.

When he got to St. Louis, he spent a full day watching the train station before concluding it was safe to buy a ticket. Once on the train headed west, he stayed alert with half his brain while the other half pondered Marie Goodloe's advice to him. She had told him to confront his problem, to take the bull by the horns, and try to change the way things were. Was that possible? For an instant that night, looking up at the stars, he had felt something, almost as though Mary were out there somewhere, willing him to come to her.

He shook his head in disgust. *Bullshit,* he thought. *You're full of bullshit.* Nevertheless, the idea remained with him, and, try as he might, he could not shake it.

He jumped off the train near Medicine Bow and made his way back to Frank Burns's ranch, having completed a three thousand mile circle in little less than a month. Proud to have played a part in the escape of the notorious outlaw Butch Cassidy, Burns greeted him warmly.

"What are you doing back here, Butch? According to the papers, you're hiding out in Michigan somewhere."

"Good! It's about time I shook them. Jesus, Jess Walker tailed me all the way to some two-bit, backwoods lousy excuse for a town ain't nobody ever heard of!"

"Read about that, too," Burns laughed. "Walker must be mad as hell after what you did to him."

"Aw, it weren't that bad. Christ, I left a god-damned note telling how to find him. Reckon he'd really be mad, if I'd just left him there to die." Butch leaned back in his chair and stuck his legs out, crossing them at the ankles. It felt good to be back with friends. "How long did it take to find him?"

"Paper said they found him at midnight, a little thirsty but no worse for wear."

"I'm telling you, Burns, them Easterners is pretty damn' thick-skulled. Hell, I shared a hotel room with one of their sheriffs, and he never had one god-damn' clue he was sleeping next to the guy on the Wanted poster! Maybe I'll go back someday and knock over one of their banks. They're so slow, it'd be like taking candy from a baby!" They shared a good laugh, and then Frank went to attend to some chores, inviting Butch to make himself at home.

Weary and dirty from his travels, he soaked in a hot tub, then borrowed more of Frank's clothes. Rustling up paper, pen, and ink, he sat down at the kitchen table. For a long while he stared into the distance, thinking. Finally he scratched out two letters, one to Elzy Lay, the other to Harry Longabaugh, telling them he was back and would meet them at their prearranged spot in a couple of weeks. He had no fear of the letters being intercepted—they were addressed to aliases, and he himself used a false name known only to his accomplices.

There was one more piece of paper left on the table. He dropped his head in his hands, unable to force his fingers to pick up the pen. Angrily, he pushed away and stomped toward the door, but then hesitated as Marie Goodloe's words came back to him. *You're a strong person, George. You can shape your own fate.*

Taking a deep breath, he sat down and started to write.

September 14, 1896
Dear Mary,

    I do not know if you will ever receive this letter or if you do, if you will decide to read it. I would not blame you if you didn't. But I write anyway in the hope that you will agree to meet me at our favorite place by the river one week from today. I will wait for you.

Yours truly,
Geo. C.

With a shaking hand, he addressed it to Mary Rhodes, Lander, Wyoming. Before he could change his mind, he rushed outside, summoned one of the young ranch hands, and sent him to town to post the letters.

The next day he rode out on a horse purchased from Frank Burns, headed west in search of his fate.

Chapter Twenty-Three

There is nothing quite as beautiful as a brilliant autumn day in the mountains of the western United States. The air, already light and crisp from the altitude, has an added tartness that hints of a change in the season; the sky is so blue it almost blinds the eye; the aspen leaves are ringed with gold and flutter like butterflies in the breeze.

Butch Cassidy—cowboy, bandit, gentleman, son, lover— reclined beneath a tall cottonwood by the side of the Popo Agie and recognized the day for what it was—a miracle of creation that surpassed all the days that had come before. He drew strength from that realization, understanding that no matter what happened, nothing could diminish this day's splendor.

Butch waited patiently, reveling in the beauty of his surroundings and feeling confident about the future. During the past week, as he crossed his adopted state heading toward this long-awaited reunion, he convinced himself that things would go well today. He loved Mary; Mary loved him; they were meant to be together; and once he straightened all this out with his beloved, they could be united once more. He would tell her everything for there could be no secrets between them now, but the strength of their love would overcome any doubts Mary might have about leaving her husband and joining him in whatever adventure lay ahead.

He let his head fall back and looked up at branches thick with yellowing leaves. The dark shape of an owl, sitting motionless on one of the highest limbs, was barely visible. It reminded him of the cabin in Circle Valley where, years ago, another owl had called down to him, bearing a message of freedom and independence and unknown worlds to conquer. A fleeting finger of doubt ran down his spine. Was he about to give all that up?

Butch's horse grazed nearby. Suddenly it raised its head, pricked its ears, and nickered softly. Butch came to his feet, and there she was, not ten feet away, looking at him with wide, dark eyes and parted lips. Nothing about her had changed, and yet he felt as though he were seeing her for the first time. He was struck again by her proud beauty that had not faded with the passing of the years.

Then she walked toward him, and he could see tears filling her eyes, and they embraced. The feel of her body and the smell of her hair were so familiar he found himself struggling to fight back his own tears. He held her close until he gained control, letting his hands remember all the hills and valleys of her strong, supple back.

Finally she pulled away and looked at him, her eyes full of questions. But all she said was: "I knew you'd come back."

Her husky voice still worked its magic on him. He wanted to pull her close and make love to her until she cried out his name over and over again. He reached for her, but she took a step back. For the first time he noticed the ring on her hand. From deep inside him, anger welled up, and, although he had meant his first words to her to be words of love, he heard himself asking: "Why did you do it, Mary?"

She lifted her head proudly. "Do you really need to ask me that?"

"Yes, goddammit!" he said, unable to temper his anger. "You lied to me. You said you'd write to me in prison, but you didn't. You said you'd wait for me, but you didn't."

"How dare you accuse me of lying, Mister Butch Cassidy!" The venom in her voice was like a slap in the face. "We lived together like man and wife, and yet you never told me the first thing about your past. Not a word about all the rustling, not a word about a certain bank in Telluride, and you can't tell me you didn't know those horses at Mail Camp were stolen."

"Did you think you was shacking up with a choirboy?" He wanted the words back the minute they were out of his mouth. This was all wrong. He had come here to declare his love for her, and yet all they could do was fight. She turned to leave, trembling with hurt and anger.

"Mary, wait! This ain't how it's supposed to go. I admit there's a lot I didn't tell you, but it was for your own good. I didn't want to burden you with things you didn't need to know. But that ain't important now." He took her arm and made her face him. The tears spilled unchecked over her cheeks. "You know all about me now . . . who I am, what I've done. I ain't going to try to tell you I'll change. It's too late for that, and, truth to tell, I don't know as I want to change. I'm my own man, free as a bird and likely to stay that way as long as I keep my wits about me. I've got more friends than I can count, and as for money, hell, all I'm doing is taking it from people who don't deserve it in the first place. It's a damn' good life, Mary, and I just want to know . . . well, I just want to know . . . where you stand."

"Why? What difference does it make?" she said, wiping the tears from her face.

"Well, I thought, that is, I hoped maybe . . . maybe we could . . . I don't know . . . start up again," he stammered.

Mary looked at him incredulously. "For God's sake, George, I'm married!"

He stepped closer and grabbed her shoulders. "That don't matter, does it? Not to us." *Tell her, you bastard,* he screamed to himself. *Tell her you love her. It's now or never.* But the words died on his tongue. Her nearness confused him. All he could see were her tantalizing, seductive lips, and, although his brain cried out at him to say what he knew he had to say, his body seemed to have a will of its own. His mouth found hers, and, for a fleeting second, he tasted her wild, sweet taste once more.

"No!" She wrenched away from his kiss, although he still held her by the arms. "Don't! We can't do this!"

"Why not? You don't love him." He tried to draw her close again, but she put her hands on his chest to stop him.

"He's my husband," she said quietly.

"So am I, darlin'. We had everything but the ring, didn't we?" He crinkled those bluer than blue eyes at her, and she felt her heart break. *Yes,* she thought, *you are the husband of my heart and the father of my child, but it's no use pretending we have a future together.*

What he called freedom, she called rootlessness. What seemed glamorous to him seemed tawdry to her. No, she could not live on the run, moving from one dismal camp to the next, constantly looking over her shoulder wondering when the law would find them. Besides, there was Mary B' Hat to think of. Her daughter still lived with Gray Hair since Ole Rhodes had turned out to have a little of Bill Boyd in him and refused to let her bastard child live with them. But Mary saw the little girl often and had vowed never to leave her again.

Mary searched her lover's face. There was so much of him in Mary B' Hat, not just in her appearance, but in the way she acted, so sunny and good-natured and kind. What if she had told him in the very beginning about the child?

Would things have turned out differently?

"What is it, darlin'?" he asked, smiling down at her with a puzzled look.

"Nothing." She shook her head sadly.

"Mary, listen to me." He tilted her chin up, forcing her eyes to meet his. "It ain't in my nature to beg, so, if you say no, I'll never bother you again. But I got to ask one more time . . . will you come with me?"

She dropped her eyes to his chest where her hands still lay. The band on her finger shone brightly, mocking her. Suddenly, she reached up and unclasped a gold chain with a tiny cross that hung around her neck. Taking his hand, she dropped it into his callused palm, closing his fingers around it.

"I guess you know how I feel about you, George. I never hid it too well." She managed a small smile. "But you and I chose different paths, and those paths aren't going to cross, maybe not ever again. I won't forget you, though, and I don't want you to forget me. So please take this"—she squeezed his hand that held the cross—"to remember me by."

She raised up on tiptoe and brushed his lips with hers, then was gone, trailing her distinctive earthy scent behind her. Butch watched her go. He did not try to stop her. He had been deluded to think she would go with him. Suddenly he felt a burning need to get away from this place.

He mounted up and urged his horse into a gallop, thrilling as always to the beat of the hoofs, the rhythm of the gait, and the feel of the wind in his face. After a few miles he slowed to a walk. He had a long way to go, and there was no sense in ruining a good horse.

Glancing down, he realized he still held Mary's chain in his hand. Clumsily, not used to such delicate things, he fastened it around his neck. *So this is how it's to be,* he thought. *This is all I'll ever have of her.* His fingers closed around the cross, and he started to tear it from his neck and throw it in the dust, but something stopped him. In the distance, the Wind River Mountains rose tall and stately, and beyond them lay the Sweetwater country, and beyond that, Brown's Hole where Elzy and Sundance and the rest of the gang waited for him. With a slight smile on his strong, open face, he touched the spurs to his mount and called: "Come on, boy, let's burn the breeze!"

Author's Note

Following the Montpelier hold-up, the Wild Bunch went on to pull seven more major robberies. Finally, in the early 1900s, things got too hot, and Butch Cassidy, accompanied by the Sundance Kid and the Kid's mysterious lover, Etta Place, sailed for South America. There the story ends, or does it? Did Butch and the Kid really die in 1908 in a shoot-out with the Bolivian army?

There is some evidence Cassidy did not. That evidence is in the form of a person, William T. Phillips, late of Spokane, Washington. In 1935, Phillips penned a manuscript entitled THE BANDIT INVINCIBLE, THE STORY OF BUTCH CASSIDY from which the title of this book and portions of its story are taken. That manuscript contained enough detail about the life of the famous outlaw that it is safe to say it was either written by Butch Cassidy himself or by someone who was very close to Butch.

What's more, many of Butch's friends from his outlaw days, including Mary Boyd Rhodes and her brother, Bill, said they saw Phillips on his visits to Wyoming in the 1930s and that he was, indeed, Butch Cassidy. Even Butch's sister, Lula Parker Betenson, maintains he came back to Circleville in 1925 to visit his family, although she declined to identify William T. Phillips as her brother.

Although I introduced the reader to Phillips in the opening chapter of this book, I have made no attempt to solve the mystery of whether he was the real Butch Cassidy. Nevertheless, having "lived" with Butch for the last few years, I am convinced that, if he had wanted to stage his death in order to return to the United States with a clean slate, he would and could have done so. The man was, in what may be his own words, invincible.

For the most part then, this is a true story. Some of the characters and situations are the product of my imagination; some are based on the Phillips manuscript. But Mary Boyd, Elizabeth Bassett, and many others mentioned in this book really lived and really knew Butch Cassidy. I have inferred much about the relationship between Butch and the women in his life, but who wouldn't? If they did not succumb to the charms of the Bandit Invincible, they were stronger women than I.

About the Author

Raised in the Midwest, Suzanne Lyon moved to Colorado at seventeen to attend The Colorado College. She worked as a lawyer for, among others, the National Park Service before turning her talents to writing. Lured by the landscapes and legends of the West, Lyon's interest is in Western historical fiction. She resides near Denver with her husband and two children. Her next **Five Star Western** will be LADY BUCKAROO, a story based on the lives of female rodeo stars in the 1920s.

About the Author